A. Vossoughi

MODERN PERSIAN PROSE LITERATURE

MODERN PERSIAN PROSE LITERATURE

BY

HASSAN KAMSHAD

IRANBOOKS
Bethesda, Maryland

Modern Persian Prose Literature
by Hassan Kamshad

Manufactured in the United States of America

The paper used in this book meets the minimum requirements of the American National Standard for Information Services – Permanence of Paper for Printed Library Materials, ANSI Z39.48-1984

Iranbooks, Inc.
8014 Old Georgetown Road
Bethesda, Maryland 20814
Telephone: (301) 718-8188
Facsimile: (301) 907-8707
e-mail: iranbook@ix.netcom.com

LIBRARY OF CONGRESS CATALOGING-IN-PUBLICATION INFORMATION

Kamshad, H. (Hassan)
Modern Persian prose literature / by Hassan Kamshad.
p. cm.
Includes bibliographical references and index.
ISBN 0-936347-72-4
1. Persian fiction--History and criticism. I. Title.
PK6423.K3 1996
891'.553009--dc20 96-1869
CIP

1 3 5 7 9 8 6 4 2

"It is the fashion with some scholars to talk as if literary and poetical talent were a thing of the past in Persia. No mistake could possibly be greater."

E. G. Browne, *A Year Among the Persians*

CONTENTS

PART TWO

Facsimile of part of Shaykh Aḥmad's letter to
E. G. Browne, facing p. 22
Reproduced by courtesy of the University Librarian,
Cambridge

FOREWORD TO SECOND EDITION

Modern Persian Prose Literature was written as a Ph.D. thesis in the 1950's and revised for publication the early 60's. It is, therefore, gratifying to see the book reprinted, nearly half a century later—if only for the perennial interest shown abroad in Persian literature.

This is particularly heartening when a variety of reasons in these recent years make it important that Iran's contributions to arts and culture should be remembered and respected.

It is hoped that the reprint of the present study, which has become a standard work for the student of modern Persian literature, will enhance the currently much needed understanding of Iran.

The quotation from E.G. Browne's *A Year Among the Persians*, with which the first edition opens, still deserves attention. As a matter of fact the manner in which this literature has been flourishing in recent decades calls for a sequel to this work, since it does not cover the period beyond 1961; however, this author does not consider himself quite up to the task.

HASSAN KAMSHAD

London
September 1995

INTRODUCTION

THE last volume of E. G. Browne's *Literary History of Persia* was published in 1924. It covers the literary developments of the country in this century up to 1921. For students of Persian literature the inducement to make an attempt at continuing Browne's work is an obvious one and the present author was so tempted when he was teaching Persian at Cambridge in 1954–9. While E. G. Browne looked with an eye equally profound and penetrating at both Persian prose and poetry, and at all the manifestations of the two, the less well-equipped continuator has, in this instance, chosen only to try to produce a study of recent Persian prose, and that only in the field of fiction. Journalism in the twentieth century in Iran requires a special study of its own. Here it is touched on only in so far as it affects the publication of fiction and serves to promote specifically modern styles of prose writing. Drama also is noticed only in so far as it has influenced modern styles adopted by the novelists and short-story writers. The excellent *belles lettres* of certain literary journals have also been excluded as being essays and not works of fiction. This is also the case with scholarly and scientific articles which fall outside the purview of this study.

The work has been written in the belief that imaginative prose writing in Persia has developed sufficiently in the past fifty years to merit study and description, and that it reflects certain salient characteristics of modern Persian culture and society. The description of the works considered in this book has had to be somewhat fuller than would be warranted in a study dealing with a literature more widely read and known outside its country of origin. The author has been at pains, not only to discuss critically the works cited, but also to describe their forms and contents for the benefit of those who are not familiar with modern Persian works of fiction. In order to illustrate the extent to which modern Persian imaginative writers have been influenced by the development of society in their country, attention has also been paid to the social and political conditions in which modern authors have lived, and in particular to the increasing contact with the West and to the ensuing state of transition in which most modern Persians live.

It may well be asked, particularly outside Iran, why should an Iranian present the prose literature of his country to the outside world, while it is generally poetry that has pride of place in the literature of Persia. Poetry was until the nineteenth century an immensely important vehicle of literary expression in Iran, but with the nineteenth century came increased contact with the modern and predominantly technological world. A poetry of stereotyped and dead conventions lacked the kind of diction modern ideas required, and Persian poetry has apparently as yet been unable to adapt itself to these new ideas. Prose therefore has become the dominant literary medium in modern Iran. Moreover, prose is by no means an entirely new literary medium in Persian. A considerable body of important prose works exists, notably historical annals which are essential to the full understanding of the development of the Persian language. Besides the numerous histories, works of fiction, principally in the form of moral and didactic tales often interspersed with verse quotations, have existed for centuries, and indeed form part of the glory of the Persian literature.

It was thus deemed necessary to give at the outset a brief outline of the historical development of Persian prose. The marked change in the type of prose that has come into use in the modern period is a feature of the works discussed in this study. Nevertheless, modern prose cannot be justly dealt with as though it were completely isolated from the prose literature of the past.

After a brief general survey of Persian prose, the modern period has been opened with the study of the early Qajar and pre-Constitutional Period. At that time modernizing influences first began to manifest themselves in Persian life and letters. Concomitant with these influences was the advent of new political factors and an increased social consciousness, with a rising middle class of educated persons, all of which had a profound effect on the Persians' attitude towards literature. On the other hand, increased social consciousness resulted in literature being used—and this use of literature was not new in Iran, though the forms employed were—as a weapon of social criticism. Further, a new type of reading public demanded a new type of literature which contained, among other things, reflections of foreign cultures and scientific progress. Hence the spread of newspapers and the beginning of extensive translations of foreign works. These resulted in developments which, even if its products were to be read by one quite unaware of the actual history of the end of the nineteenth century in Iran, would nevertheless clearly indicate that political ferment existed. After a period of comparative stagnation, a highly vocal people, never for long lacking literary articulateness in one form or another, had again been agitated into literary expression. The tone of this expression was to change as the golden hopes of the first flush of modernization were disappointed. The intensity of modern literary output has, however, remained sufficiently strong to justify calling these new developments a literary renaissance.

It is with the change of tone and accent in modern Persian literature that the following pages are concerned. In the post-Revolutionary Period there was a rather confused medley of literary production, emerging at a time when complex political issues were far from being solved in Iran, and when foreign models, eagerly snatched at, were by no means properly understood or assimilated. During the 'twenties and 'thirties of the present century a general lowering of social standards and public morality occurred, and these have been reflected in the literature of the time. It is then that writers claiming to be motivated by reforming zeal will be seen in many cases to have been indulging their public with salacious stories under the guise of exposing social evils. In the post-Riẓā Shah Period a renewal of hope is discernible in the production of literary works that have a more than ephemeral interest. The collapse of these short-lived hopes will also become apparent.

After the discussion of the above period, it has been considered essential to treat in some detail the writer whom we rank the highest among the modern authors of Persian literature. Ṣādiq Hidāyat was too complex a literary figure to be fitted in with his contemporaries, many of whom he profoundly influenced. In his work the tragedy of modern Iranian society and the weight of Iran's long history are hauntingly reflected.

If further justification than what has already been tentatively put forward were required for this study in English, perhaps it should be noted that studies of this subject in Russian have reached quite copious proportions, while in French a surprisingly large number of articles on modern Persian letters have been published by students of literature, by no means all of whom were primarily orientalists. It is hoped that the following pages will be of assistance to foreign students of Iran and will help to familiarize readers with modern trends in a great literary heritage.

Among scores of friends and university colleagues to whom goes my sincere gratitude for their invaluable assistance, my thanks are particularly due to Professor Reuben Levy, under whose guidance this study was first prepared as a Ph.D. thesis, and to Mr Peter Avery, lecturer in Persian at Cambridge University and author of *Modern Iran*, without whose help and encouragement the revision of the work in its present form would not have been possible.

HASSAN KAMSHAD

Tehran
July 1965

NOTE ON TRANSLITERATION

The system of transliteration used in this book is based on that approved by the International Oriental Congress of 1894, as follows:

الف	a	ر	r	ف	f
ب	b	ز	z	ق	q
پ	p	ژ	zh	ك	k
ت	t	س	s	گ	g
ث	th	ش	sh	ل	l
ج	j	ص	ṣ	م	m
چ	ch	ض	ẓ	ن	n
ح	ḥ	ط	ṭ	و	v
خ	kh	ظ	z̤	ه	h
د	d	ع	ʻ	ی	y
ذ	z̲	غ	gh	ء	ʼ

Vowels a, i, u lengthened ا ā, ی ī, و ū.

PART ONE

CHAPTER I

THE HISTORICAL BACKGROUND

THE Persian language, in its present form and as a written medium, was developed some two centuries after the advent of Islam and the Arab conquest of Persia in the first half of the seventh century A.D. The spoken language of the country before that time had been the dialects of *Pahlavi*, one of which was the official language of the Sasanian court and the Zoroastrian priesthood. Of the literature of the pre-Islamic period only scanty fragments are extant.

The "New Persian" that emerged after the Arab conquest has changed remarkably little since it became a great literary language in the ninth century. Poetry in particular has enjoyed continuity of more than a thousand years; this is also true of the spoken language. But prose literature has undergone many changes. In order to appreciate the trends in modern Persian prose, it is essential to look briefly at this background. Four different periods can be discerned in the long history of Persian prose before the modern phase:

(1) the Samanid period (A.D. 820–998), characterized by simple, straightforward, and laconic prose very close to the Persian spoken by an educated man today;

(2) the Ghaznavid, Seljuq, and Kharazmian period (A.D. 998–1220), when, despite the persistence of the former style, the increasing use of Arabic forms made the language highly decorative;

(3) the Mongol and Timurid period (A.D. 1220–1502), when the writing of history reached its height while prose literature in general declined; and

(4) the Safavid period (A.D. 1502–1796), when over-ornamented, arabicized ecclesiastical compositions prevailed.

The Samanid period (820–998)

The language of the people of Persia after the Arab conquest remained for some time the pre-Islamic dialects. But as the number of Persian converts to the new creed increased, Arabic, in which they had to perform their religious rites and conduct most official and commercial transactions, became more popular. And unlike *Pahlavi*'s complicated graphic system—to read and write it was a major feat—the legible, convenient Arabic characters lent themselves to literary and scientific deliberations. As a result, during the early Islamic period, Arabic predominated as the written medium, and no Persian prose work of any value written during this time is preserved.

A political and literary revival began almost simultaneously during the reign of the semi-independent dynasties: the Tahirids, Saffarids, and above all, the Samanids. The style of prose in this period is extremely simple, straightforward, and objective. No particular attention is paid to making phrases rhyme (*saj*ʿ), which, as we shall see, became popular in later centuries. Repetition of words and even of sentences was not regarded as a stylistic blemish. Sentences were short and precise and, except for official, scientific, and religious terms, contained as few words as possible.[1] On the whole, it appears that the authors' prime concern was to make themselves understood, and so they used words and expressions most familiar to their contemporaries.[2]

The Ghaznavid, Seljuq and Kharazmian period (998–1220)

This era, which covers roughly 200 years, is one of the most brilliant in Persian history for the number of poets, writers, and scientists it produced, as well as for the proliferation of their works. Thus the prose compositions of this age include some of the most important classical texts ever written in Persian.

In the development of style two distinct features can be detected. The first, the Samanid style described above, changed very little during the early part of the period, when the Ghaznavid court of Maḥmūd (998–1030) was consciously imitating the models

[1] See *Tārīkh-i Sīstān* ("The History of Sistan") (Tehran, 1314/1935), p. 209, for an interesting account of Yaʿqūb-i Layth Ṣaffārī's instruction that complimentary verses should not be addressed to him in a language he did not understand, i.e. Arabic.

[2] See E. G. Browne's elaborate article "Description of an Old Persian Commentary on the Kuran", published in the *Journal of the Royal Asiatic Society* (July 1894).

established by its Samanid predecessors. Persian was encouraged as the administrative language; scientific and *Sufi* writings of a religious and speculative nature were written in this language; literary and historical works established Persian as the seal of fine prose. Gradually, however, and doubtless assisted by Ghaznavid dependence on respectable ties with the Caliphate of Baghdad, Arabic began to reassert itself. Official correspondence reverted to Arabic. Baghdad scholars reached Khorasan and the Ghaznavid centres in north-eastern Iran bringing with them much new learning, which had originated in Greece and the Levant and was now preserved in Arabic after translation in the Baghdad schools. Thus authors began to come under the influence of Arabic diction and to use its copious terminology. Early simplicity of expression was so far lost that by the end of the first half of the twelfth century, the secretary of the Sultan Sanjar (1118–57), Muntaqib al-Dīn al-Juvaynī, in his *'Atabat al-Kataba* ("Threshold of the Clerks"), was advocating restraint in the quest for rhyming phrases and syllables.

Sentences grew in length with frequent parables, quotations, anecdotes, and elaborate narrations. Idiomatic phrases, proverbs, popular expressions of the time, and verse quotations were generously used; but there also appeared scores of newly coined Arabic-Persian words, which helped to make the language more flexible and resourceful.

Towards the end of this period, however, and compared with earlier as well as modern standards, Persian prose began to deteriorate. The habit of imitating the rhymed and cadenced style of Arab authors was taken up by the majority of writers, and the grace and spontaneity of Persian suffered. A laboured and highly artificial prose, full of word-play, symmetrical phrases, synonyms, enigmas, and even Arabic constructions, persisted right down to the middle of the eighteenth century. As the years passed, increased exaggerations reached the point of absurdity, and an almost incomprehensible style was the result.

Nevertheless, the Samanid and Arabic styles were to become the established form of prose literature in Persia, and authors down to the present time have usually chosen one or a mixture of the two for their compositions.

The Mongol and Timurid period (*1220–1502*)

The Mongol invasion brought terror and destruction to Persia, harming almost all branches of culture. Yet the literary heritage of the former period was so deeply rooted that for a considerable time many forms of twelfth-century prose survived; moreover the pagan Tartars' disregard for Islamic institutions, coupled with the overthrow of the Caliphate, reduced the influence of writers in Arabic, and this in itself proved an unexpected advantage to the Persian language. The extent of this release of the Persian language from the dominance of a culture fundamentally Arabic may be seen in the remarkably varied and, on the whole, successful experiments in prose literature that characterized this age. On the one hand there is a work like *Tārīkh-i Waṣṣāf* ("Wassaf's History"), full of tasteless bombast, vain epithets, exuberant rhetoric, and so much of the foreign element that "in many cases except for conjugations all the words are taken from Arabic". On the other hand the post-Islamic Persian prose in Sa'dī's *Gulistan* ("Flower-Garden") may be considered perfect in form and superb in its clarity of expression.

Because of the Mongol Ilkhans's keen interest in recording their campaigns and achievements, this period is notable for the number of historians it produced. The multitude, and the merit, of their books are summed up in the rather exaggerated words of M. T. Bahār: "In no other period has Persia or even the Islamic world achieved more in quantity or in quality in this craft [historical writing]."

The consequences of Mongol atrocities—their wholesale massacre of men of learning, the burning of libraries, destruction of mosques, etc.—began to appear towards the end of this period. Under the Timurids, when narrow-mindedness, lack of taste, and a sharp decline in public morality prevailed throughout the country, research and the scholarly traditions of the past were greatly neglected. Most of the prose works of this time are written in plain, artificial, and unvaried language, which has neither the ease, simplicity, and precision of the early writings nor the richness and elegance of later styles. Many delectable Persian words, idioms, and expressions are replaced by Mongol elements. The history books, for all their abundance, are often so full of lip service and flattery to patrons that it is difficult to separate truth from falsehood. Finally the scientific books of this period, except for a few written in a technical style during the Timurids' last years, are all in the traditionally stereotyped language of scientific works.

The Safavid period (1502–1796)

This period, though in many respects a great one, is notoriously poor in the field of literature, both in prose and poetry. The chief reason for this phenomenon, according to a remark attributed by Professor E. G. Browne to the late Mīrzā Muḥammad of Qazwin, is that the rulers of the Safavid dynasty "devoted the greater part of their energies to the propagation of the *Shī'ite* doctrine and the encouragement of divines learned in its principles and laws".

Persian prose during this period fell into unparalleled confusion. The religious tracts, which form the main body of Safavid literature, were either written for laymen in a plain and jejune style (none the less full of Arabic grammatical constructions), or else they were composed by *Shī'ite* doctors imported from Arabia, who had little knowledge of Persian and wrote in an arabicized style. In either case the works are usually pedantic and garrulous discourses, written merely to show off and achieve eminence as propaganda of piety. As such it is hard to regard them as Persian prose at all.

The court messages and correspondence, and the history books as well, are generally stilted. In them we notice blandishment, dissimulation, and many rhetorical devices that are devoid of sense and grace. Long and tedious sentences, with Mongol words encumbering almost every line; far-fetched metaphors, numerous synonyms, and tasteless artifices, often overladen with Arabic elements, are the characteristic ingredients of prose in this age.

After the fall of the Safavids, during the reign of Nādir Shah and the short-lived dynasty of Zand, no major improvement was made, and writers generally trod the same path as their Safavid predecessors. The degeneration of Persian prose during these troubled years is clearly displayed in a work like *Durra-yi Nādira* ("The Rare Pearl"), in which Mīrzā Mahdī Khān, the secretary of Nādir Shah, describes his military campaigns. In its excessively florid style, bombastic narration, redundant epithets, and far-fetched subtleties, this book stands unique in Persian prose.

Perhaps the only saving grace of Safavid prose was the publication of a number of story books, including four that were translated from Sanskrit and the Indian vernacular: *Razm-nāma* ("The Book of Battle"), *Ramayana*, *Mahabharata* and *Shukasaptati*. A Persian version of the latter, entitled *Ṭūṭī-nāma* ("The Book of Parrot"), had been made in 1330 by Ẓīyā'u-d-Dīn Nakhshabī. In 1793 Muḥammad Khudādād Qādirī produced in Persian a greatly abridged version of this work in a simple style, and an edition of Qādirī's abridgement, accompanied by an English translation on facing pages, was printed in London in 1801. These story books are written in a comparatively simple, smooth, and eloquent style, affording pleasant light reading. This "popular" literature can legitimately be regarded as one of the precursors of contemporary trends in Persian literature; some of the stories have been read and related generation after generation and are still quite popular in Persia. *Iskandar-nāma* ("The Story of Alexander"), *Rumūz-i Ḥamza* ("Secrets of Hamza"), *Ḥusayn-i Kurd* ("Husayn, the Kurd") and *Nūsh Āfarīn* are examples.

CHAPTER II

THE QAJARS AND REFORM (1796–1925)

WITH the Qajar dynasty's conquest of Persia, a new age began. Following the death of Karīm Khān the Zand in 1779, fifteen years of fratricidal war weakened the power he had succeeded in establishing over a large part of the former Safavid dominions. The last Zandid was Luṭf 'Alī Khān, the gallant prince defeated by Āqā Muḥammad the Qajar in 1794. But the Qajarid ruler did not officially become shah until enough of the country had been subdued for him to feel secure in the title. He was crowned in 1796. Tehran became the capital.

As with their Safavid predecessors, the new dynasty was of Turkish origin; and administrative institutions similar to those the Safavids had attempted to build up were revived. The power of the tribal nobility to influence affairs began to diminish; the men of humbler origins but broader education were able to reach the highest offices. A conscious effort was initiated to establish a strong central government. Contacts with the West were renewed. A revival began which was certain, sooner or later, to affect literature.

On the testimony of Sir John Malcolm, twice British envoy to Persia between 1800 and 1810, the first Qajar disliked rhetorical outpouring in state communications. In his *Sketches of Persia* (London, 1828), Malcolm describes how Āqā Muḥammad Shah, "who was remarkable for his hatred of ornament and show in every form, when his secretaries began with their flattering introductions, used to...exclaim, 'To the contents, you scoundrel'". What reform of official jargon Āqā Muḥammad Khān might have begun, however, was retarded by his successor, Fatḥ-'Alī Shah's interest in fine writing for its own sake, so that for another half-century, flowery expression continued to rule. Even as late as 1875 this was apparent, in Riẓā Qulī Khān Hidāyat's description of his 1851 embassy to Khiva on behalf of Nāṣiru'd-Dīn Shah (1848–96). But despite the bombast of this elderly savant's style, his minute topographical and social observation, recorded in an informative travelogue, do indicate a new spirit: a mental vitality reflected in a reform of literary style.

The main causes of this reform can be listed as follows:

(1) After the fall of the Afghans and the Nādir Shah, the collection of Safavid books plundered by the Afghans, together with the books brought from India by Nādir, found their way into the hands of the people. The publication and study of these texts left a strong impact on the minds of the new educated class arising in early Qajar times.

(2) After the victories of Āqā Muḥammad Khān and Fatḥ-'Alī Shah, and especially during the long reign of Nāṣiru'd-Dīn Shah, there was a period of peace and security, in marked contrast to the disturbed period following the Safavid decline. In this environment, interest in culture and learning developed to a considerable degree.

(3) The general policy of the Qajar rulers was to diminish the power of petty chiefs and landlords, in whose territory the Shah's writ had become almost imperceptible, and to establish a centralized government. In the course of time this policy led to a new civil service resulting in a class of professional people who earned their living as clerks and had leisure to cultivate letters.

(4) Most of the Qajar kings were patrons of art and letters who attracted many poets and writers to their court. And the religious leaders of the time, concerned about the ignorance of the masses, went out of their way to encourage the education and enlightenment of the people.

(5) From the beginning of the nineteenth century, political and commercial contacts were once again established with the European countries. With the interest of these powers in India and the rivalry among Britain, Russia, and France, European missions started to frequent the court of Fatḥ-'Alī Shah. In particular, the far-reaching plans of Napoleon Bonaparte brought Persia within the orbit of European politics. As Lord Curzon in his Introduction to an edition of *The Adventures of Hajji Baba of Ispahan* remarked: "The envoys of great Powers flocked to its [Persia's] court, and vied with each other in the magnificence of the display and the prodigality of the gifts with which they sought to attract the superb graces of its Sovereign, Fath Ali Shah."

(6) With the introduction of the telegraph into Persia in 1864 and its subsequent connection to the Indo-European lines, com-

munication between Persia and the outside world increased further. These and other contacts with Europe helped to promote the modernization of the country.

(7) Successive disastrous defeats by Russia and the conclusion of the obnoxious treaties of Gulestan (1813) and Turkamanchay (1828) also opened the eyes of Persian rulers to the weakness of their country as compared with the strength and modern equipment of powerful neighbouring states.

(8) To a lesser degree, the frequent journeys of the Qajar kings (Nāṣiru'd-Dīn Shah and Muẓaffaru'd-Dīn Shah) to Europe, though very costly for the country, were not without consequence, for they made these despotic rulers aware of their kingdom's backwardness and of the urgency of social reforms.

(9) Printing was introduced into Persia in 1812. Later a number of people were sent abroad to study lithography.

The fact that printing came into Persia relatively late deserves more attention than it has generally received, if only for its effect on literary style and on the attitude toward literary expression. In a country like Iran, where since the ninth century the art of calligraphy had been part of the practice of literature, the introduction of printing did more than simply increase the number of books available. Among the subtle changes it wrought was one in the nature of communication itself. For Persian penmanship and exquisitely decorated manuscripts with their numerous miniatures (government decrees were as carefully adorned as manuscripts of pure literature) had always accompanied an over-decorated and oblique style of communication. With lithography, the art of decorating the written word started to decline, and the movement began to make written communication simpler and more direct. Neither the printed book nor the concision required in telegraphic communication were the natural allies of a high degree of penmanship or of words chosen simply for their agreeable assonances or the beauties of rhyming prose. Books became less exquisite but more readable and more readily available. It was now the age of rapidly produced and widely disseminated pamphlets by reformists; of the reproduction of text-books and of translations of European works. All these factors, and not least the latter, played an important role in stirring the minds of progressive thinkers and bringing about the subsequent revolution.

(10) Also of great importance in the renaissance of Persia was the appearance of journalism. The first newspaper, published during the reign of Muḥammad Shah in 1253 (A.D. 1837), was a short-lived monthly publication in the form of a government bulletin, which bore the state emblem on its first page but had no particular title. The editor was Mīrzā Ṣāliḥ Shīrāzī, who had studied typography in England. Later, during the reign of Muẓaffaru'd-Dīn Shah, and under the direction of Mīrzā Taqī Khān, the *Amīr Kabīr*, a regular weekly called *Rūznāma-yi Vaqāyi'-i Ittifāqīyya* (1851) was published in Tehran. Prominent among the host of early newspapers and the one especially influential in promoting the revolution in Iran was Mīrzā Malkom Khān's *Qānūn*, which was published in London.[1]

(11) The establishment of new schools on European lines, and the teaching of science and other modern subjects marked other important phases in this development. Of particular importance was the foundation of a new state college, the *Dāru'l-Funūn*, at Tehran in 1851. Here, under the supervision of European teachers, a great number of celebrated political leaders of the forthcoming years were trained, and many technical and scientific books were either adapted or directly translated from European sources. Meanwhile for the first time a number of Persian students were sent abroad on government scholarships, bringing back with them Western ideas that undoubtedly had a substantial effect on the literary revival in Persia.

(12) The culmination of all these forces, and in itself the greatest influence on Persia's modernization, was the Constitutional Revolution (1905–9). Details of its impact on Iranian society and culture will be discussed in chapters V and VI.

[1] For the newspapers appearing on the eve of the constitutional uprising, see ch. IV, pp. 29–30.

CHAPTER III

REGENERATION OF PROSE

PERSIAN prose, as we noticed in the foregoing pages, had steadily deteriorated since Mongol times. But early in the nineteenth century, due to the influences cited above and in harmony with other developments, a great literary revival began. In prose literature the primary reforms took place in official correspondence, led by two of the greatest prime ministers Persia has ever produced: the *Qā'im Maqām* Farāhānī and the *Amīr Kabīr*. Later innovations came from two political and literary figures: Mīrzā Malkom Khān and 'Abdul-Raḥīm Ṭālibuff.

Qā'im Maqām Farāhānī

The *Qā'im Maqām* Farāhānī (1779–1835), distinguished minister of Muḥammad Shah Qajar, was a celebrated prose stylist.[1] He met his death upon the orders of the master he had faithfully served. The *Qā'im Maqām* not only introduced many reforms into the civil administration, but he was the first man to prune the florid style of the official correspondence. As his position in political and literary circles was an exalted one, his style soon set the fashion for the majority of his contemporaries. Compared with modern standards, however, his writings are not without superfluous ornament. In fact, as Dr Khānlarī points out: "Today, when we read the letters of Qā'im Maqām, words not required by the meaning will strike us. The reason is that a complete escape from accepted literary conventions was not possible so quickly."

The Amīr Kabīr

A greater and more progressive prime minister was Mīrzā Taqī Khān the *Amīr Kabīr*, who in 1852 met a tragic end similar to that

[1] The collection of the *Qā'im Maqām*'s poems and prose was first published in 1863 by Farhād Mīrzā. A second edition of his poems was brought out around 1930, edited by Vaḥīd Dastgirdī. For more information about his literary and political significance, see *Qā'im Maqām dar Jahān-i Adab va Sīyāsat* ("The Qa'im Maqam, the Politician and Writer") by B. Qā'immaqāmī.

of his master, the *Qā'im Maqām*. Trained by the latter, he carried on his work and managed to simplify the style of official correspondence still further. The illustrious though short career of this able vizier, with all his outstanding achievements, forms a notable chapter in the regeneration of Persia, and the influence of his direct, unornamented style, like many of his noble ideas and unfulfilled schemes, survived his untimely death. The mark of his style is apparent in the official correspondence of Nāṣiru'd-Dīn Shah's reign, in the works of the writers of the time, and even in the travel diaries of the king who had him put to death.

Mīrzā Malkom Khān

After these two distinguished ministers came the famous innovator Malkom Khān, who should be regarded as the real forerunner of modern Persian prose. He was born in Isfahan of Armenian parents in 1833 and in early childhood was sent to Europe for his studies. On his return to Persia he started teaching in the *Dāru'l-Funūn* and acted at the same time as interpreter to the European professors in that college. With his knowledge of Western civilization, Malkom Khān's first aim was to induce the Persian rulers to bring about necessary reforms in the country's administration. The pamphlet *Kitābcha-yi Ghaybī* ("The Oracular Notebook", 1275/1859), which he wrote shortly after his return from Europe, was in fact a guide to the rulers for the reformation of the state. In later years he formed a kind of "Freemasonry" society, consisting of students of the *Dāru'l-Funūn* and some discontented intellectuals of the time. He was eventually banished for his political views to Constantinople, where he got in touch with the circle of Persian reformers already in exile there. During his stay in that city he wrote several plays and a number of political and social tracts. Three of the plays, sketches of Persian life and institutions with social and political topics as their main theme, were published in 1340/1921–2 in Berlin: "Adventures of Ashraf Khān, the Governor of 'Arabistān", "Methods of Government of Zamān Khān of Burūjird", and "The Story of Shāh Qulī Mīrzā's Travel to Karbalā".[1]

[1] A French translation of these plays, called *Les Comédies de Malkom Khan*, by A. Bricteux, a Belgian Iranianist, appeared in Paris in 1933.

In 1871 he was recalled to Tehran, whereupon he presented the shah and the prime minister with a plan for the formation of a National Assembly. Meanwhile he was granted the title of the *Nāẓimu'l-Mulk* and was sent to England as Persian minister. But once again his critical views brought him into disfavour, and he was removed from office. He then started publishing his famous newspaper the *Qānūn* in London, which, though banned in Persia, found its way into the hands of progressive, educated Persians, who read it with zeal and enthusiasm. After the assassination of Nāṣiru'd-Dīn Shah, Malkom Khān was appointed Persian minister to Rome. He remained in this office until the end of his life. Though still alive when the Constitutional Revolution broke out, he was too old and ailing to come to the scene and take part in it. Yet his voice, calling for constitutional monarchy and individual rights, could be heard through the speeches of every constitutionalist, and the seed he had planted bore fruit in the laws and measures passed later by the first *Majlis*.

Malkom Khān was a prolific essayist, mostly on topical issues of political or social importance. His style was influenced more by European authors than by the classical prose stylists of Persia; argumentation was its essential trait, and this appealed to the younger generation as a new literary phenomenon. There are occasional grammatical mistakes and ideological inconsistencies, yet the ease and simplicity of style, coupled with the novelty of the contents, stirred the readers of his time. His writings were effective not only in arousing the constitutional movement but in setting the fashion for the younger writers who followed. After the victory of the Constitutionalist, a host of young, progressive authors, especially journalists, regarded his style as the model of effective writing.

Besides holding critical social and political views, Malkom Khān was an ardent advocate of reform in the Persian script, and he published several books and treatises in the alphabet he had invented. Another of his services to the Persian language was the new terms he employed in his writings. Often extremely accurate and expressive, they passed from his writings into the current language. Indeed, many of the terms used in civil service language today are either the same as or derived from the terms he first used in his newspaper and various tracts.

'Abdul-Raḥīm Ṭālibuff

The first writer to introduce Persians to modern science was 'Abdul-Raḥīm Najjārzāda, called "Ṭālibuff" (1855–1910), who later called himself "Ṭālibzāda", substituting the Persian suffix for the Russian. He was born in Tabriz but spent the greater part of his life in the Caucasus, where he set up business and studied literature and natural sciences. His books are generally written in a simple, readable style, covering a wide range of ethical and scientific subjects. His literary fame rests mainly on his last major work, *Masāliku'l-Muḥsinīn* ("The Ways of the Charitable", Cairo, 1905), regarded as one of the outstanding literary achievements of the period. Although an imaginary voyage in the realm of modern science, it takes the form of a close-knit story, full of vivid descriptions of the habits and manners of people from different walks of life. Among his other works were: *Pand-nāma-yi Mārkūs* ("Counsels of Marcus Aurelius") and *Hay'at-i Flamarion* ("The Astronomy of Flamarion")—both of which he translated from Russian—*Masā'ilu'l-Ḥayāt* ("Problems of Life"), *Nukhba-yi Sipihrī* ("The Select of the Universe"), *Sīyāsat-i Ṭālibī* ("Talibian Policy"), *Āzādī Cha Chīz Ast?* ("What is Freedom?"), and the two volumes of *Kitāb-i Aḥmad Yā Safīna-yi Ṭālibī* ("Ahmad's Book or the Talibian Vessel"). All achieved considerable popularity at the time. The latter is a kind of children's guidebook to modern science, in the form of a father's conversation with his son. In this, as well as in *Masā'ilu'l-Ḥayāt* and *Āzādī Cha Chīz Ast?*, which are to be regarded as a continuation of *Kitāb-i Aḥmad*, the author explains the laws of physics, chemistry, biology, and new inventions, the meaning of freedom, democracy, independence, and so on, all in everyday language, endeavouring to enlighten his readers and to intimate the need for social and educational reform in the country.

Ṭālibuff's writings were condemned by some of the religious leaders in Tabriz, who accused the author of atheism and forbade the reading of his works. Nevertheless, they had earned him so much respect and popularity in Iran that after the proclamation of the constitution, the people of Tabriz elected him, *in absentia*, as their deputy to the first *Majlis*. He accepted the honour, but because of old age and his past dissatisfactions he never went to Tehran.

CHAPTER IV

THE EVE OF REVOLT

"*Sīyāḥat-Nāma-yi Ibrāhīm Beg*"

ON the eve of the Constitutional Revolution, two books appeared in Persian that greatly influenced the coming events, the awakening of the people, and the literary revival. These were the *Sīyāḥat-Nāma-yi Ibrāhīm Beg* and the Persian version of James Morier's remarkable novel, *The Adventures of Hajji Baba of Ispahan.*

The *Sīyāḥat-Nāma*, or "The Travel Diary of Ibrahim Beg", was the first attempt to write a Persian novel on the European model. The book is in three volumes, and when the first volume was published anonymously in the years preceding the constitutional movement, it caused a great stir in Iran. Trying to prevent its distribution (for the book was venomously critical of prevailing conditions), the despotic government of the time fined anybody who was found reading it and arrested a number of people on the suspicion of their having written it. But these measures were of no avail. People became even more eager to read the book and continued reading it clandestinely. Publication in Iran being out of the question, each volume appeared in a different place abroad. The first is undated and appeared in Cairo; the second, written in 1325/1905, was published in Calcutta in 1907, and the third in Istanbul in 1327/1909. Dr Schulz's German version of the first volume was published in Leipzig in 1903, which gives some idea of the publication date of the original.

The Iranian public did not know who the author was until some years later when the third volume appeared and the name Ḥājj Zaynu'l-'Ābidīn of Maragheh, an Iranian merchant residing in Istanbul, was inscribed on the title page as the author. Included also in volume III was an autobiography of the writer, from which the following is taken:

Born in Maragheh in 1837 of Kurdish ancestry, Ḥājj Zaynu'l-'Ābidīn had as his forefathers the Khans of Sāvujbulāgh, who followed the *Shafī'ite* rites and later became *Shī'ites.* They were among the wealthy of Maragheh; or, as the writer himself puts it, because they had 5000 *Tumans* they were the Rothschilds of the district! He went to a *maktab* in childhood, but because of poor instruction and being bad at his studies he made little progress; at the age of sixteen he turned to commerce. Faced with bankruptcy, he and his brother travelled to the Caucasus. This trip was one of the turning points in his life. He became occupied with commerce there, and having made his fortune accepted the Iranian vice-consulship in Kutais. In this position he became the benefactor of the Iranian community, lent money to people, failed to recover his debts, and once more found himself penniless. He then went to the Crimea and opened a store in Yalta. Once again his fortunes prospered, and now he adopted Russian nationality. But, in his own words, in his heart of hearts he was not happy until, after fifteen years, he returned to his former nationality at the expense of giving up most of his property. He left Yalta and chose to live in Istanbul. He died in the year 1328/1910 when he was nearly sixty.

Though few people in Iran are familiar with the name of the author, his book is very well known. *Sīyāḥat-Nāma* is about a Tabrizi merchant's son born and brought up in Egypt. Having imbibed from his father an education in patriotism and a fanatical love of his country and its old civilization, Ibrāhīm Beg, in accordance with the terms of his father's will, sets out on a journey to Iran accompanied by his tutor. But contrary to his anticipation, he finds the place so often described by his father as "Paradise" full of wretchedness, poverty, and oppression. These he records in the pages of his travel diary with the wrathful indignation of a passionate and disappointed patriot, ruthlessly noting and commenting on every sign of rottenness in the state, every absurdity and injustice that came his way. He misses nothing: the arbitrary power and evil practices of the shah's entourage, viziers, and senior officials, who, with their high-flown titles, torture and extort money from the people; the backwardness of the country, seen in the total absence of law, justice, and order, in the appalling condition of schools and education in general, in the lack of health services, the habit of smoking opium, and the disruption of commerce; the hypocrisy and dissimulation of *mullahs* and religious leaders—all are bitterly criticized. Even the florid writings of the past and the Persian alphabet are not spared. In one interesting part of the book, when Ibrāhīm Beg interviews the ministers of war, of the interior and of foreign affairs, he discusses the functions of their respective departments, and this gives him a chance to enlighten the people on the real task and duties of these ministries. Constantly drawing comparisons between the prevailing conditions of the time and the past glories of Persia, he reminds his readers again and again of their outstanding historical figures, and the names of Shah 'Abbās, Nādir Shah, and Mīrzā Taqī Khān the *Amīr Kabīr* recur frequently.

Though conscious of his task ("The purpose in writing the *Sīyāḥat-Nāma* was to awaken people's minds"), and despite the reassuring success and popularity of the first volume, which adheres to his purpose, the author fails to remain consistent in the ensuing volumes. The second volume is devoted mostly to the fantastic illness of Ibrāhīm Beg (caused, we are told, by the terrible plight of Persia) and the tedious lamentations of his family. In the third volume the original theme becomes of secondary importance, and the book turns into a medley of poetry, wise sayings, and the maxims of Ḥaẓrat-i 'Alī, followed by a list of Persian saws and proverbs, fifty rules for kingship, extracts from the famous newspaper of the time, *Ḥablu'l-Matīn*, and finally a detailed chapter on Japan, her sudden rise to power and a speech made by the Mikado. Inclusion of this chapter shows how Iranians concerned with the awakening of their country in the nineteenth century were consciously comparing the processes that might, they thought, be achieved in Iran with those that were satisfactorily completed in Japan. As for the maxims of the prophet's son-in-law and the popular saws, both of these are very old devices in Persia for the dissemination of sage counsel in a manner as inoffensive as possible to suspicious censors.

Nevertheless, this diversion from the author's original theme is regrettable, especially when we remember that the third volume was published after the Constitutional Revolution, which could have furnished an ideal sphere in which to expand the main theme and even develop the flimsy plot. Indeed, the mediocrity of subject-matter in the last two volumes and the difference in style between the first volume and the other two have led many people to doubt whether they were all written by the same author; some have even declared that Mīrzā Mahdī Khān Tabrīzī, a writer on the newspaper *Akhtar* in Istanbul, wrote the first volume. Moreover, at times one encounters glaring mistakes in the book: for example, it says that the laws of European nations are derived entirely from those of Islam.

For all that, the book is written with the zeal of an ardent patriot whose sole passion is to see prosperity and advancement in his country. His patriotism is demonstrated, for instance, when he asserts that the use of Turkish as a spoken language in Azerbaijan (his own province) is artificial, and that Persian speakers who communicate with Azerbaijanis in Turkish are committing treason. Thus in his breathless impatience the author is often driven to the worst extremes, and this gives a sentimental, chauvinistic and sometimes ridiculous character to the book. One can easily notice that, although he has a fairly clear mind about the sickness, he is at a complete loss for the cure. Hence many of his ideas and suggestions, though they might have been new at that time in Persia, now seem time-worn and incoherent. What the writer has in ardour he lacks in logic and system.

Apart from the substance and tone, however, the style of the *Sīyāḥat-Nāma* is of immense importance. The author was one of the first Persians who dared to break away from the old traditional style of ornate composition and to write in the simple medium of the spoken word. His language is vivid and forceful, though not without occasional imperfections. It is suggested that the prose writings of Zaynu'l-'Ābidīn Marāgha-aī suffer in general from a Turkish influence, due to his long stay in that country. Yet compared with most writing of the time, the language of the *Sīyāḥat-Nāma* stands unique in its ease and fluency. The words of E. G. Browne—though no longer a valid description of Persian writers, since almost everyone now uses the spoken word as his vehicle of expression—are, two decades after the book's first appearance, still an indication of the novelty and importance of the *Sīyāḥat-Nāma*. He says:

> The travels [*Sīyāḥat-Nāma*] of Ibrāhīm Beg which . . . had an appreciable effect in precipitating the Persian Revolution of 1905–6 A.D. . . . is well and powerfully written in a simple yet forcible style, and I know of no better reading-book for the student who wishes to obtain a good knowledge of the current speech and a general, if somewhat lurid, idea of the country.[1]

[1] *Literary History of Persia*, IV, 467–8.

Whatever the shortcomings of his book, the author of *Sīyāḥat-Nāma-yi Ibrāhīm Beg* was one of the heralds of national unity in Iran; his book had considerable influence on subsequent events in the country, and he may justly be recognized as one of the founders of the Constitution.

Translation of "Hajji Baba of Ispahan"

The second notable work mentioned above is the translation of *The Adventures of Hajji Baba of Ispahan.* This picturesque and picaresque novel by James Justinian Morier has been a source of misapprehension and some speculation ever since it first appeared in England in 1824. This is mainly due to the dual character of the book. On the one hand the picture drawn by Morier is sometimes preposterously exaggerated, and therefore to regard Ḥājjī Bābā as a typical Persian is misleading. On the other hand the author displays such amazing knowledge and understanding of the private lives, customs, and practices of some sectors of Persian society that it is difficult to credit a foreigner with these meticulous observations. Hence the controversy about the book. Despite the author's denial in his introduction to *Hajji Baba in England* ("Here I beg to disclaim personality of any kind..."), was Ḥājjī Bābā a real person, namely, the historical Mīrzā Abu'l-Ḥasan, the Persian Envoy Extraordinary to Great Britain, who accompanied Morier on his journey to England and back to Persia? Or was he a fictitious hero (rascal seems to be a more appropriate term) created by the writer? Did James Morier write the book himself, or did some Persian friends help him? And so on. But such conjectures need not be pursued in the present work, where our main concern is with the Persian translation of the book.

Yet even when we address ourselves to the Persian text of *Hajji Baba*, we find that the realms of speculation and doubt are entered anew. Until recently it had generally been assumed that the translator was Ḥājjī Shaykh Aḥmad "Rūḥī" of Kerman, the staunch liberal opponent of Nāṣiru'd-Dīn Shah and all that constituted the political and spiritual establishment in Iran in his day. This Shaykh Aḥmad's life is briefly outlined in the Introduction to the first edition of the Persian translation, published in Calcutta in 1905 by Col. D. C. Phillott, who entertained no doubts that Shaykh

Aḥmad was the translator. Yet, such a claim, advanced on his behalf posthumously by his British editor, must now be discarded on the evidence Shaykh Aḥmad himself affords. For in a letter to the late Professor E. G. Browne in 1892,[1] Shaykh Aḥmad states unequivocally that Mīrzā Ḥabīb-i Iṣfahānī translated Morier's *Hajji Baba* "from the French" into Persian. Whether the reference to French is a slip of the pen is unclear. What is clear, as the translation of part of Shaykh Aḥmad's letter will show, is that the translator was not the Shaykh but his friend Mīrzā Ḥabīb of Isfahan. The significant portion of the letter, as rendered by Browne in his Introduction to the 1895 edition of the English version of *The Adventures of Hajji Baba of Ispahan*, is as follows:

That accomplised writer Mīrzā Habīb of Isfahan has translated the book of *Hajji Baba* from the French (*sic*) into Persian very literally, with especial regard to the preservation of those local and characteristic peculiarities and idioms which mark the speech of the common people of Isfahan and other Persian towns, thus giving, as it were, a living representation of the customs of the Persians. He wished to print it in Constantinople, but the Censor of the Press would not permit this. If you would like it, I will send a copy for you. If you could get it printed in London, it would find many purchasers and readers in Persia, and Mīrzā Habīb would make over all his rights to you, and be perfectly satisfied if he could secure the publication of the book.

According to Browne's statement in the same Introduction (in which, incidentally, he praises *Hajji Baba* more extravagantly than in a subsequent reference to this work, in volume IV of his *Literary History of Persia*), Mīrzā Ḥabīb died soon after Shaykh Aḥmad's letter had been dispatched. It appears that Mīrzā Ḥabīb left the manuscript of the Persian *Hajji Baba* with Shaykh Aḥmad, who was killed in 1896, four years after he had informed Browne of the existence of a Persian translation of this book—a piece of information upon which Browne seems never to have acted. Evidence suggests that the action was left to another: Col. D. C. Phillott. For when Shaykh Aḥmad, after being extradited from Turkey, was treacherously murdered at Tabriz on crossing the Persian-Turkish frontier, his papers (presumably including Mīrzā Ḥabīb's Persian version of Morier's book) were delivered to his family in the city of Kerman. Phillott happened to be British Consul in

[1] Browne MS. F 53^2, University Library, Cambridge (see plate).

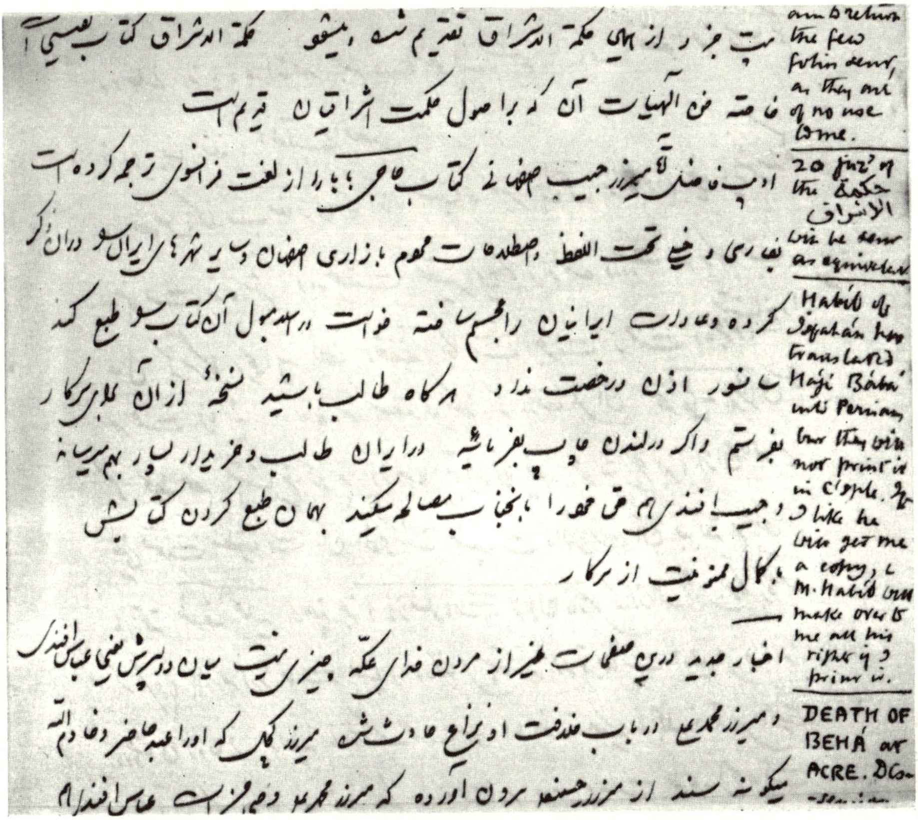

Facsimile of part of Shaykh Aḥmad's letter to E. G. Browne.
(For translation see opposite.)

Kerman at the time and came across the original MS.: "The present edition", writes Phillott in his Introduction to the first edition, "is printed from a MS. copied from, and again collated with, the original MS. that the translator [meaning Shaykh Aḥmad] sent to his native town, and is published with the permission of his heirs." We can therefore assume that the colonel took it for granted, though erroneously, that Shaykh Aḥmad was the translator. Oddly enough, Phillott does seem to have got the notion that the late Mīrzā Ḥabīb had something to do with this translation, for in his Introduction he avers that Shaykh Aḥmad while in Constantinople translated several French and English works (including *Hajji Baba*), "assisted by Mīrzā Ḥabīb, a poet from Ispahan".

In any case, Phillott accepted Shaykh Aḥmad as the translator: he even published his photograph as the frontispiece to the first, second, and third editions, all printed in Calcutta. He dates the Preface to the second edition (1923) from Cambridge, where he must have met Browne. Had Browne forgotten the letter from Shaykh Aḥmad? Or, having regard for Phillott's assertions in the Introduction to the first edition (dated 1905), did he with his customary tact and generosity decide not to correct the colonel's mistake about the real translator? In his fourth volume of *The Literary History of Persia* (published in 1924), Browne, in a cursory reference to the Persian version of *Hajji Baba*, states that the translator was Shaykh Aḥmad; yet he also refers the reader to his Introduction to the 1895 English edition where he had cited the real translator! Perhaps Browne, now old and in poor health, had forgotten Shaykh Aḥmad's plea on behalf of his friend's translation, in a letter received by Browne thirty-two years earlier.

Our knowledge of the life and career of Mīrzā Ḥabīb, the hitherto unrecognized translator of *Hajji Baba*, is very little. Born in a small village in the Chahār Muḥāl of Isfahan, he received his early education in that city, and later in Baghdad, where he studied literature and theology for four years. We know from incidental remarks by his contemporaries that he was a very erudite and accomplished scholar. He was best known as a poet, however, and had chosen "Dastān" as his *Takhallus̤* (*nom de guerre*). He was also the author of some prose works, the most notable of which is *Barg-i Sabz* ("The Green Leaf") published posthumously in Tabriz in 1900; and he edited several rare Persian texts, such as the poems of Bushāk and Maḥmūd Kārī. Among his other literary achievements were a number of treatises written on Persian grammar and caligraphy: *Dastūr-i Sukhan* ("The Rule of Speech", Istanbul, 1869), *Dabistān-i Pārsī* ("Persian School", Istanbul, 1890), *Rāhnamā-yi Fārsī* ("Guide to Persian", Istanbul, 1891) and *Khaṭṭ u Khaṭṭāṭān* ("Calligraphy and Calligraphers", Istanbul, 1888) (the last was written in Turkish). Finally, he translated Molière's *Le Misanthrope*, which he published in 1869 under the title of *Mardum Gurīz*, and a book called *Gharāyib-i 'Avāyid-i Milal* (1885) (literarally translated it means: "The Marvels of the Nations' Income") the author of which is not named. We also know that Mīrzā Ḥabīb was a resolute advocate of democracy and liberalism, that he bitterly opposed the despotic rule of the time in Iran, and that he had strong feelings against the religious hierarchy. Because of his views he was accused of atheism and had to flee in 1860 to Turkey, where he stayed, in horror and despair, earning his living as a teacher, until the end of his life in 1897.

That Mīrzā Ḥabīb-i Iṣfahānī was critical of Iran's religious and political establishments, the two most deep-rooted and powerful institutions of the time, greatly influenced his rendering of Morier's work into Persian. The original *Hajji Baba*, despite all its fame and brilliance, is a one-sided, prejudiced, and exaggerated picture of only certain aspects (and those the worst) of Persian life; and the Persian version, because of the translator's religious and political bias, is even more so.

To begin with, the Persian version is a very loose rendering of the original. The translator has shown no scruples in altering or supplementing the story whenever fancy takes him, or rather, as is mostly the case, whenever the change suits his purposes. Thus, compared with the English text, the Persian reveals many minor alterations on almost every page; there are times when a whole passage is added or omitted on the translator's own initiative; indeed, there are occasions when several pages are left out.[1] For example, chapter XXXVII, "The History of Yusuf, the Armenian, and his wife Marian", occupies thirty-four pages (pp. 249–82) of the original English. In the Persian text the story is shortened to five pages (pp. 215–19). The reason, one is given to understand, is

[1] The Persian version referred to here and in the forthcoming pages is D. C. Phillott's edition (Calcutta, 1905).

that this chapter is devoted mainly to Armenian customs and marriage ceremonies, which, since it can hardly provide any social impetus to Persian readers, serves little purpose for the translator.[1] A few random examples will further illustrate this point.

In his Introductory Epistle, Morier names or alludes to some Europeans who adopted the Mohammedan faith; the translator skips them. But wherever the original refers to Persian officials by their ranks, such as the prime vizier, minister of the interior, secretary of state, lord treasurer, etc., the translation gives actual names or titles, since it is mostly the folly and iniquities of these people that are displayed. Thus we read the *I'timādu'd-dawla*, the *Dabīru'l-mulk*, the *Mustawfīu'l-Mamālik*, and, in the case of the lord treasurer, first the *Amīnu'l-dawla* Ṣadr-i Iṣfahānī, and in later chapters the *Mu'ayyiru'l-mulk*.[2]

When describing the lives and practices of the clergy, the Persian version is almost always amplified, and the picture of the hypocrisies of this group is more lurid than in the original. With his own contributions the translator often intensifies the implications of the book's criticisms.[3] There are times when he becomes more Catholic than the pope; and if Morier happens to have a good word for the Persians, the translator reverses the whole meaning. Speaking of the political demands of the British ambassador, for instance, Morier writes:

> The latter [ambassador] was very urgent that some demands of a political nature might be conceded to him, which the vizier, out of consideration for the interests of Persia, was obliged to deny (p. 117).

In the Persian rendering of this sentence we read (p. 117):[4]

«ایلچی در رواج تجارت و گشودن مدارس و مکاتب در ایران اصرارد اشت
ومعتمد الدوله میگفت که این کارها مصلحت دولت نیست»

Translated back into English this would literally read:

> The ambassador was insistent on the flow of commerce and the opening of schools and *maktabs* [old-fashioned primary schools], but the *Mu'tamidu'd-Dawla* stated that "these deeds were not in the interest of the Government".

[1] Cf. also chapter XXVI and the end of the Introductory Epistle.

[2] Cf. pp. 47 and 99.

[3] Cf., for example, pp. 3–4, 90, 101, 119, 120, 140 and 141 of the Persian with the English.

[4] See also pp. 331 and 453.

The translator also tends to alter figures, sometimes for no obvious reason (see pp. 1, 19), and sometimes for the sake of assonance (see pp. 92, 216).

The English version of *Hajji Baba*, apart from its many other attributes, is a humorous satire. In this respect the translator has certainly excelled the author. In his description of court manners, his exposure of *mullahs*, dervishes, and so on, and with his own additions, the translator has in fact made the Persian text much more subtle and funny than the original.[1] Another great distinction of the Persian edition is the wealth of well-known and proverbial poems that are fitted into appropriate places. This, together with a multitude of popular, everyday sayings and the frequent verses quoted from the Koran and the Traditions, indicates the translator's mastery of Persia's literature, life, and language, as well as his knowledge of Islamic institutions.

But at times his literary flair gives a sudden impulse to a flow of words, so that he literally puts the original aside and, after the fashion of old Persian prose stylists, indulges in some flamboyant descriptions. Thus the original sentence "The caravan was ready to depart a week after the festival of the New Year's day" (p. 13) prompts the translator to produce about ten lines of "fine writing" on the arrival of spring (p. 11). This kind of change happens on several other occasions. For instance, on page 29 the translator suddenly embarks on a flood of decorative words, so irrelevant and recondite that, in the words of Phillott, he "loses himself in the intricacy of his own sentences". The editor advises the reader to skip the whole passage. Moreover, numerous minor faults and inaccuracies show the translator's inability to understand certain foreign words and expressions. On the other hand, there are as many instances where he has corrected the errors and completed omissions of the original.[2]

But if we forget such technical details and take the Persian *Hajji Baba* at its face value, then a new vista opens to us. Socially and politically the book had an immense influence on the awakening of the people and on bringing forth the Revolution. And from the literary point of view it was one of the most successful experiments

[1] Cf., for example, pp. 32, 42, 77, 79, 213 and 325 of the Persian with the English text.

[2] Cf., for example, pp. 3–4, 67, 86, 89, 148 and 150 of the Persian with the English text.

in the new trend of prose writing: its style is still followed by modern Persian writers, and it is acclaimed as one of the best compositions of the present century. "The writer who had the power of creating the images of the Persian *Hajji Baba*", remarked M. T. Bahār, "is one of the most powerful, precise and realistic writers of this age." Bahār continues with the assertion that for fluency, conciseness, and maturity of expression, this work in places equals even the *Gulistān*. In its realism and effect on the reader he likens it to European compositions. He praises it for simplicity, but at the same time points out its great artistic techniques. It conforms, he says, to the best stylistic canons of Persian prose, while also reflecting the new schools of writing.[1]

Finally, there are the excellent footnotes added by the editor to the Persian translation. These, apart from a few instances where he fails to apprehend the correct meaning of an expression,[2] are accurate and tremendously helpful to students who want to learn modern and colloquial Persian.

Early Translations

Besides Mīrzā Ḥabīb's *Hajji Baba*, other popular translations appeared before the Constitution and played a significant part in the literary movement of the period.

Translation from European languages had started as early as the introduction of the printing press. But the first translations, mostly text-books on history, geography and science for use in the *Dāru'l-Funūn*, had little or no literary value. Translation of novels and drama began in later years, and their novel contents, attractive form, and expressive language so enchanted readers that for many years they remained one of the main sources of family diversion throughout Persia.

Among the first story books was Mīrzā 'Abdul-Laṭīf Tasūjī Tabrīzī's translation of *Thousand and One Nights*, the famous Arabic collection of what were originally Persian tales. The Persian prose of the translation, with its forceful, sober, yet gracious tone, left a deep impress on the writings of subsequent years.

In 1288/1871 Mīrzā Ja'far Qarāchadāghī translated from

[1] *Sabk Shināsī* ("Study of Literary Styles"), III (Tehran, 1958), 366.
[2] See, for example, footnotes to pp. 289, 324 and 382.

Azerbaijani Turkish several plays written by Mīrzā Fatḥ-'Alī Ākhūnduff. Five of these were published in a collection three years later. In an interesting introduction to these plays, the translator points out the educational value of the theatre, explains the reason for the simple, colloquial language he has used (so that "both the literate and illiterate, by means of reading and hearing, may benefit from the lessons exemplified in the plays"), and instructs the players to pronounce the words as they are spoken. In 1890 A. Rogers translated three of these plays into English, printed face to face with the Persian and accompanied by an excellent glossary. With the publication of these plays, not only was a new literary *genre* presented to Persian writers, but the use of spoken words in literary works was encouraged. For the first time the problem of whether and how to represent direct speech (as it is heard) was posed before Persian authors.

Another early translator was Prince Muḥammad Ṭāhir, the grandson of 'Abbās Mīrzā, who upon the orders of Nāṣiru'd-Dīn Shah, translated some of Alexandre Dumas's novels, such as *Le Comte de Monte-Cristo*, *Les Trois Mousquetaires*, *La Reine Margot*, *Louis XIV* and *Louis XV*. The intricate tales and excitements of this new literature were so fascinating to the people that families used to gather to hear them read aloud.

Because the first groups of Persian students sent abroad on government scholarships went to France, the influence of French culture and literature was dominant during the late nineteenth century, and the majority of translations were made from that language. Some of the more well known of these were: three translations by the *Z̲ukā'ul-Mulk* (Furūghī), namely, Jules Verne's *La Tour du monde en* 80 *jours*, Bernardin de Saint-Pierre's *La Chaumière Indienne*, and Chateaubriand's *Les Aventures du Abencerage*,[1] Le Sage's *Gil Blas*, translated by Muḥammad Kirmānshāhī, Bernardin de Saint-Pierre's *Paul et virginie*, translated by Ibrāhīm Nishāṭ and Molière's *Le Médecin malgré lui* by 'Alī Muqadam, the *I'timādu's-Salṭana*. A number of Jurjī Zaydān's historical novels translated by 'Abdu'l-Ḥusayn Mīrzā Qājār also affected current literary taste and compositions.

[1] The Persian version of the last is entitled *'Ishq u 'Ifat.*

Early Newspapers

A detailed study of the history, importance, and role of the Persian press, would merit a separate volume. Yet a number of papers published on the eve of the Constitutional rising had such a powerful influence on the formation of ideas, the training of new writers, and generation of modern prose that it would be unjust not to refer to them briefly.

Before the Constitutional Movement began in 1905, very few papers had appeared in Persia. Those that had contained scarcely anything of political interest, their slender copies consisting mainly of poetry and literary articles. This was because the despotic régime of the time prohibited criticism of the government. Thus those papers that were involved in the political struggle and represented different approaches to the problems of reform, and likewise most of the books discussed above, were published abroad.

Prominent among the papers published inside the country was the *Tarbīyat* (1896–1906), edited by a man already mentioned, Muḥammad Ḥusayn (Furūghī), known as the *Z̲ukā'ul-Mulk.* As one would expect, this paper had little political weight; in fact it carried the banner of the despotic rule. As literature, however, it had a special significance, for the editor was a distinguished writer and poet; his compositions, together with many interesting biographies, scientific treatises and, in particular, a series of translations that appeared as *feuilletons* (*pāvaraqī*), made the *Tarbīyat* one of the literary precentors of the time.

But it was the papers edited abroad, and belonging definitely to the Opposition, that introduced the most startling new literary forms and exerted real ideological influence on the general public in Persia. These were generally prohibited in the country, but because of the people's eagerness to obtain them, they reached readers clandestinely. Of these papers, five are particularly worthy of mention. First there was the *Akhtar*, which appeared weekly in Constantinople from 1875 to 1897; and though it had a relatively mild tone, it served as a rallying point for the many patriotic Persians in exile. The *Qānūn* appeared monthly in London from 1890 to 1893 and was edited by Mīrzā Malkom Khān. In the political awakening and establishment of new styles of writing, this paper was of considerable significance among pre-constitutional journals. The *Ḥablu'l-Matīn* appeared weekly in Calcutta beginning in 1893. It was one of the most regular papers of the time and gained substantial support among the religious circles. With its consistent exposure of political and social evils, it influenced the course of many political events, performing signal service in the cause of the people. In addition, its press was used for the publication of a number of useful books and publications less ephemeral than a weekly paper. Finally, the *Thurayyā* (1899–1900) and the *Parvarish* (1900–1) were two papers written by Mīrzā 'Alī Muḥammad Khān Shaybānī and published in Cairo. Though short-lived, they achieved a wide fame and popularity: both "effected a great intellectual revolution amongst young Persians, stirring up public opinion and filling the creatures of the Court with consternation".[1]

These, as well as some other papers of lesser importance, did more than arouse the political consciousness that led to the Constitutional Revolution. Perhaps more than any other factor, they influenced and directed the foundation of a literary movement that has since developed into a distinctly modern Persian prose literature.

[1] E. G. Browne, *The Press and Poetry of Modern Persia* (Cambridge, 1914), p. 23.

CHAPTER V

CONSTITUTIONAL REVOLUTION

PERHAPS in no other country has the development of literature been so closely associated with social and political fluctuations as in Persia during the present century. As has already been indicated, this alliance between literary and political expression was implicit from the start of the modern literary movement at the turn of the century. The history of the country in the past sixty years may be divided into three major political phases, each of which has produced a literature strikingly in accord with its nature:

(1) the period of revolution and post-revolution until the *coup d'état* of Riẓā Khān (1905–21);

(2) the period of Riẓā Shah's reign (1921–41); and

(3) the period from Riẓā Shah's abdication down to the present (1941–65).

To understand and evaluate the literary trends of each of these periods, some knowledge of social and political conditions is essential. We shall therefore try to preface each of the forthcoming chapters with a general consideration of the main events of the period.

Increased contact with the West, accompanied by a quickening tempo of modernization, the political awakening of the people, and the propagation of a need for change in the country's political and legal life: these have been briefly described as the forces behind the Constitutional Movement (1905–11) and the period up to the *coup d'état* of 1921. By the beginning of the nineteenth century, the various ill-advised concessions to foreigners, the frequent loans and mortgages from Russia, and a general deterioration of internal affairs had increased the public lack of confidence in the régime. The first open conflict between the people and the government took place after the granting of the notorious Tobacco Concession, which resulted in the riots of 1891. The victory of the nationalists, supported vigorously by religious leaders, encouraged them to seek further reforms.

In addition to these factors, the first Russian Revolution of 1905 affected developments in Iran, for it caused agitation among the masses in the Caucasus region. Besides being close neighbours, these people were consanguineous with and co-religionists of the Persians. Consequently, any political movement among them was bound to have repercussions in Iran. Publications from Baku, notably the illustrated satirical journal *Mullā Naṣru'd-Dīn*, in which the reactionary aspects of Islamic society were held up to ridicule, also contributed to the political and social awakening of the Persian people. Finally, the Caucasian revolutionaries sent emissaries into Iran who took an active part in political developments there, particularly in the northern provinces.[1]

The Constitutional Revolution began with a meek request for the convocation of a "House of Justice" or *'Idālat-khāna*. But as the movement gained momentum, the people increased their demands, asking for a regular constitution and representative National Assembly (*Majlis-i Millī*). The despotic yet weak and inept ruler, Muẓaffaru'd-Dīn Shah, soon gave way: a constitution was granted, the rule of law was declared, and the first *Majlis* opened in 1906.

The nation-wide celebration of this epochal occasion was hardly over before the ominous Anglo-Russian Agreement of 1907 was signed, dividing the country into three "spheres of influence": a Russian zone in the north, a British zone in the south, and a neutral zone in the middle. Encouraged by foreign intervention, the new Shah (Muḥammad 'Alī Shah, crowned on 19 January 1907) attempted to re-establish the old autocratic régime in 1908; aided by his cossacks and their Russian officers, he bombarded the building in which the newborn Parliament held its meetings. Despotism once again triumphant, the rule of law was suspended, the free press suppressed, the popular leaders slain, kept in chains, put to flight, or forced to take refuge in the foreign legations in Tehran.

The people, however, having tasted of liberty, were no longer prepared to tolerate the old rule. They took up arms and rallied gallantly to the Constitutional cause. The city of Tabriz sustained a

[1] See the pamphlet *Les Socialistes démocrates Caucasiens et la Revolution Persane*, published in Paris in 1910 and republished in a Soviet work in 1925 in Moscow. See also B. Nikitine, "Le roman historique dans la littérature persane actuelle", in *Journal Asiatique*, CCXXIII (Oct., Dec. 1933).

siege of nine months; two separate forces gathered in Resht and Isfahan, and disturbances began to occur in almost all parts of the country. The struggle lasted long, with the sacrifice of many lives, but at last the Constitutionalists won. Their combined forces from south and north marched on Tehran, and the shah was deposed. The *Majlis* re-opened in 1909.

Rid of their incubus, it seemed as though the Persians were at last left free to live in peace and devote their time to the task of restoring order to their disturbed country. But the following four years witnessed a series of troubles caused on the one hand by partisans of the ex-shah, and on the other by the interference of Russia and Britain in the internal affairs of the country. The history of Persia during these stormy years consists of recurrent rebellions among tribesmen, and revolts led by princes and ex-ministers; of raids by brigands, the massacre of villages, hostile demonstrations, local brawls, and political assassinations, famine, lootings, and intrigues against the government.

Coupled with these internal difficulties was the arrival of fresh detachments of Russian troops—first sent on the pretext of raising the siege of Tabriz—who were being sent into northern Persia where their actions were becoming increasingly aggressive. Besides the Russian, there were Turkish troops concentrated on the Persian frontiers in the north-west, while in the south, on the British Government's instructions, small parties of Indian troops had been landed. These moves were followed by a series of ultimatums sent to the Persian government by Russia and Britain tabling various demands. The *Majlis* stood firm, however, and rejected concessions to foreigners, so that, as *The Times* put it, Russia came to regard "the existence of the Majlis as incompatible with her interests". Consequently, fighting broke out between Russian troops and Persians in various parts of the northern districts. Tabriz was heavily bombarded, and the Russians began a series of aggressions indignantly described by E. G. Browne in his *The Press and Poetry of Modern Persia*:

...executions of leading citizens and patriots by publicly hanging [them] on a gallows gaily decorated with the Russian colours....In most cases the houses of the victims were blown up with dynamite. ...The unprovoked bombardment and plunder by the Russians of the sacred shrine of the Imām Rizā at Mashhad on March 29th,

1912, on which occasion many innocent people, both inhabitants and pilgrims, were killed, was the culmination of these horrors, and produced an indescribably painful impression throughout the Muslim World.

Under foreign pressure the second *Majlis* was also forcibly dissolved in 1911. During the two following years of interregnum, "Persian cabinet ministers", according to Browne, were hardly "able to hold office, much less act, without the sanction of the Russian and British Legations". These political tribulations were aggravated by an outbreak of plague in 1913 and then by the First World War, in which Persia, though neutral, suffered greatly. The belligerent powers ignored the country's national sovereignty, and the already weakened authority of the central government broke down completely; large parts of Persia slipped almost entirely out of the government's feeble control, and conditions akin to anarchy prevailed.

The Russian Revolution of 1917 brought a relaxation of Russian pressure. Indeed, the treaties concluded under the tzars to regulate Russo-Persian relations were cancelled, their nature exposed and condemned by the Bolsheviks as a gesture of goodwill towards the Persian people. But this change in attitude did nothing to alleviate the actual conditions in Persia, which were being exacerbated by the revolutionary and counter-revolutionary movements in the Caucasus and on the shores of the Caspian; by the fact that Persia was for a time the corridor through which a British force to aid counter-revolutionaries in Russia had to pass; and, finally, by Persia's inclusion in those nations the Bolsheviks decided should be drawn into the vortex of revolution. Another irritant was the view held by some British observers that after the war and the defeat of Germany, and with the new policy of the Soviet Government, Britain was left without a rival in Persia. An attempt was made to urge the Iranian Government to accept the Anglo-Persian Agreement of 1919. Under this Agreement, had it been ratified by the *Majlis*, Persia's position would have resembled that of a mandated territory under British tutelage. This—it was argued by some in Great Britain and even supported by a few in Persia—would benefit Persia by providing an opportunity for organized fiscal reform, adequate social services, and the security that by 1920 was almost totally lacking. However, those who thought thus reckoned without the Persians' national sentiments and their tenacious desire to keep their independence at all costs.

In 1920, uprisings in Gilan and Tabriz brought the country to the verge of a civil war. Confusion and social collapse finally culminated in the *coup d'état* of 1921 by which the reign of Riẓā Shah was inaugurated.

Literature of Revolt

The literature of these years has been aptly described, by the *Times Literary Supplement* of 5 August 1955, as a "literature of revolt". The article states:

> Ever since the end of the 19th century, under the stimulus of European precedent, the autocracy has been the object of attack from men who felt that it deprived the people of the privileges of democracy, there has been bitter criticism of the system which permits the existing cleavage between the conditions of the rich and the poor, and grave charges of corruption and incompetence have been levelled against the bureaucracy. This literature of revolt is much to the liking of educated men in Persia, not only because it is regarded as a means of getting wrongs redressed, but also because it uses a new idiom and has the refreshing flavour of living actuality.

The literature of revolt during 1905–21 appeared predominantly in the form of poetry and journalistic essays. The years succeeding the Revolution were remarkable for an extraordinary boom in journalism: for example, in 1907, the year immediately following the granting of the constitution, no less than eighty-four newspapers were founded in Persia. Almost all these papers, whether moderate, liberal, or revolutionary in their political leanings, were anxious to open the eyes of their compatriots both to the evils of the former autocratic government and the advantages of a constitutional democracy. In this way they tried to ensure the safeguarding of the new régime.

The crux of the new situation, in the words of Professor A. K. S. Lambton, was that:

> When Persia adopted constitutional parliamentary government in 1906 she passed from the medieval Islamic theory of government to a modern system based on western theory without any of the intervening developments and understandings, or any of the checks and counter-

checks, which evolved in the West during the gradual transition through feudalism to our modern conception of parliamentary government.[1]

The leading figures of the movement were conscious of this impediment. Yet in their desire for reform and progress, they were hoping to set the people astir and rally them to the constitutional cause.

The Press and Poets

Their weapons for achieving this aim were the press, which had gained its freedom through the declaration of the constitution, and the medium of poetry, which was traditionally the most effective means of arousing the populace. This combination was so strong that most of the prominent poets of the time chose journalism as their career.[2] The names of the *Adību'l-Mamālik* Farāhānī (1860–1917), Mīrzāda 'Ishqī (1893–1924), Īraj Mīrzā, the *Jalālu'l-Mulk* (1874–1925), Adīb Pīshāvarī (1842–1931), 'Ārif Qazvīnī (1883–1934), Muḥammad Taqī Bahār, the *Maliku'sh-Shu'arā* (1886–1951) and Abu'l-Qāsim Lāhūtī (1887–1957), who all flourished during this period, indicate the literary taste of the time. In the early stages of the period the leading newspapers published almost daily poems on internal and external politics. To such an extent was this done that some of the papers have rightly been termed "a versified chronicle of the main political events" of those days.

It is not our intention, however, to discuss here either the press or poetry; for besides being beyond the limits of the present work, they have fortunately—unlike most aspects of modern Persian literature—been amply studied. To name all the books and treatises on these subjects would form an exhaustive list; many of them, being simply anthologies, carry little weight. Some of the more famous studies are E. G. Browne's *The Press and Poetry of Modern Persia* (Cambridge, 1914) and *Persian Press and Persian Journalism* (Persian Society lecture) (London, 1913); M. Ishāque's *Sukhanvarān-i Īrān dar 'Aṣr-i Ḥāẓir* ("Poets and Poetry of

[1] "The Impact of the West on Persia", p. 15, reprinted from *International Affairs*, XXXIII, no. 1 (Jan. 1957).

[2] E.g. the *Nasīm-i Shamāl* was edited by Sayyid-Ashraf; the *Naw-Bahār* by M. T. Bahār the *Maliku'sh-Shu'arā*; the *Bīsutūn* and *Pārs* by Lāhūtī; the *Nāma-yi 'Ishqī* and *Qarn-i Bīstum* by Mīrzāda 'Ishqī; and in the later years the *Ṭūfān* by Farrukhī Yazdī.

Modern Persia") (2 vols., Delhi, 1933–7) and *Modern Persian Poetry* (Calcutta, 1943); Rashīd Yāsamī, *Adabīyāt-i Mu'āṣir* ("Contemporary Literature") (Tehran, 1937); Dīnshāh J. Irānī, *Poets of the Pahlavi Regime* (Bombay, 1933); *Nukhustīn Kungra-yi Nivīsandigān-i Īrān* ("The First Congress of the Iranian Writers") (Tehran, 1947); a special edition of *Life and Letters* on Persian writers (London, December 1949), and M. Ṣadr Hāshimī, *Tārīkh-i Jarāyid Va Majalāt-i Īrān* ("A History of Press and Periodicals in Iran") (4 vols., Isfahan, 1948–53).

'Alī Akbar Dihkhudā

As an exception, special mention should be made of a series of satirical articles entitled *Charand Parand* ("Balderdash"), which appeared in a newspaper of the time, the *Ṣūr-i Isrāfīl,* and were written by 'Alī Akbar Dihkhudā (1879–1956), who signed himself *Dakhaw.* Dihkhudā, son of a prominent landowner from Qazwin, was born and educated in Tehran. After graduating from the School of Law and Political Sciences he travelled to Europe, where he studied French and spent about two years, mostly in Vienna. He returned to Iran at the outset of the Constitutional Movement and collaborated with Mīrza Jahāngīr Khān and Mīrzā Qāsim of Shiraz in publishing the *Ṣūr-i Isrāfīl,* which became one of the most influential newspapers of the time.

After Muḥammad 'Alī Shah closed the *Majlis,* Dihkhudā and a host of other Iranian democrats were exiled to Europe. In Switzerland, Dihkhudā tried to resume publication of the *Ṣūr-i Isrāfīl* but succeeded in bringing out only three issues at Iverdon. He then travelled to Istanbul and, with the help of a number of Iranian nationals residing there, published a new periodical called the *Surūsh,* of which fifteen issues came out. After the downfall of Muḥammad 'Alī Shah, Dihkhudā was elected to the *Majlis* from two constituencies, Tehran and Kerman, and upon persistent requests of the liberals and constitutionalists he returned to Iran and took his seat in the National Assembly. After the First World War, Dihkhudā held several important positions in government and public administration, including that of dean of the School of Law and Political Sciences. The later part of his life was devoted entirely to his studies and scholarship.

The *Charand Parand* pieces of Dihkhudā not only introduced a new *genre* into Persian literature, but also established a new style of writing, which was enthusiastically adopted by future writers and is still an important influence. Specimens of the satirical vein can be found in the works of Persian classics, but these normally contain personal motives; tinged with gross maledictions, they are in fact a kind of poetic invective. (An exception is the satirical works of 'Ubayd-i Zākānī (died 1371), particularly his *Akhlāqu' l-Ashrāf* ("The Ethics of the Noble"), which contain poignant criticism of his society and its rulers.)

Dihkhudā's satire was really modern in that it was not merely destructive mockery of established institutions, but also set forth a canon of social realism—and not in verse but in prose. Employing this new weapon courageously and without self-interest, Dihkhudā exposed and parodied all the elements that seemed to his contemporaries foremost in inhibiting social progress: the shah, Muḥammad 'Alī, who was plotting to overthrow the Constitution his father had so recently signed; corrupt courtiers and the ministers who paid lip-service to the new National Assembly while endeavouring to countermine its decisions; and reactionary divines (the *ākhūndhā*) whose pompous arabicized language particularly incited Dihkhudā's skill as a parodist. In attacking these, he knew that he could count on the ready response of wit and humour in his people.

Apart from the social and political significance of Dihkhudā's satirical essays, his choice of style helped greatly to liberate Persian writing from the stultifying and exhausted diction of former times. It has already been seen that such pieces as the Persian *Hajji Baba* and the *Sīyāḥatnāma-yi Ibrāhīm Beg* did a lot to effect this release. Dihkhudā continued and perfected this process. The *Charand Parand* articles were written in a lively colloquial language; more important, with their skilled parody and wordplay they introduced a new vitality into the written language: they showed once again what a master, using Persian with originality, could make that rich and flexible language do. "Once again" because this renovation of language, these new models and standards, bring to mind the service rendered to the Persian language by the poet and prose writer Sa'dī, in the thirteenth century.

Characteristic of Dihkhudā's style was the abundant use of

popular idioms and proverbial allusions. Herein lay his solution to the central problem confronting Persian writers of the new age: how to bridge the gulf between written and spoken communication. A major Iranian problem has always been to maintain a distinct and integrated civilization despite a heterogeneous ethnic composition and the frequent inroads of other peoples. Thus a standard literary language has through the centuries assumed vast importance: but for literary Persian, disuniting forces might have proceeded almost without restraint. For nearly a thousand years a great language of literature was retained almost unchanged; and this was all right so long as there remained a succession of great literary artists, whose originality lay chiefly in their ability to create something fresh and beautiful within the compass of established precedents. Such men as Sa'dī and Ḥāfiẓ could have revitalized the language without destroying it. Instead they repaired the damage of preceding periods and returned to earlier great models, whose themes and images they used to shape into something new and befitting their own times.

Once such innovators ceased to appear ("classical" Persian literature is generally taken to end with the death of the poet Jāmī in 1492), the language gradually disintegrated until all that was ultimately left was the husk of an outmoded but traditionally preserved rhetoric: the exhausted diction just mentioned. Popular speech remained alive and developing while this husk continued dead. Thus the gap between the spoken language and the written—between what people normally said and what it was *permissible* to write—widened. Consciously or not, it is with the removal of this gap that modern writers have been principally concerned. Naturally, a rhetorical written language could be used only by the educated minority; written language tended to be the exclusive possession of a few—the "writing" by which the ignorant and oppressed could be overawed; an appurtenance of power. This is why the liberal movement in politics was inevitably associated with the attack on rhetoric; why Dihkhudā, himself trained in the traditional schools, turned on the circumlocutions of the reactionaries, held their clichés up to mockery, and hammered home the idea of using the charming and expressive speech of the people as a literary medium.

Moreover, to find his expressions and style, he went beyond the lanes of the city and the places where men met and conversed; he did what some of his successors have sometimes forgotten to do: he went back to earlier literary models. This is possibly what Sa'dī and Ḥāfiẓ had done, though it is yet to be elucidated—if elucidation is possible—whether the sayings of theirs that have become adages were originally of their own coinage, or whether they used what they heard men around them say and what was already part of an old oral tradition. Dihkhudā himself compiled a four-volume lexicon of "Proverbs and Aphorisms" (*Amthāl u Ḥikam*) (Tehran, 1931), culled from the classical poets, in which the adages of popular speech were traced back to their literary homes. He also devoted many years of his life to compiling a dictionary (*Lughat-nāma*), rather in the form of an encyclopaedia, which is now being published in parts. These works say much for his approach to the linguistic-literary problems of his era.

Apart from the work of Dihkhudā, most of the development of prose literature, as opposed to journalism, between 1905 and 1921 was extremely languid. No prose work of importance appeared that was comparable to the works of Malkom Khān, Ṭālibuff, Zaynu'l-'Ābidīn-i Marāgha'ī, or Mīrzā Ḥabīb Iṣfahānī. The only notable contribution was the publication of some historical novels in the later years of the period, and of these we shall now speak in some detail.

CHAPTER VI

HISTORICAL NOVELS

THE Constitution obtained, sharp criticism of existing institutions was relaxed: former critics were themselves now partly responsible for the government of the country. The press and poetry whose burden was political were now largely devoted to the sometimes admirable, sometimes pathetic, self-examination of the new candidates for power; to a discussion of political theories and of the new leaders' capacity to carry out those duties towards the nation that the Constitution had conferred upon them; or to invective between rival groups in the new-fledged democracy. There was much writing on what the country needed and what should be done, and some enlightened exposure of Iranian political immaturity with suggestions for its cure; there were treatises on what the rule of law meant. It was a period of general hopefulness and ebullience.

The optimism was soon dispelled. For a while civil war gave journalists time and scope only for straight reporting of events, notably those in Tabriz, where the Constitutionalists were withstanding a siege by the forces loyal to Muḥammad 'Alī Shah. The politicians themselves canalized their verbal skill into the drafting of remarkable telegrams. The art of the caricaturist flourished. But these days of crisis left little time for creative literature: pens celebrated both for fine calligraphy and the production of elegant occasional verses were now employed to write manifestos and proclamations. Even with the restoration of Parliament, the problems confronting the Constitutionalists and the grave self-searching of some in their ranks, the impossibility of repairing the country's security, recently shattered by revolution and internecine strife, and the intrigues of Russia and Great Britain—all hindered any renewal of hope.

These events in the arena of politics had their effect on Persian literature. Writers began to do two things, neither of which was without precedent: they turned to purely creative writing, and they chose legendary themes. Patriotism was expressed by glorifying the country's past. A particular kind of historical novel writing came into being.[1] The most important historical novelists were Prince Muḥammad Bāqir Khusruvī, Shaykh Mūsā Nathrī, Ḥasan Khān, the *Nuṣratu'l-Vuzarā*, Badī', and Ṣan'atīzāda of Kerman. Their works appeared between 1909 and 1921. They worked in isolation, in places as far apart as Kermanshah and Kerman, Tehran and Hamadan, but all four were men of the educated class, actuated by high moral sentiments and a firm sense of the type of behaviour most conducive to a well-ordered society. It was this sort of urban, middle-class citizen, generally of either clerical or mercantile origin, whom the Constitutional Movement had brought into prominence. Today such citizens comprise Iran's sober and genuinely patriotic element, though in times of national distress they tend to withdraw into themselves and into nostalgic reveries about their country's past. The four writers discussed here revealed just such a tendency. In the tenth century, Firdawsī, author of Persia's national epic the *Shāhnāma* ("The Book of Kings"), had done something similar, though it could be shown that in the *Shāhnāma* he had indulged in far more criticism (albeit by innuendo) of existing political trends than did the modern "historical" novelists. They wrote either during the period when political controversy, which had become a national pastime to an almost inane degree, was being reacted against (1909); or in the years following, when the game of popular politics had proved to yield only disillusionment. Politics, therefore, they avoided.

Instead, their concern was public and private *morality*. This can also be attributed to events in Iran in the last decades of the nineteenth century. Islam had always been not only a religious but also

[1] This phenomenon has received the attention of several students of Persian literature. E. G. Browne, for instance, gives a brief but significant comment on the new development in his *Literary History of Persia*, IV, 464–6. K. Chaikine and the late E. E. Bertels have each dealt with it in *A Short Outline of Modern Persian Literature* (Moscow, 1928) and "The Persian Historical Novel in the Twentieth Century", respectively; Bertels's article is included in *Problèmes de la littérature d'Orient* in the proceedings of the Institute of Orientalism of the U.S.S.R. Academy of Sciences for 1932. In the *Journal Asiatique*, CCXXIII of 1933, B. Nikitine published an article, "Le roman historique dans la littérature persane actuelle"; while in 1952 in Cracow, F. Machalski published a book in Polish on the same subject. The same author has also written an article in French on one of the works in question, *Shams u Ṭughrā*, which appeared in *Charisteria Orientalia*, published in Prague in 1956. Finally the four principal exponents of this *genre* are discussed in Jan Rypka's *History of Persian Literature*, of which the German edition was published in Leipzig in 1959.

a political and legal institution. With reform in the political structure came a weakening of the religious institution, which meant a further depraving of morals already buffeted by years of social and political insecurity. While none of the four novelists was in any guise an exponent of Islam—on the contrary, they were all liberals—they shared a common disenchantment with their age, begotten of fear of the growing moral degradation around them. It was not to Islam that they looked for moral sanctions, but to an heroic past; to legendary ages of chivalry; to ancient Iranian codes of behaviour, as viewed through eyes not only romantic but also belonging to men influenced by the romantic, nostalgic literature of nineteenth-century Europe.

Muḥammad Bāqir Khusruvī

The first of the novels, *Shams u Ṭughrā*, appeared in Kermanshah in 1909. The author, Muḥammad Bāqir Khusruvī, belonged to an aristocratic family which through poverty had gradually merged into the middle class. Under the terror of Muḥammad 'Alī Shah and the mass insurrection of Constitutionalists, Khusruvī had been put in jail several times and forced to leave his hometown of Kermanshah. Written between 1907 and 1909, when the country was in the throes of a civil war, his massive book is a trilogy (the last two volumes, *Mārī-yi Vinīsī* ("Venetian Marie") and *Ṭughrul u Humāy*, appeared in 1910); but each volume is in fact an independent story with only the characters in common. It depicts Persian feudalism in the thirteenth century, the epoch of Il-khanid administration, when Sa'dī was passing the evening of his life in Shiraz, and Fars was ruled in the name of the Mongols by the famous lady Ābish-Khātūn (1268–87).

Shams, the hero, an impoverished descendant of the former Buwaihid princes of Fars, falls in love with the daughter of the Mongol lord Ṭughrā. A love story with all its typical ingredients and obstacles follows: the Mongol interdiction on marriage between their daughters and the "tajiks"; the young hero's prowess at the court; the buried treasure, the fantastic castle; captivity in the hands of pirates, and so on. The reader encounters a great many historical events, but these are merely episodes to keep the romantic action of the novel moving and to strengthen the verisimilitude which the author is at pains to preserve. As an informative work about conditions in thirteenth-century Persia, *Shams u Ṭughrā* is an invaluable book. It vividly portrays contemporary customs such as the ceremonies of marriage and mourning, as well as the lives of courtiers, nomad chiefs, *pahlavans*, and impostors of the time, while describing rivalries among them, voyages, hunting expeditions, and historical places in Iran and other Muslim countries. All these accounts are based on historical data, often quoted word for word by the author and cited by him in a bibliography. In his care for historical accuracy, Khusruvī made a completely new departure from older Persian literature: he brought to his work what may be described as a Western approach, engaging in extensive researches before committing pen to paper.

The author's attitude towards religion is not one of complete antagonism, yet he does not hesitate to criticize the outmoded customs sanctioned by Islam. In describing the religious laws permitting polygamy and what really amounts to the enslavement of women, he uses a good deal of satire and even sarcasm. His constitutional tendencies are clearly reflected in his allusions to the political and social conditions of the thirteenth century, and in his bitter condemnation of the oppressive government and the practices of its representatives, the foreign and indigenous feudal chiefs.

While oblivious to description of nature and to the artistic aspects of historical sites and battle scenes, Khusruvī shows considerable skill in portraying people and their lives. "He is the first", comments Professor Machalski, "to have created in the modern Persian novel people with natural traits and a very artistically motivated psychological character." Nevertheless, the author does falter in the task of establishing the modern Persian novel in accordance with Western examples and working along such unprecedented lines; in his characterization of the main hero, for instance, instead of the chivalresque ideal of nobility, which was perhaps part of his intention, there emerges something more like an adventurer whose motives are not always above suspicion. Yet, as has been suggested, the same could also be said of D'Artagnan and of Monte Cristo, two obvious models.

It is because of its novelty and its exceptional merits that Jamālzāda, the distinguished novelist and short-story writer, has ventured to make this somewhat exaggerated appraisal of *Shams u Ṭughrā*:

Unequalled among the literary works of the recent centuries. Without doubt the only book worthy of translation into foreign languages as the model of modern Persian literature.[1]

The language of *Shams u Ṭughrā*, though very similar to that of the Persian *élite* of the time, is rather overladen, especially when compared with the ease and fluency of more recent writings. The author has not made enough use of idioms, popular expressions, and the other rich resources of everyday language. There is little dialogue; instead, the book is full of lengthy narrations. Arabic terms also abound.

In brief, *Shams u Ṭughrā* stands at the cross-roads of ancient and modern Persian literature and must be judged as a forerunner of the modern novel in Iran.

Shaykh Mūsā Nathrī

The second historical novel, *'Ishq u Salṭanat*, written by Shaykh Mūsā Nathrī, director of the government college *Nuṣrat* at Hamadan, was originally intended to be the first of a cycle of novels depicting the history of ancient Iran. Three of these have appeared. The first volume, *'Ishq u Ṣaltanat yā Futūḥāt-i Kūrush-i Kabīr* ("Love and Sovereignty or Conquests of Cyrus the Great"), was printed at Hamadan in 1919. Its theme is the deeds of Cyrus the Great—at the dawn of Persian history—from his earliest youth until he captured Ikbātān (Hamadan) and assumed the powers of a king. Either as an extraordinary example of the national amnesia by which the Iranians had almost entirely forgotten large epochs of their country's past, or because the author deliberately chose to do so, the ancient Persian names are bizzarely transliterated into Persian from their French (ultimately Greek) forms, with no attempt to record their old Iranian pronunciations. Another criticism, made by Browne, is that the book is "overloaded with dates, archaeological and mythological notes and prolix historical dissertations".

The second volume, entitled *Sitāra-yi Līdī* ("The Lydian Star"), published in 1924–5, describes the expedition of Cyrus against Croesus, the capture of Sardis, and the inclusion of Lydia in the young Persian Empire. The main theme of the third volume,

[1] Preface to *Dalīrān-i Tangistānī* ("The Heroes of Tangistan") by Ḥusayn Rukn-zāda Ādamīyat (Tehran, 1934).

called *Sarguzasht-i Shāhzāda Khānum-i Bābulī* ("The Story of a Babylonian Princess"), which appeared in 1931–2 at Kermanshah, is a romance between Hurmuzan, the last prince of Media, and Eridis, the last princess of Babylon. These last two volumes show many improvements over the first. The author's study of history is more thorough; the Persian names, especially in the last volume, are written in a form closer to their original, and the story is more compact and readable. Though sometimes coarse and dry, the language of Shaykh Mūsā is on the whole appealing and straightforward. The characters rarely speak, and when they do, no matter what social class they belong to, their language and expressions are exactly the same. As is to be expected, there is a great deal of chronological inaccuracy in the trilogy.

Ḥasan Badī'

The third historical novel of this period was *Dāstān-i Bāstān* ("The Story of the Ancient Times"), by Ḥasan, the *Nuṣratu'l Vuzarā'*, Badī', printed in 1921 in Tehran. Like the other three, the author in his Preface claims his book to be the first historical novel in the Persian language, which, rather than a sign of vanity, should suggest the isolation in which these four writers worked.

Apart from Arabic and French sources, the story is drawn mainly from the *Shāhnāma* of Firdawsī, which indicates the combined legendary and factual nature of the book. We have the sentimental lovers, Bīzhan and Manīzha, as the basic theme, with the rise of Achaemenids and the reign of Cyrus the Great as the historical background. The story comes to an end with the conquest of Lydia and Babylon by Cyrus.

Badī' shows great skill in the description of places. His pictures of ancient palaces, historical monuments (particularly sculpture), and paintings in Babylon are all extremely realistic. There are a few minor technical and linguistic anachronisms in *Dāstān-i Bāstān*, but the accurate chronology and conception of the plot hold the reader's attention and place the story high as a work of art. In particular, the language of Badī' represents a step towards greater maturity in handling the novel in Persian, for at least this writer begins to make his characters speak, and speak in a tongue befitting their positions in society. As has been noticed, failure to do this was a feature of the other historical novels of this time. Put briefly, Badī' makes his princes speak as princes might be expected to do, in the language of the court, while his commoners speak in colloquial and provincial accents. This is a minor turning point in the literary developments that are being traced: as will be shown, naturalness of dialogue became a preoccupation of later fiction writers and afforded scope for the display of considerable skill.

Ṣan'atīzāda Kirmānī

The fourth author, 'Abdu'l-Ḥusayn Ṣan'atīzāda, one of Persia's most prolific writers in this field, is significant enough to merit fuller discussion. In his first book, *Dām-gustarān yā Intiqām-khāhān-i Mazdak* ("Trap-Setters or the Avengers of Mazdak"), published in 1921, he tries to expose the reasons for the fall of the Sasanian Empire and the Arab conquest. The outlook of the young author, though not sweepingly comprehensive, embraces a fair amount of historical facts. He shows the cowardly tyranny and cruelty of Yazdegird III and his religious intolerance towards the minorities. He emphasizes Yazdegird's lack of loyal and honest followers, since most of them were influenced by the doctrines of Mazdak and sought to avenge the killing of Mazdak by Chosroes, the Sasanian king. Bertels, in his interesting comment on *Dām-gustarān*, notices that a corrupt tyranny is shown falling to two forces: one external—the Arabs—with a message of equality and brotherhood; the other internal—the revolutionary society of the Mazdakites, who, for the sake of revenge, caused the "national independence of Persia" to perish.

The account given in *Dām-gustarān* of the fall of the Sassanids and the Arab conquest is the one popularly accepted in Iran: they were caused, it is believed, by royal tyranny supported by a repressive clergy; and these forces were opposed internally by adherents of Mazdak, who did in fact show willingness to go over to the side of the Arabs. Furthermore, as Arnold Toynbee points out, "the Sasanian Power showed itself impotent to fulfil its *raison d'être*...".

The figure of the Mazdakite chief who murdered Yazdegird, as well as the general structure of the book, are created under the influence of Dumas's *Le Comte de Monte-Cristo*. Moreover, the author pays considerable attention to painting the Zoroastrian clergy in the worst possible colours. In this picture they display the most contemptible characteristics of the reactionary Muslim clergy against whom Persian liberals were ranged early in this century, as indeed they have almost always been.

The second volume of *Dām-gustarān* appeared in Tehran in 1926, five years after the publication of the first one. According to M. Mīnuvī's Preface, it was Browne's review of the first volume that encouraged Ṣan'atīzāda, disappointed by the errors in his first volume, to embark on publishing his second (although the review was not in fact very flattering: see *Literary History of Persia*, IV, 466). However, the late B. Nikitine, on the authority of "a letter from Ṣan'atīzāda himself", states that the latter was fully aware that Browne had not rated his book very highly. It is a fact, Nikitine observes, that "modern Persian writers do take into account the comments of orientalists".

Although the first historical novel written on the European pattern was Khusruvī's *Shams u Ṭughrā*, published in 1909, many orientalists have attributed the first to Ṣan'atīzāda of Kirman. This is due to a note in Ṣan'atīzāda's autobiography where he claims to have written *Dām-gustarān* (published in Bombay, 1920–1) about 1900, when he was only fifteen years old. Though one cannot help suspecting that this statement and the autobiography are somewhat coloured, they are useful as a source of general information.

To escape the persecution of the old régime, says the Note, Ṣan'atīzāda's father Ḥājjī 'Alī Akbar left Kerman for Constantinople in 1907. There he formed a friendship with Sayyid Jamālu'd-Dīn Asadābādī and was charged with returning to Persia to arrange the clandestine distribution of revolutionary publications. In those days anyone who dared show constitutional sympathies was taxed with Babism and thus exposed to the vindictiveness of the populace. As a result, his father could not continue his business and the family was reduced to complete poverty. The son was forced to go out and sell matches on the street. But thanks to his father's enterprise, the family prospered again and opened an orphanage where foundlings were to be taught a trade; while Ṣan'atīzāda set up a bookshop. This was his school, where he used to read night and day. At the age of fifteen he wrote his first novel, which he printed at his own expense in Bombay. Ṣan'atīzāda remained a bookseller at Kerman for ten years and his shop became the centre for the intellectuals of the city. He then went to Tehran, set up a textile factory, and became a well-to-do merchant in the capital.

We have already commented on the first work of this writer, *Dām-gustarān.* In 1927 Ṣan'atīzāda published a second historical novel, called *Dāstān-i Mānī-yi Naqqāsh* ("The Story of Mani, the Painter"). This depicts the life of the famous heresiarch Mani, beginning with his early youth when he leaves his father to set out on a long journey. His uncle, a Zoroastrian priest, advises him to go to China and learn painting there. Besides falling in love with a girl, Zahīda, whom he rescues from brigands, he finds the treasures of Jehova's temple hidden in the mountains of Turkistan. By delivering these to Shapur I, he gains the king's adherence to his religious teaching and the authority to make it a universal religious institution. There is also the story of a campaign against China, described simultaneously with the conflict between Shapur and Valerian. After some digressions, periphrases, and even corruption of historical facts, all ends well: Zahīda is rescued after Mani's incredible feat of gaining the key to the treasure from the neck of a lion. Ispandīyār, Shapur's double in likeness, is rescued from the cage where Valerian had imprisoned him, and Valerian is put there in his stead. Shapur, with Mani's help, takes possession of the treasure. For the finale all the characters find themselves in a Zoroastrian sanctuary, where the services of Zahīda and Mani are recompensed by their union.

Compared with *Dām-gustarān*, this second novel is far richer in action, well plotted, and full of unexpected events and dramatic moments. The contrast between the characterizations of the two rival monarchs is interesting. Valerian is depicted as a ruthless, drunken and perverted ruler, whereas Shapur is endowed with wisdom and even democratic tendencies. There is also a very true-to-life secondary character, a feudal landowner who suppresses his peasants with great cruelty—a type still active in Persia until very recently.

Ṣan'atīzāda's third historical novel, *Salaḥshūr* ("Warrior"), appearing in 1933, deals with the rise of the Sasanian dynasty and its founder Ardeshir (Artaxerxes); the rule of Ardawan (Artabanus), A.D. 209–26, the last of the Parthians, also forms part of the historical background. The main theme of the book, besides the inevitable romance, is the rebellion of Ardeshir and his battles against Ardawan. Generally speaking, the author has created his own story from the Persian legends that have been passed down through generations. Another of his well-known historical novels is *Sīyāh-pūshān* ("The Black Coats"), which appeared in print in 1945. Once again the theme is the rebellion of a Persian national hero against oppressive rulers. This time we are taken back to the middle of the eighth century to witness the rise of Abū Muslim in support of the Abbasids, who sympathized with the Persians in their opposition to the oppressive Omayyads. In the year 747 in his native land of Khorasan, Abū Muslim raises the black standard of the house of Abbas, and after the decisive battle of the Great Zab, in which the Caliph Merwan is killed, he ends the despotic rule of the Omayyad dynasty. We then witness the growing power of Abū Muslim and the increasing fear of his popularity by the Abbasid caliph Mansur. Finally in 754, at the age of thirty-five, Abū Muslim is taken to the court of the ungrateful Mansur and treacherously put to death.

In contrast with his last three novels, where Zoroastrianism was glorified as the national religion of Iran, *Sīyāh-pūshān* shows Islam as a *fait accompli* for Persians and Abū Muslim as one of the greatest protagonists of Iran and Islam. The style and composition of *Sīyāh-pūshān* do not reach the standard of the previous works. The author makes ample use of historical sources but, like his other historical novels, draws no line between fact and fiction. Indeed, he sometimes sacrifices the accuracy and authenticity of historical events to the coherence of his story and the fervency of his patriotism.

The non-historical works of Ṣan'atīzāda include *Cha-gūna Mumkin ast Mutumavil Shud* ("How to Become Rich", 1930), *Rustam dar Qarn-i Bīst-u-dawun* ("Rustam in the 22nd Century", 1935), *'Ālam-i Abadī* ("The Eternal Universe", 1938), *Majma'-i Dīvānigān* ("The Assembly of Lunatics", in two volumes, undated) and *Firishta-yi Ṣulḥ yā Fatāna-yi Iṣfahānī* ("The Angel of Peace, or Fatana of Isfahan", 1952). The last is an imaginary work about a heroine who wanted to make war impossible; the book was sent by the author to the Nobel Prize Committee, who acknowledged receipt of it. Apart from his last printed historical novel, *Nādir, Fātiḥ-i Dihlī* ("Nadir, the Conquerer of Delhi", 1957), Ṣan'atīzāda is said to have some other historical novels still in manuscript form. These include *Mādar-i Ghamdīda* ("The Afflicted Mother"), which deals with the fate of Yazdigerd III's descendants; a book about the life of Shah Sulṭān Ḥusayn and the end of the Safavid dynasty; a third, whose theme is the deeds of Mīrzā 'Alī Muḥammad (known as the *Bāb*, the famous creator of Babism), together with those of his descendants Mīrzā Yaḥyā Ṣubḥ-i Azal, Mīrzā Ḥusayn 'Alī, and 'Abdu'l-Bahā, the founder of Bahaism, to contain many descriptions and photographs connected with Babism and Bahaism.

Ṣan'atīzāda cannot be ranked among the notable creative writers of modern Persia; yet the ingenuity and freshness of his earlier works have made his name famous. His language is simple, clear, and devoid of the redundancies and ornament formerly characteristic of Persian prose. The two striking features in Ṣan'atīzāda's writings are his idealism and patriotism, which have usually led him astray on historical facts. The rigid language of his characters is another handicap; and, finally, the excessive use of European words, especially where Persian expressions could be found, is damaging to his style.

Others

During the last four decades, historical novel writing has been one of the most productive branches of Persian literature. The reason for this is twofold. First, the historical past of the country offers ample resources to writers. Secondly, the ruling class, while discouraging discussion of everyday affairs lest their corruption and inefficiences be disclosed, has always tacitly encouraged authors to provide the nation with a mitigating dose of bygone glories. This was particularly true during the reign of Riẓā Shah, when the favourite theme of writers was—to quote their own words—to compare the "glorious past" with the "current golden era". As a result, every layman who wishes to try his hand at writing takes up a fragment of history and, twisting it according to his own fancy, produces an "historical novel". The majority of these books, crammed with distortions and anachronisms, resemble legendary tales and contain no historical value. And apart from the earlier works, which pointed the way to European realism, none of them has achieved any special literary distinction. Compared with the best works of their time, they cannot be regarded as important works of art.

Because they are entertaining, however, they have been, and to a large degree still are, popular with the Persian public. Scores of these novels are being serialized in the weekly papers of Tehran at present. In this way, history serves many hack writers as an instrument for amusing their readers with thrilling adventures, crimes, and lasciviousness. Another important reason for their popularity is that they carry an air of nostalgia, serving as a kind of antidote to a nation's suppressed ambitions. Nevertheless, it would be wrong to discount all of them, since some, of course, are more substantial and better written than others. To do them justice, since the scope of the present study does not allow a full review, we shall try to give a comprehensive list of those most worthy of attention.

Ādamīyat (Ḥusayn Rukn-Zāda), *Dalīrān-i Tangistānī*, solar 1310 (Tehran).
Ārīyān-Pūr ('Abbās Kāshānī), *'Arūs-i Madī*, 1308 (Tehran).
Āẕarī ('Alī), *Upirā-yi va'da-yi Zardusht*, vol. 1, 1313 (Tehran).
Bihrūz (Ẕabīḥ), *Shāh-i Īrān va Bānū-yi Arman*, 1306 (Tehran).
Fāẓil (Javād), *Lārījān: 'Ishq u Khūn*, 1329 (Tehran).
Gulshan (Ḥusayn-'Alī), *Parīvash-i Nā-Kām* (1st vol.), 1307 (Tehran).
Ḥujat (Riẓā), *Sitāra-yi Kārvān*, vol. 1 (2nd ed.), 1334 (Tehran).
Humāyūn Farukh ('Abdu'l Raḥīm), *Dāstān-i Tārīkhī-yi Bābak u Afshīn*, 1328 (Tehran).
Kamālī (Ḥaydar 'Alī), *Maẓālim-i Turkān Khātūn*, 1307 (Tehran).
Kamālī (Ḥaydar 'Alī), *Afsāna-yi Tārīkhī-yi Lāzīkā*, 1309 (Tehran).
Kasmā'ī ('Alī), *Zībā-yi Ḥasūd* (2 vols.), 1330 (Tehran).
Khalīlī (Muḥammad 'Alī), *Dukhtar-i Kūrush*, — (Tehran).
Khalīlī (Muḥammad 'Alī), *Nigāristān-i Khūn yā Qīyām-i Khurāsān*, 1321 (Tehran).
Khalīlī (Muḥammad 'Alī), *Bahrām-i Gūr*, — (Tehran).
Khalīlī (Muḥammad Riẓā 'Arāqī), *Bānū-yi Zindānī*, 1319 (Tehran).
Kurdānī (Muḥammad Taqī), *Dalīrān-i Khārazm*, — (Meshed).
Lārūdī (Nūru'l-lā), *Nādir Pisar-i Shamshīr*, 1319 (Tehran).
Masrūr (Ḥusayn Sukhan-yār), *Dāstān-i Tārīkhī-yi Maḥmūd-i Afghān*, — (Tehran).
Masrūr (Ḥusayn Sukhan-yār), *Dah Nafar Qizilbāsh*, — (Tehran).
Masrūr (Ḥusayn Sukhan-yār), *Qurān yā Sar-guẕasht-i Luṭf-'Alī-Khān-i Zand*, 1332 (Tehran).

Maymandī-Nizhād (Muḥammad Ḥusayn), *Zindigī-yi Pur Mājirā-yi Nādir Shāh* (1st vol., 2nd ed.), 1335 (Tehran).
Mudarisī (Ibrāhīm), *Panja-yi Khūnīn*, — (Tehran).
Mudarisī (Ibrāhīm), *'Arūs-i Madāyin*, — (Tehran).
Mudarisī (Ibrāhīm), *Payk-i Ajal*, — (Tehran).
Mu'tamin (Zaynu'l-Ābidīn), *Āshīyāna-yi 'Uqāb* (in 6 vols.),— (Tehran).
Nafīsī (Sa'īd), *Ākharīn yādigār-i Nādir*, 1305 (Tehran).
Nafīsī (Sa'īd), *Yazdgird-i Sivvum*, 1321 (Tehran).
Nafīsī (Sa'īd), *Bābak-i Khuram-Dīn, Dilāvar-i Āzarbāyijān*, 1333 (Tehran).
Nafīsī (Sa'īd), *Sar-guzasht-i Ṭāhir-ibn-i Ḥusayn*, — (Tehran).
Najmī (Nāṣir), *Dāstānhā-yi Tārīkhī*, 1327 (Tehran).
Partaw A'ẓam (Abulqāsim), *Bābak*, — (Tehran).
Qarīb (Yaḥyā), *Khūn-i Sīyāvush*, 1310 (Tehran).
Qarīb (Yaḥyā), *Ya'qūb-i layth Ṣafārī*, 1314 (Tehran).
Ṣafavī (Raḥīm-Zāda), *Dāstān-i Shahr-Bānū*, 1310 (Tehran).
Ṣafavī (Raḥīm-Zāda), *Dāstān-i Nādir Shāh*, 1310 (Tehran).
Ṣafavī (Raḥīm-Zāda), *Yād-dāshthā-yi Khusru-yi Avval Anūshīrvān* (Translation), 1310 (Tehran).
Ṣafavī (Raḥīm-Zāda), *Bīzhan u Manīzha*, 1334 (Tehran).
Sālūr (Ḥusayn 'Alī, the *'Imādu's Salṭana*), *Juft-i Pāk* (in 2 vols.), 1311 (Tehran).
Sālūr (Sabuktakīn), *Nasl-i Shujā'ān* (in 3 vols.), 1336 (Tehran).
Shādlū (Nuṣratu'l-lā), *'Azm u 'Ishq*, 1306 (Tehran).
Shādlū (Nuṣratu'l-lā), *'Ishq-i Pāk*, 1306 (Tehran).
Shafaq (Riẓā-Zāda), *Sattār Khān*, 1330 (Tehran).
Shāh-Ḥusaynī (Naṣīru'd-Dīn), *Sharāra-yi Khāmūsh Shuda*, 1327 (Tehran).
Sharīf ('Alī-Aṣghar), *Khūnbahā-yi Īrān* (2 vols.), 1305/6 (Tehran).
Shīn-Partaw (Shīrāz-Pūr), *Pahlivān-i Zand*, 1312 (Tehran).
Sigharī ('Alī), *'Arūs-i Marv, Kīyānūsh Dukhtar-i Yazdgird*, 1334 (Tehran).
Suhaylī (Aḥmad Khunsārī), *Maḥmūd u Ayāz*, 1333 (Tehran).
Yaghmā'ī (Iqbāl), *'Ishq u Pādishāhī*, 1325 (Tehran).
Zanjānī (Shaykh Ibrāhīm), *Shahrīyār-i Hūshmand*, — (Tehran).

CHAPTER VII

THE REIGN OF RIẒĀ SHAH (1925–41)

A BLOODLESS military *coup* on the eve of 21 February 1921 opened a new chapter in the history of Persia. Under the command of Riẓā Khān, the Cossack Brigade stationed at Qazwin marched into the capital and overthrew the weak government. A new cabinet was formed, headed by Sayyid Ẓīyā'ud-Dīn Ṭabāṭabā-'ī, a young reforming journalist who had taken a leading part in the *coup d'état.* Riẓā Khān held the office of commander-in-chief of the Army and minister of war. Soon a clash broke out between these two main protagonists, and Sayyid Ẓīyā'ud-Dīn was forced to resign and leave the country. During the next two years several governments were formed, but Riẓā Khān retained the Ministry of War and control of the army until 1923, when he became prime minister. In October 1925 the *Majlis* deposed the last Qajar king, Aḥmad Shah, and entrusted Riẓā Khān with provisional power to conduct the affairs of the state. Two months later, on 12 December, Riẓā Khān was crowned the first ruler of the Pahlavi dynasty.

A man of forceful character, with little formal education and a limited knowledge of international affairs, Riẓā Shah's strength lay in his military training and capacity to build up a strong national army. His reign was essentially dependent on this army, which he cherished with the utmost care. He emerged as a staunch patriot determined to restore the unity of Persia, to establish a centralized government based on modern social and economic institutions, and to end foreign influence and intervention in the internal affairs of the state. With many nationalist and former Constitutionalist leaders backing him, Riẓā Shah made remarkable progress towards achieving these aims in the early stages of his rule. But as his personal power increased, his handling of affairs became correspondingly more arbitrary. Under the compelling pressure of the army, the tribes were made obedient to some extent, but attempts to settle them permanently did not quite succeed.

As the first steps aimed at diminishing foreign influence, the system of capitulations that had been in force since the middle of the nineteenth century was abolished in 1928; and foreign advisors in various government departments were dismissed. These moves were logical and politically sound. Ultimately, however, policies began to bear signs of xenophobia. A. C. Millspaugh wrote:

Rezā's dislike of foreigners went to such extremes that he forbade his people to visit the embassies and legations and practically terminated social contacts between Persians and the foreign diplomats.... Books imported from foreign countries were censored, in some cases banned, in many cases burned.[1]

Yet he did establish, especially in the later years of his reign, close diplomatic, economic and cultural ties with Nazi Germany. Not only did Germany top the list in Persia's foreign trade, with German goods dominating Persian markets, but German teachers, professors, and advisors were employed by the Ministry of Education. In sharp contrast to his phobia of foreign books a collection of 7500 books called the German Scientific Library was presented by the German Government to Iran in 1939.

These carefully selected books were destined to convince Iranian readers of the cultural mission of Germany in the East and of the kinship between the National Socialist Reich and the "Aryan culture" of Iran.[2]

On the home front the nationalists, who had first come out in support of a "strong man" capable of giving Iran the security it needed, began to feel disillusioned as their leader grew increasingly self-dependent. For his part, Riẓā Shah's suspiciousness made it sometimes difficult for him to discriminate between the good and the bad among the country's leading class of statesmen and civil servants. On the whole the shah lacked good lieutenants and was burdened with tremendous responsibility, for only on his orders could any policy be initiated or executed. He surrounded himself with a group of sycophants who, while flattering the shah, and under cover of his protection, betrayed him by indulging in corrupt practices. The following account taken from

[1] *Americans in Persia* (Washington, 1946), p. 28.

[2] George Lenczowski, *Russia and the West in Iran, 1918–1948* (New York, 1949), p. 161.

George Kirk's *The Middle East in the War* (Oxford, 1952) is an interesting example of this point:

It was significant of the outlook of the Shah and his adulators that in 1940 the Swiss journalist Walter Bosshard found in a Tabriz hotel a calendar illustrating the greatest men of all time: in the centre were Rizā Shāh and Napoleon; somewhat to one side Mussolini, Hitler and Ataturk; while Theodore Roosevelt and several Bourbons were shown in the company of Caesar and Alexander the Great; over all sat Moses with the Tables of the Law.

Thus Riẓā Shah's rule, which had begun with promises of democratic policy, gradually assumed the guise of absolutism. Critics of the régime and personal opponents of the shah were seldom able to escape unscathed. The press was muzzled; political parties disappeared. The *Majlis* consisted of appointees, rather than elected representatives of the people, who automatically passed every measure dictated by the sovereign.

Some of these measures were beneficial: a number of its methods might be criticized, but the shah's policy cannot be condemned out of hand, for it was aimed at making Iran a viable modern state with a place in the world commensurate with its size and history. To some extent Riẓā Shah, almost single-handed, succeeded: during his reign Iran ceased to be moved at will by Great Powers who regarded it as a mere pawn in their wider interests. He was able to instill into his people, especially some of the younger generation, a renewed sense of confidence in their country's destiny and a self-confidence that soon outgrew his paternalism; but by an ironical process beyond his control, the shah's paternalism was to cause some of the tensions of the later years of his reign.

To meet the criticism that his policy of rapid reform inevitably produced, the shah established an office for the "guidance of public opinion". Among his positive internal achievements, a great number of public buildings, factories, hospitals, hotels, roads, and streets were built; transportation facilities were improved immensely, and the construction of the Trans-Iranian Railway was justly a source of pride to the shah. Public health and education received greater attention than ever before. Numerous modern schools and the University of Tehran came into being. Finance and the system of civil administration were considerably reformed, commerce and foreign trade increased, and bold steps were taken towards the industrialization of the country. The power of the Muslim clergy was notably reduced. Worthwhile attempts were made to emancipate women. In fact, in certain spheres of public life rapid progress was made, but the pace was not maintained. Iran on Riẓā Shah's abdication had in some respects advanced appreciably. Nevertheless, it remained an unhappy land, for there was not sufficient justice or liberty, and Iranians value both very highly.

Hence the achievements of Riẓā Shah, however progressive and benevolent, did not in the end comfort the intelligentsia. They were the first and indeed foremost to suffer from the tightening grip of dictatorship. Writers in particular, as we shall see in the following pages, having little access to free expression, either became advocates of the régime, producing stereotyped writings and receiving their reward, or else they retired, frustrated and resentful.

CHAPTER VIII

EARLY WRITERS OF THE RIẒĀ SHAH PERIOD

AT the outset of the period two works appeared, one a collection of short stories, the other a two-volume novel. Both were critical of social conditions, both introduced new literary styles and attracted much attention. But whereas one treated its subject-matter with realism and represented a genuine move towards literary regeneration, the other was only a poor imitation of European romantic fiction. Significantly the two works offered a choice between two different paths for the coming generation of Persian writers.

The first one, *Yakī Būd Yakī Na-būd* ("Once Upon a Time", Berlin, 1921), by Muḥammad 'Alī Jamālzāda, was written in lively, deliberately colloquial language. Although new in form and content, it was strikingly Persian. In a preface to the book, which served as a kind of manifesto of a new literature, the author recommended a simplification of literary language and invited others to write in a style closer to colloquial speech with copious use of everyday expressions. He appended to his collection of stories a short glossary of popular idioms that are not found in ordinary dictionaries.

The style advocated by Jamālzāda, though now prevalent in some form in the writings of every author of distinction, was not at first taken up by popular writers of the 1920's. Jamālzāda did not become a model until later, with Ṣādiq Hidāyat, in whose works the new style reached perfection: it is due mainly to the influence of Hidāyat that the present generation of writers has turned wholeheartedly to an uninhibited use of popular speech.[1]

[1] For a more detailed discussion of Jamālzāda and Hidāyat and their writings, see below, pp. 91–112 and 137–201 respectively.

Mushfiq Kāẓimī

The language and style adopted by the majority of writers during Riẓā Shah's time were those of the second book, *Ṭihrān-i Makhuf* ("The Horrible Tehran", 1922) by Murtaẓā Mushfiq Kāẓimī,[1] a two-volume romantic novel dealing mostly with the unfair position of Persian women in the early 'twenties. The hero, Farrukh, and his cousin, Mahīn, having grown up together as childhood playmates, are in love and wish to marry. But Mahīn's father, avaricious, mean, and conscious of Farrukh's limited means, opposes them. Without any regard for his daughter's feelings, he has arranged that she should marry a scoundrel, who happens to be the son of a prince; in return he is promised a seat in the *Majlis* during the coming parliamentary election. A struggle ensues. On one side are the mutual devotion of the young lovers and their eagerness to be united. Against them are the intrigues of their opponents, and these form the main elements of the plot. The story comes to a tragic end with Mahīn's death and Farrukh' banishment.

The basic theme of the novel, involving questions such as the rights of women, outmoded marriage customs, prostitution, etc., deserves attention. The author also makes frequent allusions to a number of other social evils of his time: for example, the corruption of the ruling circles, police tyranny, and social depravity in general. He condemns reactionary elements and tries, by a kind of reportage, to open his reader's eyes to the realities of the modern age. Certain fragmentary episodes, such as scenes in a brothel, are skilfully sketched. But the picture as a whole remains unconvincing, partly because the author's language is far from the real speech of people, and partly because he does not distinguish between what is essential and inessential. There is too much superfluous and subsidiary detail, so that the main thread of the narrative is sometimes lost. Moreover, the plot-building is primitive: situations are often clumsily contrived; the characters seldom appear true to life. Farrukh is supposed to personify the virtues and ideals of the

[1] The other works of this author, *Gul-i Pizhmurda* ("The Faded Flower", 1929), *Rashk-i Pur-bahā* ("Precious Envy", 1930) and *Yādigār-i Yak Shab* ("Reminiscence of one Night", 1961) have not gained much success. The last book is a continuation of *Ṭihrān-i Makhuf*.

younger generation, yet the man we encounter is an idler who considers it humiliating to join the civil service and thus, as though there were no other openings for a young man, does nothing. His time is devoted entirely to his love affair. A good deal of the book is taken up by the question of young girls, especially from respectable families, becoming prostitutes, and in describing the miseries of these victims of society the author is at his best. But when it comes to reasoning, he fails. His analysis of prostitution and other social problems shows little understanding of basic economic and social factors: his approach is descriptive rather than deductive. There is a constant appeal to the emotions with plenty of platitudinous moralizing.

The language of *Ṭihrān-i Makhuf*, though simple, lacks the force of that in *Yakī Būd Yakī Na-būd*, because it does not sufficiently adapt itself to popular speech. In composition and style it resembles more recent journalistic essays, which, in order to display their pseudo-modernism, avoid the resources of the national culture and grow increasingly dependent on European expressions. In a language as rich in expressive idioms and apt proverbs as Persian is, few habits could be more unjustified than the literal translation of European idioms and their over-usage in a literary work.

The faults of Kāẓimī's *Ṭihrān-i Makhuf* are mentioned in some detail because they characterize a great deal of inferior literature produced, perhaps inevitably, by a nation struggling to achieve modern expression. An exception among the early writings of the period were the works of Aḥmad 'Alī Khudādāda: *Rūz-i Sīyāh-i Kārgar* ("The Black Fate of Workers", 1926) and *Rūz-i Sīyāh-i Ra'īyat* ("The Black Fate of Peasants", 1927), which describe the life and poverty of Iranian workers and peasants. But most writers were devoting attention, not to the problems of the masses, but to the position of women specifically.

'Abbās Khalīlī

In the numerous works of 'Abbās Khalīlī, editor of the daily *Iqdām*—e.g. his *Insān* ("Man", 1924), *Intiqām* ("Vengeance", 1925), *Asrār-i Shab* ("Night's Secrets", 1926), and *Rūzigār-i Sīyāh* ("Black Days", 1931)—the chief themes are women's rights, compulsory marriages, prostitution, and moral lapses of youth. This author also published a number of other works containing a hotchpotch of odd topics, stories, and ideas translated directly, or taken indirectly, from foreign writers and journals. The style used by Khalīlī in these writings—the prime example is to be found in his *Rashaḥāt-i Qalam* ("The Effluence of Pen", 1932)—is, as one critic has said, "an unhappy blend which has emerged out of the prose translations of European poetry and Persian romantic classical element".[1]

Rabī' Anṣārī

Rabī' Anṣārī was another writer who gained some success with his first book, *Jināyāt-i Bashar* ("Man's Crimes"), published in 1930. The theme is the familiar problem: prostitution. Two girls from respectable families are kidnapped by a gang of white-slave traffickers and sold to a brothel in Kermanshah. The brutal manner in which they are entrapped, the abominable treatment they and other victims receive, and finally their tragic end are described with the compassionate and fastidious pen of an emotional chronicler. This author tends to attribute most social ills to the spread of modern civilization, hence the sub-title of the book: *Ādam-Furūshān-i Qarn-i Bīstum* ("Human Traffickers of the Twentieth Century"). The story itself is moving, but the author's pauses for preaching and his dead-earnest style make it heavy reading.

Anṣārī's second book, *Sīzda-yi Nawrūz* ("The Thirteenth Day of the Year", 1932), opens in the festive mood of a Persian New Year but becomes progressively grimmer as we learn about the dismal sufferings and humiliations of the poverty-stricken Kurdish families living in north-western Persia. The subject, apart from its literary novelty, is of special political and sociological importance, for it throws light on the inner life of a desolate minority community; a community that has been the cause of many political disturbances during more recent times. This work could have served as a timely alarm bell had the author treated his rare material with sufficient discretion. It contains a fair amount of criticism directed against government officials and the way in which they handle the machinery of laws they are supposed to be applying.

[1] M. Shaki, *Charisteria Orientalia* (1956), p. 309.

Yet because of the slovenly composition and structure of the story and the author's unrestrained indulgence in overdramatizing events, the book as a whole fails to leave a deep or lasting impression on the reader.

Still another book on problems concerning women was Yaḥyā Dawlat-ābādī's romantic novel *Shahrnāz* (1924), which advocated love as the natural basis for marriage and condemned marriages based on the decision of parents.

CHAPTER IX

LATER WRITERS OF THE RIẒĀ SHAH PERIOD

THAT prose literature during the first decade of Riẓā Shah's reign declined may be chiefly attributed to political conditions, not least of which was the despotic nature of the régime. Riẓā Shah grew increasingly ruthless, both in promoting reform and suppressing criticism. Among other things he cherished a desire for the emancipation of women. This progressive aim, as well as the shah's obvious will to strengthen his country, was reflected in the literature of the first half of his reign. Whether mesmerized by his patriotism or frightened of his harsh measures, most writers avoided social and political criticism. Yet they wholeheartedly supported his programme for the emancipation of women. This afforded a safe topic in literature, and those with literary ambitions began to produce variations on this theme. But by and large, conditions in the 'twenties were inimical to serious creative writing. Gifted authors like Jamālzāda and Hidāyat, who would not accommodate themselves to the prevailing circumstances, either left off writing until the collapse of the régime or printed their works in limited editions to be circulated among a circle of intimates. To Jamālzāda's clarion call for "literary democracy", which meant bringing the literary language closer to popular speech, writers subservient to the régime turned a deaf ear. In short, the number of writers in this decade could be counted on the fingers of one hand, while the fragmentary works they produced were, as a rule, the repetition of one theme.

During the 'thirties, a new group appeared. These writers, though much more gifted and versatile than their predecessors, would not, or perhaps could not, break away from the established norms: in their works, too, women, portrayed as fallen or excessively virtuous, occupy a prominent place. As artistic creations, however, their writing shows notable signs of new departures. Whereas crudeness, lack of sound composition, absence of imagination, and particularly want of method characterized the writings of the 'twenties, a good deal of subtlety, a relative maturity, and above all progress in composition and stylization mark the works of the later writers. Among the crowd of authors who followed the popular trends and style of Riẓā Shah's period (as distinct from the school of writing advocated originally by Jamālzāda and upheld brilliantly by Hidāyat until it became the undisputable medium of literary expression during the 'forties and 'fifties), these four, J. Jalīlī, M. Mas'ūd, 'A. Dashtī, and M. Ḥijāzī, came to prominence in the 'thirties. The first two are now dead, but the last two, despite their political preoccupations, have continued to carry the banner of what is now regarded as an old and flowery style, although they remain popular writers in more conservative circles.

Jahāngīr Jalīlī (1909–38)

Jalīlī began writing in early youth. After finishing his higher education in classical Persian literature and accountancy (he had also acquired a knowledge of French and English), he published a number of poems and literary articles in various journals. His first book, which showed a high degree of sensitivity and intelligence, was *Man-ham Girya Karda-am* ("I Have Cried As Well...", 1933), appearing first as a serial under the pen name of J. J. Āsīyā'ī in *Shafaq-i Surkh*, a prominent newspaper of the time. It soon caused a stir: the young author immediately became famous. His two later works, *Az Daftar-i Khāṭirāt* ("From the Author's Memoirs", 1935) and *Kārivān-i 'Ishq* ("Caravan of Love", 1938), though less successful than the first book, were sufficient indication of a talent capable of maturing. Jalīlī's sudden death at the age of twenty-nine was a regrettable loss to modern Persian letters.

Man-ham Girya Karda-am is the work of a young man. The theme is the familiar one of prostitution, but a seriousness coupled with deep insight make the book less coarse and more sincere than earlier books on the same subject. Once again we are introduced to a "fallen" girl from the educated class. Vehemently attacked as the basic causes of this social evil are schools for their inefficient programmes, writers for their failure to open the eyes of the public to social depravity, translators for propagating cheap romantic novelettes that poison the minds of the young, and the superficial onslaught of westernization in the country. A moving tale, written with an eloquent pen and coloured by a fertile imagination, brings home the message of the book quite efficiently. Nevertheless, the writing is not entirely free from the characteristic flaws of the time. Apart from incessant preaching and moralizing, which interrupt the progress of the story, occasional outbursts of emotion give rise to faulty reasoning and extreme idealism, revealing the author's naïveté. Still worse is his habit of repeating foreign names and "citing" European men of learning, sometimes with little or no relevance, as if to show off his knowledge of world culture. However, the unfair status of women in society is demonstrated and their rights strongly supported.

If, as has been suggested by Dr Khānlarī, Jalīlī's first book was written in protest against M. Mas'ūd's treatment of prostitution in his *Tafrīḥāt-i Shab* ("Night Diversions"), then it could also be taken as a protest against his own second book, written two years later. Not only the form of *Az Daftar-i Khāṭirāt* but the subject and situations are strikingly similar to those found in the early works of Muḥammad Mas'ūd. Here, too, the main theme revolves around the vagaries and frustrations of youth, especially if they have a claim to the rank of "intellectuals". Unlike his first book and the third and last one, *Kārivān-i 'Ishq* (a commonplace love story), which were each single, complete stories, *Az Daftar-i Khāṭirāt* is a collection of sketches and episodes based on the reminiscences of a group of young people who do not know what to do with their lives or how to combat their dejection and ennui. There are the usual preoccupations—prostitution, defence of the rights of women, corruption in the civil administration, deficiencies in the educational system, trivial novels, vile translations, poisonous films, and so on. But a new and timely theme is the advocacy of a literary revival and criticism of the works of so-called scholars.

Jahāngīr Jalīlī was basically an idealist, but passages of sheer realism appear in his work. His passionate sympathies, especially for the social grievances of women, resulted in a vigorous exposure of many of the worst facets of a changing society that was not yet furnished with new, stabilizing traditions to replace those that modernity had deprived it of.

Muḥammad Mas'ūd (Dihātī)

What is the world? A dirty midden! A horrible charnel house! A huge bedlam that up to now has never been properly organized or run according to any fixed rules or regulations!...In this chaotic, confused world everybody has opened his maws to gulp another down, their teeth kept sharp to tear each other in pieces....

These few lines sum up this author's dismal outlook on life. In his trilogy, *Tafrīḥāt-i Shab* ("Night Diversions", 1932), *Dar Talāsh-i Ma'āsh* ("In Quest of a Living", 1932) and *Ashraf-i Makhlūqāt* ("The Noblest of Creatures", 1934), he presents gloomy, at times nauseating, passages of the blackest pessimism and misanthropy, chiefly concerned with the decline of morals and composed in a language that sometimes sounds like the cries of a man under torture. The characters are a number of school friends, who for one reason or another have failed to continue their studies and are struggling to live. They idle away the daytime at their work: in offices, schools, factories, etc., and spend their nights wandering from one bar to another, getting drunk, looking for women, and ending up in brothels. They have no hope, no ambition, and no moral scruples. They are the products of their society—a society portrayed with the utmost spite. Not only do these colleagues in debauchery suffer from various kinds of venereal disease but, as the author sees it, the whole body of the nation is similarly ailing. People from every walk of life lie, cheat, and try to rob each other. Money reigns supreme. It is Hegel's "animal kingdom" where "dog eats dog".

Mas'ūd is a rebel without a cause, a pessimist with no faith in human nature. In his view, people are fundamentally vicious, debased and wretched, deserving whatever misery befalls them. Altruistic concepts such as love, friendship, humanity, public spiritedness, etc., are no more than a mirage. Not surprisingly, therefore, his trilogy contains more invective and destructive criticism than sober and rational analysis. His particular hatred is reserved for the wealthy and prosperous, and with an almost frantic anguish he attacks the power of money and those who enjoy it. But his enmity for the latter bears the mark of a personal grudge rather than a studied social conviction. One of his morbid preoccupations is the question of inheritance:

In the arena of life there exists this hazard and lack of order, that not all the runners for the goal of success begin at one starting-line nor move by the same means....After the ineffable claws of death cut the arteries of the life of one stupid idiot, his stupid progeny mounts the steed of success in his father's place and counts the leagues by which he is ahead of the others as due to his own capability and talent....

Muḥammad Mas'ūd was, as might be suspected, of humble origin, having spent his childhood in a small provincial town. In his early twenties he reached the capital and became a teacher in an elementary school. At this time he wrote some unsuccessful articles and literary essays for different newspapers. Then came his first major work, *Tafrīḥāt-i Shab*, published under the pen name of M. Dihātī in the newspaper already mentioned, *Shafaq-i Surkh.* The book and its two successors had a mixed reception. To many, among them the "upholders of literary tradition", they seemed a manual of debauchery and malicious ribaldry, written in a disgusting language.[1] Others believed that the author had skilfully put his finger on some of the worst ills of society. Accordingly, they regarded Mas'ūd's writings as a bold literary innovation that put an end to the old style as well as to outmoded subjects.[2] The storm of criticism provoked by his first novel helped the author a good deal in establishing himself.

A cabinet minister, attracted by the talent and adroitness of the young author, sent him on a government scholarship to Europe to study journalism. But on his return Mas'ūd saw no chance under the prevailing political conditions of continuing his career as a savage critic of society. Instead he set up a small business. In 1941, after Riẓā Shah's abdication and the restoration of freedom of the press, he started publishing a vociferous weekly paper called *Mard-i Imrūz* ("Man of Today"). The paper soon gained a wide circulation. Its harsh, even slanderous, editorials, which stopped at nothing and spared no one who had any influence in the affairs of the state, won the editor the admiration of a large secion of the public (who saw themselves revenged by the lash of his tongue), while

[1] It is interesting to note that Mas'ūd gave most of his books an "X. cert.", by asking boys and girls under twenty to refrain from reading them.

[2] See Jamālzāda's article, "Muzhda-yi Rastākhīz-i Adabī" ("News of a Literary Movement") published in *Kūshish* (Isfand 15, 1311/1933) and quoted by B. Nikitine in "Les thèmes sociaux dans la littérature persane moderne", *Oriente Moderno*, XXXIV (May 1954).

it also gained him a number of powerful and vindictive opponents. The latter resorted to an old device. Muḥammad Mas'ūd was assassinated in 1947. The assassin has never been discovered.

After resuming his literary activities in 1941, Mas'ūd published several new books. Prominent among these were *Gul-hā'ī-ka dar Jahanam Mī-rūyad* ("Flowers that Grow in Hell", 1942) and *Bahār-i 'Umr* ("The Spring of Life"), the first two volumes of an unfinished project. In these disturbing volumes we see a master craftsman, mature and accomplished, using his medium with great vision and realism. The story is in the form of an autobiography: an Iranian student, having finished his studies in Europe, goes back to Persia in the hope of finding a job, settling down and bringing home the European fiancée he has left behind. After many frustrations, unforeseen difficulties, and disappointments, he writes to the girl about life in "hell" and explains why conditions there compel him to abandon her.

The first chapter opens with an impressive description of Riẓā Shah's reign and includes occasional flashbacks to some of the calamities Iran has suffered throughout her long history. This is followed by a meticulous and fascinating account of the author's childhood. His playmates: half-naked children wandering about the town, the seat of a holy shrine, in dust and mud under the hot summer sun or winter rain. Their playground: the graveyards with the continuous caravan of incoming dead. Their amusement: watching dervishes and snake-charmers, religious mournings, and passion plays. Their education: treatises on obscure subjects and the brutal floggings from ignorant teachers. Then comes the outbreak of the First World War, the ensuing famine, and the cholera epidemic. All these and a host of other matters are described in simple yet piquant and moving language. Furthermore, they are quite factual. As in his earlier works, considerable space is devoted to criticism of school programmes. And there are some very interesting passages comparing the life, customs, and characteristics of Eastern and Western societies. *Gul-hā'ī-ka dar Jahanam Mī-rūyad* is a fine work of art; had the author lived long enough to complete it, the book would have been a notable contribution to modern Persian literature. Perhaps it would even have earned Mas'ūd the deserving fame of a serious, objective writer, instead of the "scurrilous journalist" that his fellow-countrymen, not unjustly, call him.

'Alī Dashtī

'Alī Dashtī is one of the most controversial figures in the letters and politics of modern Iran. He was born into a middle-class family with a strict religious background. His first contact with public life was through journalism. *Shafaq-i Surkh*, which he founded in 1921 and remained editor of until 1930, soon became one of the leading daily papers of the time and played a major part in shaping public opinion throughout the 'twenties. Apart from valuable literary discussions and a genuine attempt to open the eyes of its readers to progressive ideas, to the realities of the modern age, and to Western culture and civilization, the chief attraction of the paper was its passionate editorials, written in an unusually vigorous and expressive style and directed chiefly against government policy. As a result of his editorials and the political candour Dashtī showed in his youth, he was often, during Riẓā Shah's time, sent to prison or exiled. Later, however, he acquired more discretion: on curbing his language he became a recognized politician with a seat in the *Majlis*, a seat he retained for several sessions. After the Second World War he served as Persia's ambassador to Egypt and Lebanon for several years. Still a bachelor in his seventies, and well versed in Arabic and French, Dashtī was later rewarded with a seat in the Senate, where he has remained a witty speaker.

Dashtī's first book, *Ayyām-i Maḥbas* ("Prison Days", 1921), appeared when the author was still a struggling young man and is therefore very different from his later works. After the *coup d'état* of 1921 a number of politicians, and pressmen, and other public figures, of whose support the new régime was not certain, were detained. Dashtī was one of them, and *Ayyām-i Maḥbas* includes his reflections during imprisonment. To the fourth, enlarged edition he has added notes, political essays, and memoirs written during his later arrests. In addition to the easy and graceful style characteristic of all Dashtī's work, a common feature in all these pieces, written over a number of years, is their rebellious and angry spirit. The writer appears a militant revolutionary, using the extraordinary power of his pen against the rich and privileged, the crimes and intrigues of the police, and the general corruption in civil administration. Pages are devoted to the condition of prison cells and the maltreatment of political prisoners by the warders. His arguments about life imprisonment and capital punishment, coming down ultimately in favour of the latter, seem equivocal. Here, as when criticizing the consequences of modern civilization and condemning man as little better than a ferocious beast, the author goes to such extremes that he seems more of a nihilist than the freedom-loving democrat he claimed to be.

Written with considerable skill and appeal is the section on Riẓā Shah's policies and his morbid suspicion of able men, which resulted in the death of many political leaders. The reader is stirred as the terror in a cowed society comes to life.

Apart from *Ayyām-i Maḥbas*, Dashtī has other ruminations on society and politics, usually in the form of articles written for various journals. A number of these can be found in his *Sāya* ("Shadow", 1946). Here, in contrast to earlier pieces, the author speaks in mild tones, treating his material soberly and conservatively, while passing judgements that the younger generation could easily term reactionary.

The second group of Dashtī's works, and one that has gained him much respect in recent years, is about Iran's classical literature. These writings include some essays of literary criticism published in the collection *Sāya*, and a series of books elucidating Dashtī's views on the personality, works, and ideas of some of the great Persian classical poets. Four of the series have so far appeared, under the titles: *Naqshī az Ḥāfiẓ* ("A Portrait of Hafiz", 1957), *Sayr-ī dar Dīvān-i Shams* ("An Excursion into the Poems of Shams", 1958), *Qalamru-yi Sa'dī* ("Sa'di's Realm", 1959) and *Shā'ir-i Dīr-Āshnā* ("The Poet it's Hard to Know", 1962), which is about Khāqānī. These books are a new departure in the evaluation of Persia's great classical heritage. They also represent a somewhat surprising development in the literary activity of an elderly author. Adopting the techniques of European classicists, an increasing number of Iranian scholars spend time examining manuscript sources for new literary information on texts and the lives and inspirations of poets. Dashtī, however, has chosen to present the poets of his imagination: to give his personal, and learned, reactions to a classical literature which for his people is still very much a living entity, and not exclusively a field of scholarly research.

There is hardly any new scholarship in these studies. Rather, the author is popularizing the classics, assisting the student to appreciate them. Dashtī's argument is that old methods of scholarly research—delving deep into rhetorical treatises in search of dates and the poets' places of birth, genealogy, age, and so forth —left to us by historians, have done little to further our understanding of the merits of classical literature. He states that the historians' interest has centred mainly around rulers and their conquests; the incidental references they have made to poets are not infallible, for they are not immune from personal prejudice. In his view the criterion for passing judgement on a poet must be his works, not the hearsay of chroniclers. Thus, Dashtī is not concerned with how these classics have come to be known to the outside world. Instead he attempts a realization of the poets through their verses.

There may be many men of learning in Iran and elsewhere with a far deeper knowledge of Persian poetry, but very few have shown Dashtī's sensitivity, breadth of imagination, and skill in appraising their findings. Besides his general remarks about the poetical talent, language, style, and ideas of these poets who have been a source of constant inspiration to him, there are informative chapters on the translation of Ḥāfiẓ (which Dashtī considers impossible); reasons why the *Dīvān* of Shams has been hitherto comparatively unknown; and some enlightening comparisons between the poets in question and a number of other great poets of Persia. In this respect the chapter in *Qalamru-yi Sa'dī*, comparing this poet with Nāṣir Khusraw, is of particular interest. Nāṣir Khusraw's personality, as well as his social, political, and religious ideas, are depicted with great charm and acumen. In the same book there is a close scrutiny of the philosophies and counsels contained in the *Gulistān*, and Dashtī has daringly attacked Sa'dī's attitude to life by disclosing the weak points and contradictions latent in the masterpiece of this revered Persian sage.

In the books discussed above, 'Alī Dashtī has not only reached the peak of his career as a writer, but has opened a new vista in the study of Persian literature. No matter how thorough our acquaintance with these four poets, Dashtī's contribution, written in exquisite language, furthers our knowledge and appreciation of them.

There are few critics in Persia who differ on the merits of the above works of 'Alī Dashtī. There is a great deal of controversy, however, over the social virtues of a third type of his writings, which, to say the least, constitute a pretty *chronique scandaleuse*: books like *Fitna* (1949), *Jādū* (1952) and *Hindū* (1955). These colourful *tableaux vivants*, depicting the caprices of certain promiscuous women who move in high society, are immensely popular among certain upper-class circles and teenage schoolgirls. To the former they serve as a mirror reflecting aspects of their own lives; to the latter as a window through which they see glimpses of the forbidden world. Sex is the predominant theme. And the characters in these works are all identical.

The man—always a bachelor, smart and handsome, sociable, genteel, and well mannered—is seen at every important function of the *beau monde*. He is fond of poker and dancing, throws frequent parties, and is obviously well read and familiar with Western culture. His main interest in life, however, is the fair sex. He is the subject of rivalry among the drawing-room ladies of modern Tehran society and invariably displays a great passion for possessing what does not belong to him. The woman—always married, good looking, and part of the gay world of high society—moves in chic and fashionable circles, where she cuts a distinctive figure. In her view men who do not seek adventure and lack a capricious heart have a defect in their manhood.

These two people easily find each other and fall in love. The rest of the story describes their secret meetings, their emotional experiences, joys and sorrows, disloyalties to one another, and finally their inevitable separation. At no time is there any suggestion of a social contract being violated or indeed any mention of the unfortunate husband. On the contrary, the narrator often poses as an experienced tutor instructing the ladies of society in the art of seduction. Not only the characters but the theme and overall texture of the stories all follow the same pattern. It is ironical, therefore, when in one of them we read:

> Jādū...was too discriminating to attach any importance to or regard as worthy of record these repeated and trivial events of which one was generally a copy of the other.

One wonders why a man of Dashtī's acumen and calibre should display so little discrimination in registering trivialities that one of his own "heroines" did not deem worthy of attention.

Still, if we can overlook the social level of these pieces and suppose that the author wrote them for the sake of writing only, then the novelty of his language, especially in psychological analysis, and the beauty of his style in revealing the characters' innermost mental processes are worthy of praise. In his choice of elegant and poetical words—unique among contemporary writers—he moves in a diametrically opposite direction to Jamālzāda, Hidāyat and their followers. Refusing to descend to colloquial, everyday language, he selects words and phrases for their rhythm and musical lyricism, and tries to give his compositions a kind of decorous and *distingué* flavour. To achieve this, however, he finds it necessary to resort to a wide range of foreign and arabicized terms, which are a serious detriment to his graceful style.[1]

Apart from writing numerous essays, short pieces, and stories, Dashtī has translated three major works: from the French, Samuel Smiles's *Self-Help* and Gustave Le Bon's *Navāmīs-i Rūḥīya-hi Taṭavur-i Millal*;[2] and from Arabic Edmond Demolins's *A quoi tient la supériorité des Anglo-saxons*. His style in these works is rather simple and straightforward, without the flamboyance that characterizes most of his later writings.

Muḥammad Ḥijāzī

Quite understandably, most contemporary writers in Iran shun government affiliations. But Muḥammad Ḥijāzī (*the Muṭī'ud-Dawla*), both as a writer and an individual, has been closely connected with official life ever since his early youth. He entered the literary field at the beginning of the 'twenties and was one of the most popular novelists and essayists during the period of Riẓā Shah. This alone should indicate the nature of his writings; yet a glance at his whole career will help us in assessing the success and failure of his literary achievements.

[1] Besides the arabicized constructions in these three books, one finds more than once such European words as: aisance, ambiance, collectionneur, compliqué, conscient, coquette, coquetrice, excentrique, exposition, fatuité, féministe, femme de ménage, femme fatale, formuler, gentleman, homme charmant, idée fixe, inconscient, indifferent, objective, originalité, passion, réservée, subjective, sexualité, subconscience, sadique, sentimental, surprise, tact, tactic, théâtral and vulgaire.

[2] Presumably *L'homme et les Sociétés, Leurs Origines et leur Histoire.*

Born in 1899, Ḥijāzī was educated at the "Islām" and "St Louise", the first an indigenous free school, the second a French Roman Catholic missionary institution in Tehran. He then travelled to Europe, studied political science for some time in Paris, and later took a degree in telecommunications—a typical example of the vagaries of scholastic careers of Persians sent abroad for higher education. Returning to Persia, he occupied several government positions in the Ministry of Posts and Telegraphs and was for some years the editor of this ministry's monthly magazine. In 1937 he was appointed head of the press section of a newly established government institution called "Sāzmān-i Parvarish-i Afkār" (The Bureau for Public Enlightenment: literally, "The Bureau for the Training of Thoughts"), intended to direct and develop the "collective mind" of Persian citizens. In this capacity Ḥijāzī was charged with editing the journal *Īrān-i Imrūz*, which was the mouthpiece of this organization; subscription to this journal was obligatory for senior government officials. Since the events of August 1941 (Shahrīvar 1320) and the abdication of Riẓā Shah, Muḥammad Ḥijāzī has occupied several high positions, including directorship of the state-controlled Radio and Propaganda Department. He has also had a seat in the Senate for several years now.

Ḥijāzī's writings can be grouped into three categories: novels, essays and short stories, and miscellaneous works.

His novels established Ḥijāzī's fame as a writer, beginning with the publication of *Humā* (1927), *Parīchihr* (1929) and *Zībā* (1931). The fate and the characteristic traits of Iranian women, as the author sees them, form the substance of all three: the titles themselves are all women's names.

In *Humā* two virtuous persons are the main characters. Humā, an educated girl of the middle class, has deep respect for her guardian Ḥasan-'Alī Khān, who secretly loves her but cannot declare himself because of old age, his sense of responsibility and the fact that he is already married. Humā falls in love with a young man, but Ḥasan-'Alī Khān's implicit objection makes the girl realize his desire for her, whereupon, with extraordinary self-sacrifice, she decides to dedicate her life to him. However, the young man refuses to give her up, and with the help of a wretched *Ākhund* (divine) he starts intriguing against his rival. The rest of the story describes the struggle that follows, with treachery on one side and magnanimity on the other. Finally comes a far-fetched climax: the capture of Ḥasan-'Alī Khān by Russian officers and an unconvincing though happy ending.

The author is at pains to present Humā as a paragon of virtue, the symbol of modern, emancipated, and progressive Iranian womanhood, with Ḥasan-'Alī Khān as the honest and modest intellectual. Neither character seems real, nor do their saintly virtues make any sense. They both appear extremely weak, shedding tears or fainting away when confronted with any difficulty, and suffering because of timidity and irresolution. An exception among the minor characters is the colourful Shaykh Ḥusayn, a deceitful, cunning rascal, prepared under the cloak of religion to commit any crime for self-interest. In his brief appearance, he forcefully and vividly personifies his type. Perhaps this short, successful sketch gave Ḥijāzī the idea of creating the other memorable Shaykh Ḥusayn, in his third novel *Zībā*, some years later.

The second novel *Parīchihr* is much inferior to the first in composition, character delineation, and realistic detail. The author intends to depict a spoiled and capricious woman, but Parīchihr is so vague and colourless that her real nature remains a mystery to the reader. As a kind of addendum in the closing pages, however, there appears a letter informing the husband—and the reader for that matter—that Parīchihr was really vicious and wayward. The author seems equally bewildered. He ends up by saying:

I was wondering what caused all this calamity! Inevitably, I came to the conclusion that the answer to these puzzles and problems should be sought in the next world.

Still more reprehensible than the weak structure of the story is the author's indulgence in exaggerated emotions, out-of-context details, and, above all, long didactic discourses.[1]

Ḥijāzī's fame as a novelist rests mainly on his third novel, *Zībā* (1931), which, though not immune from the faults of the other two, is among the best products of modern Persian literature. The story (three volumes have so far appeared, and it may still be continued) is so rich and eventful that it defies any attempt at abridgement.

[1] In later revised editions the author has tried to prune the book, omitting many superfluous passages. Nevertheless, the text is basically unchanged.

The two main characters are Zībā, a young, attractive, whimsical wanton, with wide connections in official circles, and Shaykh Ḥusayn, a poor provincial student of divinity who becomes a prey to Zībā's charms and ends up a formidable rascal, shuffling through life as a parasite in high society.

In the course of a moving and well-plotted story, while watching the *Shaykh*'s rise to fame and high position by means of deception, charlatanism, and the unstinting blandishments of his mistress, the reader is skilfully introduced to the alarming corruption of the country's civil administration. Having spent a lifetime in the midst of a venal bureaucracy, Ḥijāzī knows it well and therefore writes with authority on his subject. The book is almost a compendium of the lies, crimes and machinations of senior government officials and other notables to achieve their personal ends. In a galaxy of interesting characters, all alive and extremely well defined, each illustrates a particular social type. Ḥijāzī's courage in exposing the vices of his characters and in depicting a corrupt administration, despite his own association with it, deserves admiration. As for his overall views on politics and politicians, he writes:

> Politics keep a man from the delights of learning and art and from the comprehension of beauty, and restrict the scope of thought and limit the field of vision. They cast to the winds any hope for friendship, decency, goodness and justice—the most valuable assets of life; they make the world full from end to end of deceit and double-dealing. Any pure and tranquil mind that applies itself to politics becomes corrupt and distracted.

As if describing the author's predicament, Ḥijāzī's hero adds:

> What can I do? My destiny was that I should be caught up for a whole lifetime in politics and not behold the face of good fortune.

Zībā was the culmination of Ḥijāzī's talent as a novelist. During later years, as he ascended the official ladder and became more and more involved in politics, his literary talents as well as the tone of his utterance changed accordingly. Going through his later works, we notice traces of a painstaking effort to remain always on the safe side and not to be provocative. The following extract from a Persian newspaper, though written sardonically and in imitation of his own style, touches on this change of attitude as seen by his compatriots today:

. . . Now, when I came back to my own country, so long as my heart and my pen remained free of the colouring of the age, I used indeed to write beautifully and delighted in this sweetness of expression and freshness of style. My works were sought by young and old: my books purchased by both sexes. But I don't know what happened. Either I conceived a lust for position, or opportunist rogues became jealous of my success. Either I changed or they changed me. Suddenly I saw that in the "Hall for the Public Enlightenment" I had loosed a rash tongue. Even as 'Unṣurī uttered a *qaṣīda* about the conquest of Sūmanāt, I too broke into eloquent speech on the subject of the actions of the late Dictator. Whatever fitting words and agreeable modes of expression I remembered from the Old Master, I flung onto the wheel, but. . . they gave me a magazine and told me I must write, vividly recreating the state of Iran as it was before. Write I did, but, like one walking in a dream who never reaches a destination, my writings were all colourless and unproductive: the mirror of my imagination had become clouded.[1]

In the early 'fifties, almost twenty years after the appearance of his last novel, *Zībā*, Ḥijāzī published two new novels, *Parvāna* and *Sirishk* ("Tears").[2] The first is the story of a romantic schoolgirl who falls in love with a poet, without knowing or even having seen him, but simply after reading his works. She corresponds with him, and a kind of pen-friendship grows between them. Years later, when the girl has married, they meet but fail to establish any intimate relationship because of her matrimonial barriers. In the end, distressed by the thought that her love has made the poet heartbroken and miserable, Parvāna commits suicide. This sacrifice, according to the author, opens the eyes of the poet to "spiritual love. . . a love which has no need for regard, affection, friendliness or even a beloved". He leaves the girl's deathbed, confident that: "the earthly beloved is of no use to the poet, the poet's beloved is in heaven not on earth".

In the course of the story the author makes a desultory effort to glorify poetry and condemn the pursuit of gain (symbolized by Parvāna's husband). But as he points out at the beginning, his book is devoid of action and plot; nothing happens: we have only an album of word painting before us, coloured by sentimental lamentation and poetical diction.

[1] From the newspaper *Bābā Shamal* (printed in Tehran), no. 86.

[2] According to the Iranian press Ḥijāzī received the first Royal Prize, 50,000 Rials, for these new novels.

The same "theme", rather elaborated and carried into psycho-pathological analysis, forms the substance of the second novel, *Sirishk*. The story takes place in America and describes the life, love affairs, and marriage of an American youth. After associating with numerous young girls of different looks, character, and social aptitude, William meets the girl-friend of his cousin and marries her forthwith. It soon turns out that the girl is under the strain of a morbid imagination and suffers from chronic jealousy towards other women. She sees treachery in every action, even in her husband's thoughts, and she hires private detectives to spy on him. At last, suspecting him of renewed relations with his former associates, she brutally blinds him in his sleep. A trial follows, but the loyal husband appeals for the acquittal of his wicked wife and they live together peacefully thereafter. In a closing chapter the author tries to apply the moral of his tale to a newly wed Persian pair. He dedicates the book to them, expressing the hope that it might also serve as a warning to its readers, and might help to increase the happiness of families and consequently the well-being of the Iranian society!

In an article about Muḥammad Ḥijāzī written by D. S. Komissarov, a Russian orientalist, considerable space is devoted to these two novels, particularly to *Sirishk*. Mr Komissarov's comments on the first novel should be regarded as rash conjecture: in his opinion, Ḥijāzī has written *Parvāna* under the influence of Zola, and he sees a "surprising similarity between Parvana and Therese Raquin". The influence of Zola's naturalistic traits can be detected here and there in Ḥijāzī's works as a whole. But it is hard, even by a stretch of the imagination, to see an identity between Ḥijāzī's puritanical ineffectual book and the gruesome but forceful novel of Zola. Even harder to trace is a similarity between the two main characters, Parvāna and Therese Raquin. Zola's heroine is a frustrated woman who enters into an adulterous union as soon as she finds herself a lover, and then takes part in his plot to kill her husband. After the murder, filled with agony and repulsion, and facing an impossible situation, she and the lover resort to suicide as their only solution. Ḥijāzī's heroine, Parvāna, is just the opposite. In her attachment to the poet there is no physical urge: she simply loves his poetry and his spiritual merits (a situation typical of Ḥijāzī towards passion) while she will not even allow him to kiss her hand. Incomprehensible and puerile though it appears, her death is depicted as martyrdom, and is meant to display her virtuous devotion to the poet.

Though coloured by his political and ideological bias, Mr Komissarov's assessment of the second novel, *Sirishk*, is more apt. In this story he sees reflected the morals of American society, "which are governed by eroticism leading man to complete nervous disorder and crime". He rightly emphasizes that all the actions of the novel are subordinated to subconscious biological craving. In the "feast of spirits", where the guests are entertained by deformed bodies, cut-off heads, corpses in their coffins, babies nailed down on sharp spikes, vipers, crocodiles, scorpions, etc., creeping on walls and ceilings, while screams of horror and anguish echo all over the place, Komissarov discerns the "depraved tastes of the West" and the representation of a sad reality, daily emphasized by "horror" films and papers.

In addition to his novels, Ḥijāzī has published several collections of essays and short stories, such as: *Āyina* ("Mirror", 1932, 6th enlarged edition 1951), *Andīsha* ("Reflection", 1937), *Sāghar* ("Goblet", 1951), *Āhang* ("Melody", 1951) and *Nasīm* ("Breeze", 1961). These include some 250 miscellaneous pieces. Although a prolific essayist and short-story writer, Ḥijāzī suffers from lack of versatility. His themes generally revolve around the negative aspects of human nature and how to cure them with the author's evasive nostrum. In his short stories, as indeed in his novels, the majority of characters belong to the urban middle class. They are normally depicted with considerable skill; and their private lives are especially well portrayed. But in the portrayal of situations the author goes astray, appearing naïve and idealistic. Social and material elements play hardly any part in the solution of his problems. To him, human ills are the direct result of corrupt morals and can be remedied by exhorting and persuading evil-doers to correct their failings. It is useless to look for realistic inferences, logical reasoning, or analysis of social factors in these brief and often fugitive pieces. Instead the reader is confronted with an abundance of poetical dreams, diversified only by tedious moralizations. In fact, as Mr Komissarov points out: "He substitutes abstract moralizing and medieval didactics for the realistic method of disclosing reality."

The composition of these story-like essays is rather conventional: there is usually a prefatory discourse, illustrated by a simple story and a final categorical deduction to be read as a gospel.

All these characteristics are especially noticeable in the collection *Andīsha*, a book written for high school students at the behest of the Ministry of Education. In the story "Majma'-i Zindānīyān" ("The Company of Prisoners"), for example, well over one-third of the piece is taken up by the author's observations on the ugliness and horror of a prison cell, then on the necessity for safeguards for society, and finally by the bitter assertion that it is the downtrodden innocents who fall victims of the law. The story itself is very short. The author is about to visit an imprisoned friend, and he imagines that his friend must be suffering from a frightful loneliness. But when he is taken inside the prison, he notices to his surprise that true equality, brotherhood, and comradeship obtain among the prisoners. When he comes out he visualizes the world as an enlarged prison and wonders why human beings do not love and help one another.[1]

In "Pand-i Rūstā" ("Farmer's Advice") a group of friends on a picnic meet an old farmer and start teasing him about his shabby appearance. The old man tells them that he happens to be the owner of a large estate with plenty of victuals and livestock, and he invites them to visit him there. On hearing this, the attitude of the young picnickers suddenly changes. They become polite and respectful, asking the old man to join them for lunch. After the meal he informs them that he is no more than a poverty-stricken man, but will repay them with a piece of advice: they should regard every individual as they would a rich landowner and treat all people with kindness and good manners.

The theme of the "Ṣaḥrā-nishīnān" ("The Nomads") is an old feud between two rival tribes. After years of enmity and bloodshed, a wise man among them thinks of a solution. On false pretences he goes as the representative of one tribe to the other, and, loaded with presents, he apologizes for the past and promises future friendship. The rival group accepts the offer heartily and thus ends the long-standing feud of the two tribes. The moral: "The distance between love and enmity can be bridged with a

[1] An English translation of this piece appeared in *Life and Letters* (Dec. 1949), pp. 223–5.

smile. The well-being and misfortune of men and the world depend ultimately on one word, only uttered by a drunkard or one in possession of his senses."

Another story, "Āsānī" ("Easiness"), is in praise of poverty and deprivation: "In the search for happiness, poverty makes us without need of wealth and other means; why then complain of such a teacher?"! In "Dāstān-i Nīyākān" ("Ancestors' Tale"), Persian hospitality and patriotism are praised. "Dād-bakhshī" ("The Giving of Justice") and "Ḥāfiẓa" ("Memory") are about helpfulness and regard for other fellow beings, especially those in need. The rest of *Andīsha* is based more or less on the same lines.

The other three collections, *Sāghar*, *Āhang* and *Nasīm*, include stories, short essays and literary pieces, with love and moral deductions as their predominant themes. Other short stories are to be found in the massive collection of *Āyina*. Noteworthy among them are "Shīrīn Kulā", "Shā'ir-i Bilzhīkī" ("Belgian Poet"), "Fātiḥ-i Rūmī" ("Roman Conqueror"), "Munājāt" ("Prayer"), "Andūkhta-yi Safar" ("Gains of a Travel"), "Mahtāb" ("Moonlight") and "Naqqāsh" ("Painter").

Apart from his novels, essays and short stories, Ḥijāzī has also published a number of translations, including *The Interpretation of Dreams* by Sigmund Freud, *How Personalities Grow* by Helen Shacter, *The Pursuit of Happiness* by R. MacIver, *The Mind Alive* by Harry and Bonaro Overstreet, *The Wisdom of Living Religions* by Joseph Gaer, and Cicero's *De Amicitia* and *De Senectute*. These works are all rendered into Persian rather freely. The translator has at times omitted a whole chapter or altered the substance or the names of the characters, trying on the whole to "Persianize" the texts as far as possible.

Among his other works are: *Kamālu'l-Mulk* (a biography), *Tiligrāf-i Bīsīm* ("Wireless Telegraph"), *Khulāṣa-yi Tārīkh-i Īrān* ("A Summary of the History of Iran"), and a number of plays for the stage, famous among which are *Ḥāfiẓ*, *'Arūs Farangī* ("European Bride"), *Jang* ("War"), *Ḥājjī-yi Mutujaddid* ("The Modernist Hajji"), *Musāfirat-i Qum* ("A Trip to Qum") and *Maḥmūd Āqā rā Vakīl Kunīd* ("Vote for Mahmud Aqa"). The last was staged in 1949 in one of the Tehran theatres and had a very successful run. Technically the play has numerous shortcomings: there are no descriptions of the characters, their movements and costumes, of the *mise en scène*, or any other prerequisites of a stage-play. But as far as the subject-matter is concerned, it is one of the author's most decisive and positive works. In it he exposes the corruption of the state apparatus and the bribery, graft and black-mail of certain decadent elements that are trying to penetrate the *Majlis*. He daringly shows how, in the interest of their private gains, the politicians abuse the mandate of the electorate and turn the parliament into an instrument for political intrigue.

Commenting on *Māḥmūd Āqā rā Vakīl Kunīd*, Komissarov draws an interesting comparison between this play and Ṣādiq Hidāyat's famous novelette, *Ḥājjī Āqā*.[1] In his opinion the substantial difference between the two works lies in the kind of evil that each exposes. Hidāyat subjects to withering criticism the reactionary nature of a dying class, and shows how this class, by all the means in its power, tries to stifle the rising democratic movement. In opposition to Ḥājjī Āqā, the political charlatan, he puts a young idealist. But in Ḥijāzī's play, continues Komissarov, we have a different picture. Here the author exposes only the rogues who try to enter the *Majlis* with selfish, opportunistic aims. But their anti-national character and their hostility towards the people remain untouched. Thus Ḥijāzī, unlike Hidāyat, does not expose a social evil, but tries to show that it is enough to remove "depraved" individuals and allow scope for the actions of the government. In other words, Mr Komissarov sums up, this play merely reflects the struggle for power between political groups, and the author's sympathy lies on the side of those who rule the country.

Ḥijāzī has been acclaimed by Henry D. G. Law as the Steele or Addison of Persia today. There is perhaps some slight justification in such an analogy, because these two English authors held important public offices and expressed sentiments that were pleasing to the Whig politicians, i.e. the ruling clique of their day. The middle class was their hero; and comment on civilized life, including guidance on public conduct, was essential to their writings. More or less the same kind of pattern applies to Ḥijāzī. But Steele and Addison sought their public in the coffee-house assemblies of the time, among ordinary people "who did not talk like a book"; they were successful because they reflected the spirit

[1] See below, pp. 192–7.

of the times and spoke for a new and civilized urban life. The case of the Persian writer is quite different. In the words of Mr Law himself, "Hejazi writes for the cultured classes; and if he describes the life of the humbler folks he does so rather as an observer albeit a sympathetic wise and kindly observer". Between the lines of this sentence may be read the purport of another, about William Saroyan: "He writes of the poor for the rich."[1]

Nevertheless, the style and language of Ḥijāzī have a special significance in modern Persian literature. His straightforward, and melodious style, imbued with classical lyricism and a kindly philosophy, finds suitable ground among young students, ambitious to take pen in hand. In his essays, especially in the collection *Andīsha*, Ḥijāzī tries to imitate—or, rather, to modernize—the style of Sa'dī's *Gulistān*, but despite such attempts at modernity, his style remains somewhat archaic and artificial, lacking the everyday idioms and popular expressions used by Jamālzāda and Hidāyat. In comparison with theirs, his best compositions, e.g. "Bābā Kūhī"[2] (*Āyina*, p. 357), sound florid and prolix.

Speaking of Ḥijāzī's short stories and occasional pieces, Dr Khānlarī states:

> Ḥijāzī's style in these works is what is known as "literary". He exaggerates in the use of metaphors and tropes. His descriptions are full of ordinary well-known allusions, mostly borrowed from classical literature. In this manner Ḥijāzī displays a certain amount of restraint and stiffness in his phraseology. He does not insist on recording the natural idioms and expressions of the people; he makes them speak in his own turn of phrase.

Among the host of modern Persian writers Ḥijāzī is interesting because he is so representative of what can happen to the sensitive, educated Iranian who comes into contact with the West. Almost all the authors of this period show some symptoms of this sudden exposure to Western political and cultural ideas—and in the artist the symptoms accentuated are those of a whole society. There is, for instance, a tension in their writings that is typical of the age, during which deep-rooted political, social, and religious traditions were either being obliterated or else sustained the shock

[1] Howard Fast, *Literature and Reality* (New York, 1950).

[2] This story has been translated by Rudolf Gelpke into German and published in a collection called *Persische Meistererzähler der Gegenwart* (Zürich, 1961).

of impact with modern Western institutions and theories. Sometimes this tension disoriented the writers, and this is particularly noticeable in Ḥijāzī. Both as a stylist and thinker Ḥijāzī is weak because he fails to evince any definite principles or to take up a position. He shows an inclination to describe the hard life of his countrymen, but his official affiliations inhibit him. When he takes the risk, at best he confines himself to the description of how, not why, things happen.

As a literary artist and an educated Iranian, Ḥijāzī endeavours to hold on to what he regards as the Iranian artistic tradition: hence his romanticism and poetical passages. But these tendencies in his work are generally a blemish, because even here this westernized writer has lost a proper realization of what traditional Persian poetry is. That too much and too sudden contact with the West ravages the sensitive Persian mind is seen in Ḥijāzī's not-altogether-successful attempt to reproduce Persian style, poetic sentiment, and descriptions in a westernized form which might be termed Persian romanticism. Ḥijāzī wants to be Persian and at the same time to write as a novelist or essayist after the great foreign models. His failure to reach the class of writers who continue a country's literary tradition corresponds to his failure to have the best of two worlds, one of which he never properly assimilated and the other whose true nature he has forgotten.

CHAPTER X

AFTER RIẒĀ SHAH: THE PERIOD OF POLITICAL EXPERIMENT (1941–65)

THE German invasion of Russia in June 1941 accentuated the importance of Persia to the Allies. During the following months, numerous notes were exchanged between the Soviet and British governments and Iran demanding that the Iranian Government should expel the large German colony then resident in the country, and on 25 August Anglo-Soviet forces occupied the country. On 16 September Riẓā Shah abdicated, and his son Muḥammad Riẓā Pahlavi was proclaimed shah by the *Majlis*.

With the accession of the new ruler, the rule of democracy was loudly heralded: the release of political prisoners, freedom of speech, and removal of government censorship on the press, on postal services and publications were the first tokens of the new era. As a result of a general amnesty, many left-wing elements and progressive intellectuals kept in check during Riẓā Shah's time were freed. These, ambitious to carry out fundamental reforms, began to organize political groups—as did a number of professional politicians of the former régime who were apprehensive of losing their influence. Thus numerous parties were soon in existence; simultaneously many new newspapers and periodicals appeared. Barely two years after the abdication of Riẓā Shah, according to an observer, about fifteen parties and some 150 newspapers and periodicals had emerged on the political horizon of Tehran. Most of these were created merely on political impulse and had no background, specific programme, or real organization. Great impetus was given to this "democratic" holiday of political parties and journalism by the subtle support of shrewd members of the old ruling circles, who were adroit enough to use the currently fashionable mediums of publicity and political campaigning to create a situation in which they might reacquire the influence denied them throughout Riẓā Shah's reign. The followers of these groups were generally wealthy merchants, landowners, members of the religious hierarchy, and the reactionary elements of the extreme right.

Concurrently, on the left wing, a revolutionary socialist party, called the Tūda ("Mass"), was formed in 1942. It was well organized and indoctrinated, with extensive press facilities, a comprehensive programme, calculated tactics, and considerable unofficial backing from Russia. This party advocated a series of new ideas and radical reforms extremely attractive to the younger generation, who saw no prospect of fundamental social and administrative reforms under agents of the pre-Riẓā Shah régime who were now back in the political arena. Thus the more politically conscious elements—university students and many young, Western-educated intellectuals—were among the first to join and take a conscientious part in the activities of this party. The success of the Tūda in its early stages was due among other things to the fact that, unlike other political organizations of the time, it was not the party of a personage: it was the party of an idea. In 1944 the Tūda party was represented in the *Majlis* by eight members, and in 1946 it had three ministers in the Cabinet.[1]

The basis for Persian relations with Britain and Russia from 1942, following the Occupation, was the Tripartite Treaty. According to this, the Allies undertook to withdraw their forces from the Persian territory not later than six months after hostilities between Germany and her associates and the Allied Powers ceased. When this deadline came, the Russians failed to comply. In the meantime, inspired by Russia and backed by her troops stationed in the northern provinces, two autonomous republics had sprung up in Azerbaijan and Kurdistan during 1945. In 1946, after about two years' struggle and negotiations with Russia, and through United Nations intervention, Iran emerged victorious. The Soviet-sponsored régimes in the north collapsed and the Red Army divisions left Persia.

[1] For a detailed study of this party, see G. Lenczowski, *Russia and the West in Iran, 1918–1948* (Ithaca, 1949), pp. 223–35 and his "The Communist Movement in Iran", *M.E.J.* I (1947), 29–45. Also A. Kapeliouk's "Tudeh Party in Iran", in the 1953 summer issue of *Hamizrah Hehadash* (vol. IV, no. 4/16, pp. 244–54), a quarterly published by the Oriental Society of the Hebrew University of Jerusalem, and S. Ẕabīḥ's "Iranian Communism: A Case Study in Scope, Appeal, and Prospects" (unpublished), presented to a Conference on Near Eastern Politics, UCLA, June 1964.

In February 1949 there was an attempt on the life of the shah, and as a result the Tūda party was declared illegal, its publishing houses were closed, and a number of party leaders arrested. These measures, however, did not seriously impair the party's activities. On the contrary, through their underground network the leaders managed to bring more discipline and solidarity to their rank-and-file and especially to reach a wider section of the educated class.[1]

Meanwhile, a movement for nationalization of the oil industry was gathering momentum. In 1948 negotiations had begun for revision of the Oil Agreement between the Anglo-Iranian Oil Company and the Persian Government; but the resultant Supplementary Agreement was rejected by the *Majlis*. After a series of political assassinations, party agitations, and other disturbances, that created an atmosphere of terror, a single-article Nationalization Law was passed unanimously in March 1951 by both houses of Parliament. In the following month, Dr Muḥammad Muṣaddiq was chosen prime minister by a substantial majority.

The story of the stormy years of Muṣaddiq's premiership—with its political rallies, demonstrations, strikes, futile negotiations and mediations, economic pressures, rivalries of international power politics, etc.—cannot yet be assessed. His government was overthrown by General Zāhidī and his military supporters in August 1953, in circumstances that still require a thorough investigation. In October 1954 the *Majlis* ratified an agreement reached between the Persian Government and a consortium of eight large oil companies with interests in the Middle East. In October 1955 Iran joined the Baghdad Pact, the alliance that was renamed the Central Treaty Organization (CENTO) after the withdrawal of Iraq in 1958.

Certain stern measures taken by the government during the years immediately after Muṣaddiq's downfall brought some degree of internal order and stability between 1955 and 1960. Like their predecessors in the post-war period, the twin political parties "Millīyūn" and "Mardum" that came into being during these

[1] "According to the Rector of Tehran University, in 1951 up to 75% of the students of the Tehran University, numbering some 5000, had pro-communist leanings. Many lecturers, too, were under the influence of the Tudeh; the Tudeh had its sympathisers even in the secondary and primary schools and among Government officials" (V. Courtois, "The Tudeh Party", published in *Indo-Iranica*, vol. VII, June 1954, no. 2, pp. 14–22).

years failed to gain any following among the people, for the simple reason that they were created by individuals with the ultimate aim of safeguarding the interests of the ruling class. The "National Front", consisting of the various political groups who support Dr Muṣaddiq, has been the centre of political opposition during recent years; but lack of proper organization, discord among its leaders, and the absence of a clear-cut, positive policy have kept the Front from being effective.

In May 1961, after appointing Dr 'Alī Amīnī as the head of government, the shah dissolved both houses of Parliament, enabling the new premier to rule by decree. The principal item on Dr Amīnī's programme of reform was redistribution of land throughout the country—not a new phenomenon in Persia's recent history. In 1950 the shah had announced his intention of distributing the Crown estates: about three million acres estimated to contain some 3000 villages. (It is helpful to remember that out of the country's total population of nearly 20 million, an estimated 12 million are peasants living in some 45,000 villages. Only 5 per cent of the villagers are literate.) Other sweeping social reforms included in the government's latest programme, whose main body was approved by a near-unanimous majority of Iranian voters in a referendum on 26 January 1963, are:

(1) abolition of the landlord–peasant system on the basis of the Land Reform Law and its amendments;

(2) sale of government-owned factories to underwrite the land reform;

(3) nationalization of forests throughout the country;

(4) endorsement of the Profit-Sharing Law, whereby the workers will share in the profits of industrial and productive units;

(5) amendment of the electoral law; and

(6) creation of the Literacy Corps, designed to help administer compulsory national education.

As a later addition to these measures, Iranian women were given suffrage, beginning in the elections of 1963; as a result, six prominent ladies were seated in the *Majlis* and two in the Senate.

The above discussion should suggest that there are two "nations" in Iran, a literate minority and an illiterate majority living on a subsistence level. The latter cannot be expected to effectively influence the course of events because its mental horizon is limited to the satisfaction of immediate needs. But the former, now impregnated with men who have received education abroad and are hostile to many of the traditional patterns of life, provides a dynamic and promising element for the future, even though the present phase of transition may wear an uncertain aspect.

At the time of writing, with the government's intensive reform programmes being proclaimed in every paper and broadcast of the country, it is easy to forget the numerous ills that have long harassed this land. And it cannot be gainsaid that the era of real difficulties, calling for great effort and devotion, has only just begun. But the resilience of this ancient nation suggests that this period of reform may be won through to a future of more evenly distributed well-being, with power so disposed among the people that a constitutional régime can successfully operate. If the intellectual resources Iranians undoubtedly possess were given their proper scope, then this happier future could be safely anticipated.

CHAPTER XI

POST-WAR WRITERS

The architects of to-day, despite all the facilities at their disposal, have apparently lost good taste as well as the sense of fitness. Things they produce are neither in an Iranian nor European style; each part of the building [they construct] is a separate entity—for example, the pillars are Greek, the arches Persian and the fenestration an imitation of English models. The impression created is that they are about to fall to pieces and one wants to take the structure in one's arms to prevent them flying apart.

ṢĀDIQ HIDĀYAT's description of present-day Persian architecture can also be applied to the post-war literature where, side by side with original works, there are attempts to introduce modern tendencies as well as to imitate inferior Western models. The political, social, and moral flux of recent years, reflected in an erratic and ill-formulated literature, has been described in recent pages. An outline has also been given of political developments since the abdication of Riẓā Shah. It remains to be emphasized here that political awakening, especially in a political-minded country like Persia, can in no way be divorced from a literary revival. Thus most of the original works of the post-war period appeared when a feeling of freedom and hope prevailed among the people; and Persian history during the past two decades has frequently passed through such phases, with her literature flourishing considerably. On the other hand, there have been numerous periods of oppression and political stringency, when no one would write honestly about human situations, and social problems. Then, the country remained outwardly silent, the literary compositions were peculiarly debased, and gifted authors temporarily muted.

The medium chosen by the majority of younger writers since the war has been the short story, and in this mode some of the best works in recent Persian literature have been produced. Not that there is anything new about this choice of medium: the short story, in the broad sense of the term, is probably the oldest form of narrative in Persia. For the modern literary movement really to start, it needed only a man like Jamālzāda to show that this popular and principally oral form of narrative—about the adventures, passions, and ludicrous situations of ordinary people—could be produced in the language of the people as good *written* work. And the best modern Persian stories are about ordinary people, told in the sort of language they use and set in the variety of situations anybody may experience. This language has brought back to Persian the same charm that characterized its great classical poetry: the same brilliant capacity for summing up a whole situation, a tremendous amount of atmosphere and passion, in a few words or a forceful image.

Muḥammad 'Alī Jamālzāda

Sayyid Muḥammad 'Alī Jamālzāda holds a place of singular distinction in contemporary Persian literature. In his remarkable role of bringing about a renaissance in Persian letters, he is one of the innovators of the modern literary language, and was the first to introduce the techniques of European short-story writing. He also stands alone among today's Persian authors in having produced the entire bulk of his work outside Persia. And yet the striking thing about him is that in his compositions one senses the life, spirit, and atmosphere of Persia more than in those of any other writers now living in that land. He was only twelve when he left his country, but the impression left upon him by his childhood training and environment has proved indelible.

His father, Sayyid Jamālu'd-Dīn Iṣfahānī, was one of the more enlightened preachers of the constitutional period. His outspoken lectures, well remembered to this day not only for their vigorous attacks on despotism but also for the charm of his simple, everyday language, won him thousands of admirers throughout the country. His followers even founded a newspaper called *Al-Jamāl* and published all his lectures and sermons in it. During the constitutional movement he fought with faith and courage for the cause of the people and met his end in a prison cell, where he was poisoned. He is regarded, in the words of Ḥ. Taqīzāda, as "one of the founders of our political freedom".

Jamālzāda, the son, was born in Isfahan at the close of the last century and began his secondary school education at Antoura, a

Catholic school run by a Lazarite mission near Beirut in 1908. It was in this school that the first gleam of his literary talent was noticed. In a school newspaper, edited by one of his classmates and himself, he wrote various pieces in French, among them "La Neige". In an essay on "Whom would you wish to be like?", he wrote that he wished to be like Voltaire—hardly a desirable hero for a Catholic-trained schoolboy! This was not, he now informs us, because he knew much about Voltaire, but mainly because a French journal had called his father "the Voltaire of Iran".

From Lebanon, after a short stay in Egypt, he travelled to France (1910), then to Switzerland where he started reading law in the University of Lausanne and later in Dijon, where he took his degree. Due to his father's death, he received no money from home at this time and lived in abject poverty. Only the care and assistance of his friends and occasional fees from pupils saved him from starvation.

During the First World War, Jamālzāda joined the group of nationalists in Berlin who were engaged in a political and cultural campaign directed mainly against foreign influence and intervention in Iran. The first mission entrusted to him was the founding of a newspaper in Baghdad (1915) and some precarious activities among the tribes living near the Iraqi-Persian border. The newspaper, *Rastākhīz*, which soon appeared under the editorship of Ibrāhīm Pūrdāvūd, now an emeritus professor of the University of Tehran, fulfilled the first part of the mission; but the second part, despite Jamālzāda's sixteen-month stay in the north-west provinces and his friends' endeavours to win the friendship of tribal clans, failed to produce any positive result. Eventually, with the approach of Russian troops, they all fled to neighbouring countries.

Back in Berlin in 1916 Jamālzāda found his friends busy with the publication of the famous journal *Kāva*. His first contribution to this paper was an article entitled "When a nation is reduced to slavery", a translation of which appeared in some German newspapers of the time. It was during this time that he published his first book, *Ganj-i Shāyigān yā Awẓā'-i Iqtiṣādī-yi Īrān* ("The Worthy Treasure, or the Economic Situation of Iran", 1916–17), which deals with such matters as the physical geography of Persia, her commerce past and present, her customs, transportation, mines, arts and crafts, reforms, finances, weights and measures, post and telegraph system, life in the capital, and a great deal of other useful information. It is entirely a non-fiction work, and that is probably what prompted the *Journal of the Royal Asiatic Society* (January 1921) to write of it:

This well-arranged and beautifully printed volume of more than 200 quarto pages is a good specimen of the modern practical handbooks which, under the pressure of fifteen agitated and eventful years, young Persia, no longer content with philosophical speculations and mystical reveries, is beginning to produce....

This book has been translated into German.

Jamālzāda's second book, *Tārīkh-i Ravābiṭ-i Rūs u Īrān* ("The History of Russo-Persian Relations"), which appeared serialized in *Kāva*, was in fact never completed because of the journal's closure.

Meanwhile the Persian nationalists in Berlin chose him to represent them in 1917 at the World Congress of Socialists in Stockholm, where, in a message to the Congress and some articles in newspapers, he violently attacked Anglo-Russian policies in Iran and condemned their interference in the internal affairs of the country.

Jamālzāda's career as a storyteller began with the publication of "Fārsī Shikar Ast" ("Persian is Sugar"), the first modern Persian short story to enjoy an enormous success. This, together with five other stories of the same kind, appeared later in the celebrated collection *Yakī Būd Yakī Na-būd* (1921). Apart from laying the foundation of modern prose and indicating the direction towards which the present generation of writers is moving, this book throws light on Jamālzāda as a literary figure. For it shows the young author's amazing gift, as well as his painstaking care and devotion, in producing a masterpiece despite his apparent handicaps. The magnitude of his achievement can be judged by his own testimony:

My knowledge of the written language was slight and I used to write Persian with utmost difficulty. When, still very young, I left Iran, Persian was not properly taught in Iranian schools and my Persian was extremely weak. But as I was passionately fond of it, I used to read and practice a great deal. Gradually writing became easier for me and I was deeply imbued with a zest for writing things which has never flagged in me. In other words, without any preliminary, without any teacher or lesson, I learnt Persian entirely on my own by whatever means came to hand. Still, day and night, I continue to be engrossed in this process: from every book or article I read in Persian, pencil in hand, I extract notes. I note idioms, expressions and even words and phrases, which I generally con afterwards.[1]

After financial difficulties forced *Kāva* to close down, Jamālzāda found himself a job in the Persian Embassy in Berlin. He spent a couple of years there looking after the welfare of Iranian students sent to Germany on government scholarships. In the meantime, apart from contributing to a student paper called *Farangistān*, he and some friends set up a magazine, *'Ilm u Hunar* ("Science and Art"), of which he was the editor; despite its comparatively short life, several of his earlier short stories were first published there.

The next and longest stage of Jamālzāda's life has been his stay in Switzerland. In 1931 he accepted a post in the International Labour Office in Geneva, where, until his recent retirement, he worked for nearly twenty-five years. While in that office his duties took him to Persia several times, and during his last visit the prime minister of the time asked him to stay at home and take part in his Cabinet as the minister of labour. This offer he politely refused. Jamālzāda has been teaching Persian for some years in the University of Geneva. At present he is leading a rather quiet life in that city, devoting most of his time to intensive studies and literary compositions.

After the success of his first collection of short stories in 1921, Jamālzāda refrained from literary activities for the next twenty years (which coincided with Riẓā Shah's entire reign). The reason for this silence went deeper than the antagonism of the political régime towards critical and creative writers: the publication of *Yakī Būd Yakī Na-būd* had caused a tremendous stir and controversy among the reading public of Persia. At variance with the young intellectuals and progressive elements, who regarded it as a work of genius, there were some reactionary religious circles and literary dunces who condemned it as a piece of blasphemy offensive to national pride. A newspaper editor who had published one of the stories in his paper was publicly denounced by *mullahs* and threatened with exile and prosecution. Political conditions encouraged the sophistry of the latter group, and Jamālzāda's

[1] See his autobiography in the *Nashrīya-hi Dānishkada-yi Adabīyāt-i Tabrīz*, no. 3 (Azar 1333/1954), p. 274.

brilliant lead in regenerating Persian prose did not gain much following during this time. Conversely, the hue and cry raised against his book made the young author lose heart, and for a while his mind and heart were not in writing. Furthermore, as he himself admits, during this period he had given himself body and soul to the joys of life and the temptations of youth: "I thought it would be a pity to pass the brief span of my life entirely with pen and paper and be the narrator of the pleasures and wassails of other people."[1]

Thus, except for *Yakī Būd Yakī Na-būd* and a few other short stories published here and there in the early 'twenties, all Jamālzāda's literary works have appeared since the war, which is why, despite his seniority and leadership, he is included among the post-war writers.

The first story of *Yakī Būd Yakī Na-būd*, "Fārsī Shikar Ast" ("Persian is Sugar"), is about the encounter in a prison between an ordinary provincial Iranian and two notorious types of his countrymen—one a religious-minded, pompous *ākhund*, the other a Western-educated modernist just back from Europe—who confuse the simple man by the jargon they fling at him as Persian. The high-flown Arabic-Persian phrases of the divine, then the strange foreign terms used by the frenchified youth, flabbergast and bewilder the poor simple man who has been put in jail for no reason and is seeking an explanation from these eminent characters. It is a clever and extremely funny story with exquisite parodies of the modernist's and the *Shaykh*'s modes of speaking Persian. Its linguistic subtleties defy translation.

"Dūstī-yi Khāla Khirsa" ("The Friendship of Aunt Bear") is the tragic story of a kind-hearted, gay, and gallant café waiter who, despite the advice of travelling companions, saves the life of a Russian cossack lying wounded in the snow on the road to Kermanshah. (The incident takes place during the First World War.) The wounded soldier learns that his rescuer is carrying a small sum of money with him, and when he is conveyed to safety he incites a group of drunken Russian troopers to arrest the waiter and have him shot by a firing squad. Except for some inessential details, the movement and pathos make the piece as good as some of the best short stories of European literature.

In another story, "Dard-i Dil-li Mullā Qurbān-'Alī" ("The

[1] See his autobiography, *op. cit.*

Grievances of Mullah Qurban-'Ali"), an infatuated *mullah* tells us about his reckless love for the daughter of a neighbouring merchant. The girl dies and the unfortunate Qurbān-'Alī, of whose love the girl's family knows nothing, is invited to spend the night beside the coffin praying for her soul. During the night he cannot quench the temptation to see the beautiful face of his beloved once more. He is caught kissing the lips of the dead girl and ends up in jail.

"Bīla Dīg Bīla Chughundar" ("Everyman to his Deserts") is a piquant satire on the despotic order, way of life, ruling circles, and class distinctions of the late Qajar times. Fate takes a European bath-attendant to Persia, where he becomes adviser to a minister, and his memoirs about life in Persia remind one of some of the saltiest passages of Morier's *Hajji Baba*. It was mainly the remarks made in this story that disturbed religious and state dignitaries in the early 'twenties, when the book was first published.

After his silence of more than twenty years, Jamālzāda resumed his literary activities in 1942; and since then he has always had too many irons in the fire, proving himself one of the most prolific authors of modern Persia. The first of his new books was *Dāru'l-Majānīn* ("Lunatic Asylum", 1942), the engaging story of a mad-house in which some interesting characters, each with his own philosophy, habits and idiosyncrasies, are in custody. While throwing light on the abnormalities of his characters, the author also tries to criticize the conditions of a society in which sensitive men prefer taking refuge in an asylum rather than being at large. But this critical note is only incidental: it is droll humour that forms the driving force. Among the crowd of bedlamites the reader can recognize one unmistakably: a certain Hidāyat-'Alī Khān, known as *Monsieur*, who calls himself "Būf-i Kūr". He is a writer, and some of the passages and hallucinations of Hidāyat's *Būf-i Kūr* ("The Recluse")[1] are given as samples of his writings. The allusions are clear enough, and the author's love and respect for the late Ṣādiq Hidāyat are touching. The book also contains a good selection of quotations from classical Persian poetry about wisdom and insanity.

Jamālzāda's second novel, *Qultashan-Dīvān* (1946), concerns the age-old struggle between good and evil. The book opens with a neat description of a little street in Tehran that resembles "thou-

[1] See below, pp. 165-81.

sands of other streets in Iran", and of its inhabitants, whose life is shared "exactly by millions of other peoples in that country". The following chapters scrutinize the life of two inhabitants of the little street: first the hero, Ḥājj Shaykh, a wholesale dealer in tea and sugar; a virtuous, patriotic man with a good reputation among the people, he has been a deputy in the first *Majlis*. Then the villain, Qultashan-Dīvān, a cunning, and ruthless opportunist who would stop at nothing to attain his personal aims. In his first attempt to use the good name of Ḥājj Shaykh for his own ends, by marrying off his own compromised daughter to the son of old Ḥājjī, the villain fails. Embittered by Ḥājjī's refusal, he waits for an opportunte moment to take his revenge. During the First World War, when Ḥājjī's trade and financial strength are badly disrupted, the villain reappears asking for a huge consignment of sugar to be bought and kept for him. In the following months the acute shortage of provisions brings the people to the doorstep of Ḥājjī, who they know has a whole store loaded with sugar. But he cannot sell the stuff and the real owner refuses to show up. Cursed and despised by everybody, defamed as a vicious hoarder, Ḥājjī dies in grief and misery, without being able to defend his innocence. The villain, on the other hand, having made his fortune in this bargain, builds an orphanage and throws a lavish party for ministers and notables in his newly constructed, sumptuous house. At the height of his career Qultashan-Dīvān dies peacefully in his sleep of a stroke. The newspapers devote their front pages to the glorification of his benevolence and service to culture; his name is whispered on every lip as that of a great man, and all the dignitaries mourn his death as a grave national loss.

The principal characters of the book, like many other characters created by this author, belong to the middle class; and their ideas, ambitions, and personal dilemmas, as well as the tragedy of an honest man entangled in an unbalanced society, are skilfully portrayed.

> *Qultashan-Dīvān* [writes M. Borecký] is Jamalzada's most mature novel...satire, humour, social criticism and condescending love for feeble human beings are well weighed throughout the book, and the discontent with the lighter lot of the unjust only strengthens the elegiac tuning of the novel. The picture of Tehran and its inhabitants in the first twenty years of this century is vivid and appealing.[1]

[1] "Persian Prose since 1946", *M.E.J.* VII, no. 2 (1953), 237.

Ṣaḥrāy-i Maḥshar ("Plain of Resurrection", 1947) is a fantasy about the day of resurrection, possibly inspired by the pamphlet *Ru'yā-yi Ṣādiqāna*" ("A True Dream") composed by Jamālzāda's father and a group of friends some fifty years before. His father's "Plain of Resurrection" had a serious intention: to prophesy the hard times that were awaiting certain despotic rulers and political opponents of the time when they finally reached the presence of their Maker. The son's flight of fancy, however, is primarily in the realm of humour and satire: he is amusing himself by visualizing the position of people of various walks of life when they stand before the divine scales in which their deeds are to be weighed. Implicit, however, is a traditional Islamic dogma, which runs through the medieval Persian works that offer counsel to rulers and princes: the dogma that we are answerable for all our misdeeds in this life. So to understand the salient points of this satire, the reader should have a fair knowledge of *Shī'a* doctrine. But even then he is likely to be confounded by some of the things happening in the heavenly kingdom. We learn, for example, that influential connections, string-pulling, and even bribery play a considerable part in the placement and promotion of angels and other ministering spirits. The prophets, on the other hand, are dispatched to heaven straight away without any demur or interrogation. Some smart sinners, by reciting an appeasing Koranic verse or an apostolic tradition, are let off lightly; and a great number of people escape the blazing fires of Hell by reciting an appropriate line of poetry or even by cracking a joke that amuses God. But, in general, moderation and compromise seem to be the order of the day: moral issues and human values, not the religious dogmas, are the criterion of divine justice.

But when it comes to *ākhunds*, *mullahs*, and other religious pretenders, the handling of affairs takes a different turn: the gates of mercy are shut, for the sins of this group weigh much heavier than their good deeds.

Among the crowd who line up for questioning, the reader may recognize some familiar faces. One delightful moment is the appearance of Omar Khayyām. Despite his apparent mischiefs, the celebrated poet-philosopher is not only granted celestial bliss, but his plea for an investigation into the case of a fallen maid, mentioned in one of his quatrains, receives proper attention.[1] A rather sentimental story follows, resulting in the innocent girl's accompanying Khayyām to Paradise and the wretched *shaykh* getting his due punishment.

In the final section the narrator meets Satan in a lonely corner, and after some exchange of views on a number of scriptural topics, Satan, who is on good terms with God, obtains permission to take him back to earth endowed with eternal life. But before long the narrator grows tired of this troublesome gift and asks to be given liberty instead; liberty in its fullest sense, including that of dying when he chooses.

For social criticism, a study of the characteristics of different social classes, for humour and excellence of style and language, Jamālzāda's *Rā-āb Nāma* ("The Drainage Controversy", 1948) stands high above his other novels. The framework of the book is rather similar to that of *Qultashan-Dīvān*: the scene is a cul-de-sac in Tehran, the characters are members of the six households living there. But the problem this time is the repairing of a blocked water channel, without which they cannot have a drop of water—so precious in the days before the capital was equipped with a piped water system.

The hero is a European-educated Persian student spending his summer vacation at home. Having learned about the hitch in the drainage he calls a meeting of the neighbours, who unanimously authorize him to make arrangements for the necessary repairs. He thanks them for their confidence in him and promptly sets to work. After endless troubles with the architect, the mason, and other workmen, with all expenses having been paid from his own pocket, the job is completed and he sends the neighbours the bill. But they, unfamiliar with the principle of "business is business", find it hard to lend themselves to such extravagance. They start dilly-dallying, each one making various excuses and all refusing to pay their share. With his meagre allowance floating down the drain, the kind-hearted, civilized student is unable to return to Europe to resume his studies. He leaves his ancestral home and finds shelter in a cosy little room in the courtyard of a holy shrine, away from any

[1] A *Shayk* chided a harlot: you are always drunk,
And continuously carry on with different men.
She said, o *shaykh*, everything you say I am.
But are you in fact what you pretend to be?

neighbours, disillusioned at all the lectures he had received on good neighbourly relations, and cursing his compatriots for their moral degradation.

Contrary to the general pattern of Jamālzāda's novels, *Rā-āb Nāma* is concise, coherent and very much to the point. Three sketches at the beginning of the book—the unbearable heat of a Persian summer day, the active life of the bazaar and the peaceful atmosphere of the holy shrine—are portrayed with mastery. There are many other pages of skilful writing; and the author's knowledge of and deep insight into the inner lives, habits and thinking of middle-class Persian families deserve every praise. The unrestrained criticism of the national character with which the book ends, however, is not entirely free from exaggeration.

Generally speaking, there appears a sharp distinction between the early stories written by Jamālzāda and his later compositions. Conciseness, novelty of form, originality of ideas, a biting sense of humour, and, above all, observance of the conventional divisions in story writing (development, climax, and denouement) mark the earlier writings. His more recent works, however, show a tendency toward prolixity, sage remarks and mystical and philosophical speculations; there is frequent use of classical poetry and at times a lack of shape and order. Common to all his compositions is the language he uses: the charm of his prose discourses cast in a familiar yet individual style. Everyday expressions adorn almost every line, to the extent that his care for juxtaposing idioms seems to override other considerations. Years of hard work have equipped him with masses of slang and colloquial proverbs, and he has the gift to use them with skill; but his indiscreet dwelling on these terms appears over-righteous at times. A single idea is normally expressed in a variety of ways, in as many roundabout phrases as the author happens to remember; as if the flow of the story mattered less than the recording of expressions. The frequently synonymous phrases render a kind of superficiality to his description and a certain amount of immobility to the progress of the narrative. Moreover, Jamālzāda believes in tinging his stories with incidental acts of personal perception, which again hold up the plot. From the technical point of view, then, the majority of his novels lack a firm and continuous narrative: they are episodic, and in this regard he displays more gift for short- than long-story writing. In his more recent works he has grown increasingly keen on abandoning fiction for erudition.

Most of these traits are discernible in a two-volume novel called *Sar u Tah-i Yak Karbās* ("All of a Pattern", 1956). In his introductory remarks the author informs us that the book is "almost entirely the story of his childhood"; but apart from the first chapter, which is autobiographical, the rest of the book is devoted to episodes in the life of a friend, which, though immensely rich and interesting, deny us the pleasure of learning more about the later years of the author's life.

Javād Āqā is the son of a merchant, and after the death of his father he becomes interested in mysticism and ascetic teachings. After divorcing his wife and abandoning his home, he joins a Sufi *murshid* (guide) whose daily life is full of spiritual sublimities. What follows is an account of the adventurous life these two, the guide and follower, go through. Their tireless wayfaring, their experiences with people of different creeds and social standing, all imbued with the recollections, beliefs, and instructions of the dervish, form the chapters of the book. But the book is not a close-knit, consistent piece: several stories, some historical details, and many mystical speculations are woven into the overall texture of the narrative.

The first chapter, about the childhood of the author, is written with a sincerity and innocent candour rare, if not absent, in the works of any writer living inside Iran. In two other chapters, one on the history of Isfahan and the other a description of the old Persian palestras, their amiable ceremonies and traditional customs, plenty of valuable information is offered with obvious glee. Of the various stories and anecdotes included in both volumes, some (in particular, "Jahanam-i Taʿaṣṣub" ("The Hell of Fanaticism"), about the hypocrisy of an *ākhund*, and "Bāj-i Sibīl" ("Extortion"), illustrating the ruffianism of army officers) are in fact independent pieces superimposed on the narrative.[1] Taken as a whole, *Sar u Tah-i Yak Karbās* is the most erudite work of Jamālzāda. Meditations on philosophy, metaphysics, religious instructions, mysticism, and their expression in Persian ethics and literature are to be found throughout.

[1] *Bāj-i Sibīl* was rewritten as an independent play and published in the journal *Sukhan* (Murdād 1337/July 1958).

In addition to his novels, Jamālzāda has published four collections of short stories during the post-war years: *Sarguzasht-i 'Amū-Ḥusayn-'Alī* ("The Story of Uncle Husayn-'Ali", 1942), *Talkh u Shīrīn* ("Bitter and Sweet", 1956), *Kuhna u Naw* ("Old and New", 1959), and *Ghayr az Khudā Hīchkas Na-būd* ("There was no one but God", 1960). The first was republished in 1957 in a two-volume enlarged edition called *Shāhkār* ("Masterpiece"). Some of the pieces in the second volume of this collection had been written in the 'twenties and published in the periodicals of the time. Among them "Kabāb-i Ghāz" ("Roast Goose"), "Palang" ("Leopard"), "Naw-Parast" ("Modernist") and "Dushman-i Khūnī" ("Blood Enemy") are famous either for their abundant humour or for the freshness, vigour, and pathos that characterized Jamālzāda's earlier writings. But save for the title-piece "'Amū-Ḥusayn-'Alī", written with ingenuity and brilliance, the contents of the first volume exemplify some of the author's recent trends: prolixity, effusion, and reverie laden with poetic and proverbial quotations.

These tendencies are also detectable in the second collection, *Talkh u Shīrīn*, especially in the first three stories, "Yak Rūz dar Rustam-ābād-i Shimīrān" ("A Day in Rustam-abad of Shimiran"), "Ḥaq u Nā-ḥaq" ("Just and Unjust") and "Darvīsh-i-Mūmīyā'ī" ("Mummified Dervish"), where the main emphasis is on poetry and philosophical speculation. Other pieces in this book, together with six stories collected in *Kuhna u Naw*, deal with social problems such as the uneasiness of life for honest families living in a corrupt society, and the credulity of young intellectuals when they first come in contact with the rough and tumble, resulting in their bitterness and disillusionment later.

Mention should finally be made of sundry works compiled, composed, or translated by Jamālzāda as side lines to his creative writings: *Gulistān-i Nīkbakhtī yā Pand-nāmā-yi Sa'dī* ("The Garden of Prosperity, or the Counsel of Sa'di", 1938), published on the 700th anniversary of publication of the *Gulistān*, is a compilation of the prose-counsels laid down in that immortal book. *Qiṣṣa-yi qiṣṣa-hā* ("The Tale of Tales", 1948) is a compendium of the biographical work *Qiṣaṣu'l-'ulamā* ("Stories of the Learned"), written by Muḥammad-ibn-i Sulaymān of Tunukābun in 1873. It throws light on the life and works of some *Shī'a* doctors who lived between the tenth and nineteenth centuries of the Christian era. *Hazār Pīsha* ("The Pigeon Hole", 1948) is a kind of work-box containing a thousand interesting and amusing notes made from the author's reading of various books and articles. This, the first of two volumes, includes part of the first thousand jottings; the second volume, containing 309 different items, appeared in 1960 under the title *Kashkūl-i Jamālī* ("Beggar's Cup of Jamal"). Since then, Jamālzāda has been preparing the remainder of these oddments. In the words of Borecký, the collection, especially when completed, will represent: "a modernization of the old 'Beggar's Cup' and 'Baskets' as its curiosities are derived from western and eastern sources".

Bāng-i Nāy ("The Note of the Reed", 1959) is one of the novel literary activities of this author. As everybody acquainted with Rūmī's great *Dīvān* knows, the stories in the *Mathnavī-yi Mawlavī* do not always have a strict continuity. Sometimes one story is interrupted by another, or by allusions, parallels, or poetical images, and then often resumed somewhere else. In this book Jamālzāda has tried to collect these scattered pieces, and by putting them together he has produced one smooth amalgam of all the verses related to each story.

With his excellent knowledge of French, German and Arabic, Jamālzāda has also translated a large number of books and articles into Persian. The best known among these are the following: Bernardin de Saint-Pierre, *Le Café de Surat*; Molière, *L'avare*; Henrik Ibsen, *En folkefiende*; Friedrich Schiller, *Wilhelm Tell* and *Don Carlos, Infant von Spanien*; and Hendrik Willem van Loon, *The Story of Mankind*. Appended to the second edition of the last is a chapter on the history, character, political developments and people of Persia, which partly embodies the translator's personal views about his country.

Throughout his literary career Jamālzāda has been either closely associated with or an ardent contributor to the Persian press inside or outside the country. To provide a full list of the articles and shorter pieces he has written for various journals is beyond the scope of the present study. Yet a note on some of his major contributions does not seem out of place here.

During the early years of his stay in Germany he published many articles in *Kāva*. Of particular interest is "Bulshivīsm dar Īrān-i

Qadīm" ("Bolshevism in Ancient Iran"), a study of the beliefs and preachings of Mazdak, which has been translated into Russian and published in Moscow. To introduce European men of letters and their way of thought to the Persian public, he has written articles in various papers; his subjects include Maxim Gorki in *Yaghmā*, Nietzsche and James Joyce in *Sukhan*, and a comparison between Khayyām and Anatole France in *Farangistān*.

Besides his articles in *Sukhan* and other magazines, Jamālzāda's ideas about the new trends in Persian poetry have been expressed fully and candidly in his introduction to Muḥammad Ishāque's *Sukhanvarān-i-Īrān dar 'Asr-i-Hāzir* ("Poets and Poetry of Modern Persia", vol. I, Delhi, 1933), and more recently, in a detailed review of the work of one of the younger poets, in the *Journal of the Book Society of Persia* (*Rāhnamā-yi Kitāb*). During recent years Jamālzāda has been a member of the editorial board of this journal. His book reviews and scholarly essays on various literary controversies are read with keen interest by the bulk of Iranian intellectuals, who are the main readers of this publication.

Translations of Jamālzāda's works

Because of his colloquial style and the wealth of idiomatic phrases in Jamālzāda's works, the translation of his books into foreign languages is a formidable task. This is probably why, despite the literary value and the great significance of his writings for modern Persian letters, attempts at introducing him to foreign readers have been so few. The untidiness of his novels and the impeccable "Persianism" of most of his compositions are two other problems facing the translator. Hence, apart from a German translation of *Ganj-i Shāyigān*, only some of the short stories published in the collection *Yakī Būd Yakī Na-būd* and a few other stories of his have appeared in foreign languages. An English translation of "Dard-i Dil-li Mullā Qurbān-'Alī" was printed in the magazine *Ahang* (Delhi, April 1944). In his book *Kulturskitser fra Iran* (Copenhagen, 1931), Arthur Christensen included a Danish translation of "Rajul-i Sīyāsī" (pp. 179–84). Christensen praised Jamālzāda as "undoubtedly the most talented contemporary writer of Iran"—a view more readily acceptable in 1931 than now—and compared him with Ludvig Holberg, the founder of Danish literature. This story has also been translated into German, entitled "Mein debut in der Politik", and published in Austria in *Die Reise zum wonnigen Fisch*, an anthology of humorous short stories by contemporary writers all over the world. In addition, an Austrian professor, Dr Karl Stolz, has translated "Vaylānu'd Dawla" into German. This piece was also broadcast from Vienna Radio in October 1951 under the title "Der Tod des Vagabunden". Another of Jamālzāda's stories translated into German is "Namak-i Gandīda", which appeared in the German press under the title of "Die fünf Herren von der Bauchsippe".

In the first issue (1945) of the journal *Fikr u Naẓar*, published by the "Association of Letters of Aligarh in India", there appeared Dr Munibur Raḥmān's translation in Urdu of the short story "Dūstī-yi Khāla Khirsa". R. Gelpke's German rendering of this and another of Jamālzāda's stories were included in a collection called *Persische Meistererzähler der Gegenwart* (*op. cit.*), which appeared in 1961. One of Jamālzāda's short stories, "Murgh-i Musamā", has also been translated into Indian (by Tilak) and published in the magazine *Kahani* for March 1955. A slightly abridged French translation of four of the short stories of *Yakī Būd Yakī Na-būd*, made by Shāhīn Sarkīsīyān, was published in the *Journal de Teheran* (1950).

The Russian translation of *Yakī Būd Yakī Na-būd* by B. N. Zakhoder appeared in Moscow in 1936. The book contains some useful explanatory notes and a detailed preface by A. Bolotnikoff about the writer, the stories in the collection, and some general observations on the modern literary revival in Persia. Discussing the influence that Jamālzāda's first collection of stories had on Iran's contemporary literature, Bolotnikoff, quoting K. Chaikine, says:

Only with *Yakī Būd Yakī Na-būd* did the school and style of realism find a beginning in Iran. And this school and style in fact laid fresh and new foundations for the art of story-telling in Persian literature; and it is only from the time of their inception that it is possible to discuss the appearance of the novel, tale and romance in the thousand-year old literature of Iran [*sic*]....Jamālzāda's name, on account of *Yakī Būd Yakī Na-būd*, stands first among the best names in present day Persian literature—not only for his historical precedent, but also on account of his vividness and the weight and significance of his works....In brief it must be stated that Jamālzāda is for us without doubt a writer who ranks equal to the best novelists of Europe. Furthermore he successfully accomplished a formidable task, in that he introduced into the thousand-year old framework of the Persian language the spirit and technique of European prose and its power of characterization and unusual expressiveness.

Finally, a collection containing eight of Jamālzāda's better known stories appeared in French in 1959. The book, entitled *Choix de Nouvelles*, is translated by S. Corbin and H. Lotfi and published by UNESCO. It has a preface by A. Chamson, member of the French Academy, and an informative introduction about Jamālzāda's work and life written by Professor Henri Massé, the celebrated French orientalist who is an expert on Persian folklore himself.

Reflections on the works, ideas, and personality of Jamālzāda

Jamālzāda's pre-eminence is due mainly to his timely clarion call for a regeneration of Persian prose. But modest and unpretentious as this author has always been, he makes no extravagant claims to greatness. In an interview with a Persian journalist in 1938, he stated that he was very proud of his *Yakī Būd Yakī Na-būd*, for it was the origin of a new school of prose; yet he rightly affirmed that "this innovation had been in the air and it was his belief that if he had not started it someone else would have".

In this interview he also expressed his strong opposition to the tendency to imitate foreign models:

> We ought to remain Persian, think Persian and write for the Persians. The Persian writer has nothing to do with those astonishing and bizarre schools which are called surrealism and existentialism.... Persian literature is over a thousand years old and includes in its varied corpus all the known *genres*, be they "realist", "symbolist" or even "surrealist".

Similar remarks are made in his foreword to the fifth edition of *Yakī Būd Yakī Na-būd*, where he warns young authors against succumbing to the attraction of the "literary schools imported into Persia as gifts from Europe and America". Wide and promiscuous imitation of Western ways, especially rife among the younger generation, has always been a source of concern to Jamālzāda. Apart from frequent references in his works, he has expressed these apprehensions in the Preface to *Sar u Tah-i Yak Karbās*, where he indicates that not only the cultural products, but names, manners, even foods and drinks are being indiscriminately influenced, or often replaced, by their European counterparts.

Similarly, there recurs in Jamālzāda's writings the dilemma of Western-educated Persians who return to their country. Numerous characters of this type appear in his work, all in different situations and with different potentialities, but none of them is able to tolerate the prevailing conditions, accommodate himself to the requirements of his milieu, or even to feel at home once he returns to his own country. Not only in their social environment but often in their own family circle they seem like outsiders. All of them, even if endowed with exceptional learning and capabilities, fail in whatever they take up and generally end as morbid and useless members of society. For example, there is the strange creature in "Fārsī Shikar Ast", the Frenchified youth, a type "whose conduct and manners will tickle to death audiences in Persian theatres for a hundred years to come". Then the hero of *Rā-āb Nāma*, who wants to be civil and helpful to his neighbours but is easily swindled by them. Or Raḥmatu'l-lā, in "Ātash-i Zīr-i Khākistar" ("The Fire under Ashes"): trained as a skilled carpenter in Germany, he opens a factory in Tehran after his return home. As he is a master-craftsman, his trade flourishes rapidly. But rival firms cannot tolerate the success of their young colleague and their plotting loses Raḥmatu'l-lā both the factory and his profession. Later he becomes an interpreter to a Persian military mission in Germany, but once again his honesty brings him to grief. Upon the instigation of the officers, of whose embezzlement he disapproves, Raḥmatu'l-lā is forced to return to Persia, where he is immediately put under arrest and charged with communist activities. In the end he and the other members of his family are reduced to misery and complete destitution.

The hero of "Darvīsh-i Mūmīyā'ī" is another outcast. Though a learned and conscientious student, he has locked himself up in his room in Geneva, and without proper food or sleep is brooding on abstract ideas such as the existence of God, the secret of creation, and free-will and predestination. In contrast to this bookworm living like a hermit, we have the son of a wealthy merchant in *Dāru'l-Majānīn* who is sent to Paris to study commerce;

but after three years' stay in that city, he cannot yet identify the building of his school.

A slightly happier situation can be found by looking at another of Jamālzāda's heroes, one who finally did achieve a position of honour, though in an unorthodox manner, after going back to his country. Aḥmad Āqā, the hero of "Khāna Bi-dūsh" ("Vagabond"), returns to Iran from Europe with a Ph.D. degree in education. But the job he is given by the government is that of sticking labels on bars of opium! Even in this menial employment he finds occasion to complain of the prevailing bribery and corruption. His complaints are ridiculed by his friends and his own father. He feels an absolute stranger at home and finally, giving up the attempt to settle down with his own people, finds a teaching job among the wandering tribes. He completely identifies himself with the nomads, living and moving with them and winning their love and gratitude for teaching their children. When he dies his tomb becomes venerated and a place of pilgrimage to the tribes-people.

Jamālzāda's preoccupation with the tragedy of the returned student points to a major sociological problem in Iran, much of whose present unhappiness comes from its being in a state of transition. Moreover, the theme of the unhappy westernized, idealistic and ambitious young student returning to a country where prejudice and the predominance of selfish, influential classes with no sense of civic responsibility still exist, is one that Jamālzāda is most admirably suited to handle: for he is the archetype of that Iranian student who can never again adapt himself to prevailing conditions in his own country. In this regard, Jamālzāda speaks for his time and for a growing number of young Iranian intellectuals.

Another theme that looms large in Jamālzāda's works is criticism of Muslim divines and the religious institutions. Jamālzāda was brought up more religiously, so to speak, than the majority of today's young writers; and the *'abā* (cloak), *'amāma* (turban) and *minbar* (pulpit) occupy a more prominent place in any vision of Iran he may have than they would in the mind of the Tehran University graduate of the post-war period. But unlike Hidāyat, who hates the religious institution as something alien, as part of the evil resulting from the Arab conquest, which suppressed true Iranian ideals, Jamālzāda is, as B. Nikitine suggests, slightly more sympathetic or urbane towards the clergy. For it is not, he believes, that the institution they represent is evil, but that the clergy themselves fall short of its ideals and requirements. It is on the last count that Jamālzāda exposes the clergy to ruthless satire—which is not the same thing as Hidāyat's numbed horror at everything associated with them. Perhaps Jamālzāda cannot forget that supporters of popular causes during the Constitutional Rising were generally found among the divines, whom he cannot help seeing as an essential element in the life of his people. His own background conditions him to adopt a different attitude from that of Hidāyat. Jamālzāda is thoroughly middle class and by birth a member of the clerical-professional element of the middle class. Thus he can portray middle-class people with an accuracy and vividness born only of the most intimate acquaintance; and he can beat the *ākhund* with the *ākhund*'s own stick, defeating him with the cleric's own techniques and terminology, as in the argument with the *mullah* in "Jahanam-i Taʿaṣub". This the majority of more recent writers cannot do, for they do not know enough about the clerical mind and terminology. They limit themselves to the bare statement that the clergy are a vile collection of reactionary hypocrites who bar progress; while Jamālzāda, rather than abuse them, makes them actually appear in word and gesture as reactionary, ignorant, prejudiced, selfish and a blight on society. With the skill of a Molière, he makes them fulfil the worst charges against them.

An allied theme in Jamālzāda's works is social criticism, with general observation of conditions that prevailed three decades ago. (A feature notable in Jamālzāda's works is that he remains a little behind the times. It is as if he were still seeing Iran as it was in the time of his father; or, if not entirely so, as if it remained as it was several decades ago. Of this fact, which can be related to his long sojourn abroad, he himself is fully aware; see his introduction to *Sar u Tah-i Yak Karbās*.) In his social criticism he is again principally concerned with middle-class elements. And again it is not an evil middle class that Jamālzāda grapples with; instead, he probes with sympathetic insight into this class's shortcomings. He blames the young middle-class students for their *naïveté*. He shows them victimized by old charlatans of power and influence, thwarted by fear and seduced by vain fancies. In this he is speaking as the Iranian middle-class person who has lived abroad many years: he is in the happy position of the onlooker who sees the most —and who, moreover, knew the game before the players took the field. Naturally, also, he is concerned about the outmoded institutions of marriage, rights of women, etc., and here he is bordering on the question of the reactionary aspects of the religious institution. His attitude towards the social ills of his country may be summed up in the following, taken from the conclusion of his story "Namak-i Gandīda" ("Rotten Salt"), where he discusses the corruption in professional circles and what the ordinary middle-class government employee thinks about it:

...An essential reason for corrupt morals is, on the one hand, indigence, poverty and deprivation; on the other hand, the absence of security of person and property. So long as people's stomachs remain empty, and they fear the horror of oppression and injustice and lack a refuge or protection, fearing the shepherd as much as they do the wolf, having no assurance about the next day in their lives, and not being masters of their own life or property, fighting against corruption will be to measure water in a sieve and to collect air in a wicker basket.

Finally, Jamālzāda's preoccupation with language. When he left Iran for good, before the First World War, the state of the language was chaotic. Some practised the traditional style of writing, and others, supporting the idea of a literary revival, were pushing for a simpler and more concise mode of expression. With literacy gaining ground, the written word was ceasing to be the preserve of a traditionally educated few; here the press was an important factor. Contacts with the modern and technically more advanced states of the West were on the increase. People educated abroad, like the young man in "Fārsī Shikar Ast", went too far in a pretentious use of foreign terms and suffered from either having forgotten, or never having learnt, the resources of their own tongue. The reactionary clergy indulged in the grossest and most pretentious use of an Arabic jargon associated with *Fiqh* and *uṣūl*. Government circles were not sure what style to use.

Against this background Jamālzāda began writing his *Yakī Būd Yakī Na-būd*, and the Persian *literati* of Berlin, with whom he was associated in the 1920's, began consciously, through their *Kāva* and other publications, to reform the language and establish a suitable modern medium. None did this more than Jamālzāda himself; followed by Ṣādiq Hidāyat. But because Jamālzāda still tends to harp on circumstances that no longer obtain as much as they did four decades ago, he continues to write and discuss language as if the old battle of styles were still being fought with its former intensity, whereas, in fact, due to him and to Hidāyat more than others, the young writer of today commits neither the linguistic solecisms nor the anachronisms that Jamālzāda was criticizing in "Fārsī Shikar Ast" (and later in certain passages of *Rā-āb Nāma*, "Khāstgārī", "Ru'yā", *Ṣaḥrā-yi Maḥshar*, etc.). The contemporary writer is equipped with a settled brand of modern Persian, with which he can be intelligible and inoffensive to the majority of readers.

In its overall effect, Jamālzāda's writing is powerful enough to conceal his defects of style; yet these defects are serious, and should be mentioned. In introducing his characters, for instance, he often uses the method of a dramatist: depicting them at the outset of the story rather than letting them develop gradually. (See, for example, *Dāru'l-Majānīn*, *Qultashan-Dīvān*, *Rā-āb Nāma* and *Namak-i Gandīda*.) He also presents them as types rather than as individuals through whose actions their type may be perceived. This is almost like Bunyan's Mr Worldly Wiseman, Money-Love, Say-Well, etc. The comparison may not be unjust: both Bunyan at Bedford and Jamālzāda at Geneva have written as critics exposing the ills of their respective societies.

Another aspect of Jamālzāda's technique, and one mentioned briefly above, is his almost Dickensian flow of words, with adjectives piled up, numerous repetitions, and popular phrases never omitted where they can possibly be squeezed in. Also, particularly in his recent works, he seizes every opportunity for quoting maxims, poems, proverbs, and popular sayings, as well as Koranic verses and quotations from the Traditions. He allows his copious literary memory to run freely when he takes pen in hand.

Another serious defect is his negligence in revision and his careless disregard for form. Minor oversights occur in his works not infrequently. (See, for example, *Namak-i Gandīda*, pp. 8–9, and *Sar u Tah-i Yak Karbās*, vol. 1, p. 161, where the person of the narrator suddenly changes. Also his conflicting statements in *Ṣaḥrāy-i Maḥshar*, pp. 92 and 109–10, about "Murgh-i Vara'".) The impression left is that he never looks over a manuscript once he has completed it.

In conclusion, while the author of *Yakī Būd Yakī Na-būd* must always remain one of Iran's greatest writers who, despite (or perhaps because of) long years of residence abroad, is still the most absolutely Persian of writers today, nevertheless the golden touch displayed in his first work has not quite reappeared in the later writing. All the same, his importance can scarcely be over-estimated: he has just claims to his position as the elder champion of modern Persian writers.

CHAPTER XII

BUZURG 'ALAVĪ

AMONG the new generation of writers, Buzurg 'Alavī has shown outstanding ability in adopting European techniques of storytelling while at the same time creating works of art still strikingly Persian.

He was born in 1907 of an old merchant family. In 1922 he was sent to Germany, where he received part of his secondary and university education. On returning to Persia he joined an illegal Marxist group under the leadership of Dr Taqī Arānī. In 1937 'Alavī and fifty-two other members of this group were arrested; and they remained in prison until the Allied Occupation in August 1941, when in a general amnesty many political prisoners were released. It was the hard core of this small group which, after their release from prison, formed the nucleus of the Tūda Party of Iran. 'Alavī was among its founders, and his social, political, and literary activities have since been closely associated with the policies of this party. In 1953 he was made a member, and awarded the Gold Medal, of the World Peace Council. After the fall of Muṣaddiq, 'Alavī left for Europe. He is now a visiting Professor at Humboldt University in East Germany.

Unlike other leading Persian writers today, whose fame rests on a wide range of literary works, 'Alavī has attained distinction with only a few compositions. His major published works consist of three collections of short stories: *Chamadān* ("Portmanteau", 1934), *Varaq-Pārihā-yi Zindān* ("The Scrap-papers of Prison", 1941) and *Nāma-hā* ("Letters", 1952); a moving account of his prison experiences called *Panjāh-u-sa Nafar* ("The Fifty-three Men", 1942); and a novel, *Chashmhāyash* ("Her Eyes", 1952). He is also the author of "Dīv...Dīv" ("Demon...Demon"), written in collaboration with Ṣādiq Hidāyat and Shīn-i Partaw, and published in the collection *Anīrān* ("Non-Iranian", 1931); of a travelogue called *Uzbakhā* ("The Uzbegs", 1948) appearing after his visit to the Soviet Union as a member of a Persian cultural delegation; and two recent works in German, *Kämpfendes Iran*

(Berlin, 1955) and *Geschichte und Entwicklung der modernen Persischen Literatur* (Berlin, 1964).

His first published work, *Chamadān*, shows that 'Alavī was strongly influenced by Freudianism during his early years as a student in Germany. Later on, after adopting Marxist philosophy, he tried to bring to his writings what may be called socialist realism; but, as we shall see, Freud and his psychoanalysis remained a predominant part of 'Alavī's work. *Chamadān*[1] is a collection of six stories. All are subtle psychological studies, and the actions of characters are, as a rule, conditioned by their extreme sensibility and by various kinds of psychological abnormality. It is the only book of the author in which his leftist political views are not reflected. The best tales of the collection are "'Arūs-i Hazār Dāmād" ("The Bride of a Thousand Grooms") and "Sarbāz-i Surbī" ("The Lead Soldier").

The scene of the first is a modern European-style night-club, examples of which are now numerous in Tehran. The central figure is a wandering violinist who, fascinated by a song sung by a girl called Sūsan, has taken to music. After mastering the art in Europe, he returns home and marries the girl who was his source of inspiration. But Sūsan's songs do not touch the artist's heart any longer, and they separate. Years later the couple meet again (without, one is given to understand, recognizing each other) as entertainers in a disreputable night-club. Sūsan, now styling herself as Sūskī, sings the old song: a line from one of Ḥāfiẓ's odes, which had inspired as well as ruined the poor violinist:

> Seek not a valid contract from the weak-wayed world,
> For that old hag is the bride of a thousand husbands.

This stirs the violinist, and the couple start dancing to a mad tune interrupted by the singing of Ḥāfiẓ's line. The memory of the past, revived in their ecstasy, enrages the girl and she smashes the musician's violin.

Three striking points about this story are: first, the author's painstaking care over minutiae, then the brilliance of his character

[1] A detailed and interesting comment on the various stories of this collection by G. M. Wickens was published in *The University of Toronto Quarterly* for October 1958, XXVIII, 116–33.

depiction, and, above all, his ability to create and describe atmosphere. As Professor Wickens says:

The crowd effect is superbly managed throughout this story...and, over and above the constant noise and movement, we are offered two very clever punctuations of the violinist's playing and musing... : one takes the form of remarks in realistic broken Persian by the fat European proprietress of the establishment, the other is the periodic cacophany of a gramophone that certain customers prefer to the musician's own art. Mounted grotesquely on the spindle of this machine is the symbolic figure of a revolving doll, the word for which in Persian ("little bride", *'arūsak*) bears an undoubted relationship to the "bride" of the title (*'arūs*). There is something quite terrifying about the sheer pointless idiocy of this gaily dressed, whirling figure in the context and atmosphere of the story. This is, it will be realised—even from these few comments, and even by a reader who knows little or nothing of Persian literature—a type of phantasmagoria rarely attempted in the West outside drama or poetry.

The second story, "Sarbāz-i Surbī", is by far the most polished of the collection. It is forceful and bears the least traces of foreign influence. For example, it is the only story of the collection in which foreign characters or imitation of foreign ways of life do not appear. It describes the idiosyncrasies of an impotent opium-addict (who is also a minor civil servant) and his peculiar love for a housemaid. The story of their strange relationship and their fetishistic obsession with a lead soldier is told with amazing ingenuity and insight. First we hear the story bit by bit from the lips of "F", the opium addict.

Opium smokers [the author reminds us] have a special way of speaking. They begin a sentence and, at the same time, stick a fresh piece of opium on the end of the pipe: the sentence does not reach a conclusion till the piece of opium is completely smoked. The listener needs to be patient and not be put off by the sizzling of opium.

Then we hear a second version of the same story, though with different emphasis, from the girl, who, as Professor Wickens puts it, "in her own way, and in her animal boorishness, is every bit as demented and incoherent as F". The extreme sensitivity of the opium addict, his odd suspicion, jealousy, and attachment to the girl finally drive him to strangle her, while he himself mysteriously disappears.

Apart from the life, habits, mental processes, reciprocal passions, and aversions of the two main characters, which are depicted very skilfully, the development of the story—especially its beginning and end—has a special significance: the story opens in a bus, with the author telling us that he has learnt more about people and life in these buses than during his eight years in elementary and two years in secondary schools; and it closes in similar circumstances—on a bus ride, as though nothing unusual had happened in between.

Other pieces in this collection are the eponymous "Chamadān", the story of the love of a father and his son for a White Russian girl; and "Qurbānī" ("Sacrifice"), in which a sensitive and talented but cynical young man, dying of tuberculosis, marries a girl who is fond of him and then commits suicide while they are on their honeymoon. "Tārīkhcha-yi Uṭāq-i Man" ("The History of my Room") has almost all the ingredients that go to make an "exciting story": a psychosomatic husband, an attractive wife, a young lover, and a murder scene as the climax. And finally there is the satirical and humorous piece, "Mardī-ka Pāltu-yi Shīk Tanash Būd" ("The Man who Wore a Smart Overcoat"), which ridicules the modern, Frenchified, pseudo-intellectuals, in a language that is a conscious parody of the old classical style of panegyrical poetry. The writing, style, and characterization of this last piece is obviously influenced by Ṣādiq Hidāyat and Mas'ūd Farzād's celebrated *Vagh Vagh Sāhāb*.[1]

The second collection of 'Alavī's short stories, *Varaq Pārihā-yi Zindān*, was published immediately after his release from jail, in 1941. As the name of the collection suggests, they are tales of fellow-prisoners scribbled on old sugar and cigarette packets or on any small scraps of paper the author could lay hands on while in prison. The musical quality of the language is one of this book's most haunting features. The brilliant character study and the abundance of images surpass those of the first work and show vividly how much the artist has refined his craft. Despite the political bias that colours nearly all the stories, here, too, psychological probing is a major theme.

The first story, "Pādang" ("Pestle"), while relating the tragedy of an unsuccessful marriage and a resultant murder, also acquaints us with the toil and hardship suffered by peasants in the northern

[1] See below, pp. 162–4.

provinces of Iran. Like the other pieces of the collection, the story contains a good deal of criticism and innuendo directed against the conditions during the later years of Riżā Shah's reign. The author's emphasis on his own term of imprisonment, seven years, sounds as a refrain throughout the story, and has the effect of a whip, with which he lashes the ruling circles. And yet the grace, sobriety, and forbearance of 'Alavī's pen, even when describing the brutality of the warders or enraged by animosity and spite, are most striking.

"Sitāra-yi Dunbāla-dār" ("Comet") is the touching story of a young political prisoner who has been arrested on his wedding day. In "Intiẓār" ("Expectation") the tragedy of another fellow-prisoner, who eventually becomes insane in his prison-cell, is portrayed with extraordinary compassion and great conviction. In this and the story after it, "'Afv-i 'Umūmī" ("Amnesty"), where a political prisoner writes to his wife about his sufferings, and his feelings of nostalgia as he recollects past memories, there are many passages illustrating with remarkable realism the agonies of solitude in a prison cell. Here is an example:

When one is in prison one is not free. The greatest affliction is not that all contact with the outside world is cut off and that one lives far from one's family and people, far from the pleasures of life, beneath the boot and whips of a ruthless gaoler—oh, one perforce submits and grows used to these torments—the greatest misfortune and affliction is that even within this limited environment one is not free. There too one is in shackles: you must share your bed, your food, and your entire life with a number of others with whom you have nothing in common on the moral or intellectual plane. For how many years can you relate your favourite stories and experiences to your dearest friend? For how many years can you tell your companion how sick you are of this tedious existence, sick, and that your only desire is to wake up one day and open your eyes without the first thing that catches your eye being his patched old underpants? At meal-times how noisily those more unfortunate and more wretched than you gobble away morsels of food adhering to their chops, while you have not the face to ask them to eat their food a little more slowly. Just when some desire or regret is occupying your mind, the talk of the others is filled with salacious hints and allusions—and you are obliged to listen. When you close your eyes and try, from behind the iron bars, to steal a distant glimpse of mountains, snow and freedom and with this view there comes to mind a gentle and moving tune which just escapes you, and you gaze on at the mountains and the snow and freedom, trying to recall the tune—just at this very moment a lunatic cackle suddenly sets your whole body shuddering; but you are obliged, you are compelled to listen to it, condemned. All these tedious trivialities have not to be endured once, or for a day, or a week, but for months, for years—if the world does not catch fire or the flame of war does not overspread the whole earth, we must endure them for ever.

'Alavī's flair for scene-painting, the breadth of his imaginative vision, and his tender treatment of whatever material is at his disposal are all best exhibited in the last story of this collection, "Raqṣ-i Marg" ("Dance of the Dead"). The plot is a commonplace one: a love story and a murder at the end, interwoven with a piece of music, the "Danse macabre", which the girl plays on her piano. It is when the narrator conjures up the vision of this frightening dance that 'Alavī's fertile imagination does wonders:

The clock strikes twelve. From this hour till dawn the dead are free, free. Free.

It is midnight!

What a night of horror.

Every night is thus terrible; because our life is terrible and heart-rending. But they no longer have hearts to be rent. The dead have no hearts.

For we are not alike; but dead men are alike.

From midnight till cock-crow the dead hold their revels, celebrating freedom and release from the afflictions of mortal life.

All are equal.

Here is neither king nor beggar, neither old nor young, girl nor boy, man nor woman—all are dead. All are skeletons.

No head bears a plume; no back wears rags; hand in hand they dance.

Death, common to all, a part of their being, indeed, their whole being—death makes the skeletons dance.

Death, with a shin-bone that was once the leg of a tall young girl, drums for them on a thick-boned skull.

When it is twelve, the skeletons come up the steps out of the grave and dance.

Death which is they themselves—for here there is no commander and no commanded—plays a gentle melody.

The throng of the dead move their hands and feet in the dance.

He whose facial bones still retain a grin was in life a judge and used to sneer at the afflictions and plaints of the condemned. But his is newly dead. This vestige will soon vanish from his skull; between jaw and cheeks no trace of it will remain. For now he is dead and free.

He whose back-bones are bent used to incline his back in life and bow his head. Here he has no need; that which separated him from others, the needs of everyday life, no longer exist.

Here is no laughter and no weeping, no joy and no grief, no anxiety and no hope. There is no pride and no humiliation, no oppression and no helplessness or supplication, no hunger and no satiety.

There is nothing. Only death. Only freedom.

Is not death better than a judge sneering at the misery of the condemned?

Is not death better than a pauper bending his back?

Is not death better than humanity in chains?

That is why they are revelling.

They dance, because they are free.

Death with a girl's shin-bone, plays for them on a broad-pated skull the Dance of the Dead.

Alas, even this freedom is limited.

The cock heralds the approach of dawn.

All the dead, the skeletons, disperse.

'Alavī's *Panjāh-u-sa Nafar* (1942) is an actual account of what happened to the author and his comrades from the day they were put under arrest until the general amnesty. The maltreatment they suffered from the warders, their struggle for survival, the oppressions of various government agents, their trial, etc., are meticulously reported. Published during the political turmoil of the post-Riẓā Shah period, the book had an immense impact, especially on the younger generation. Yet despite its provocative power and some moving episodes, the importance of *Panjāh-u-sa Nafar* for 'Alavī's literary career remains inconsiderable.

The third collection of short stories, *Nāma-hā*, was published in 1952. It contains nine stories. Among them, "Gīla-mard" ("The Man from Gilan") stands out, if not as the best, then without doubt one of the finest short stories ever written by a Persian author. The style, the economy of words, the construction, balance, originality, and above all the piece's stirring quality are reminiscent of the work of Western writers like Hemingway. Two armed gendarmes are escorting a Gilanian farmer, accused of taking part in anti-feudal disturbances, to their headquarters. Walking barefooted in the rain, through the mud and swamp of the northern forests, with wind and thunder roaring overhead, the "culprit" remains quiet and unprovoked by the malicious accusation and abuse of one of the gendarmes, who unwittingly reveals that he has murdered Gīla-mard's wife. On the way, they rest at a teahouse. The other gendarme (who himself had formerly been a highway robber), after receiving fifty *tūmāns* from Gīla-mard, returns his pistol and creeps quietly away. Gīla-mard disarms the abusive gendarme, but, hearing his plea for his wife and children, takes pity on him and spares his life. Then he makes for the jungle. But hardly has he stepped out into the open when he is shot in the back by the first gendarme.

In "Nāma-hā", the first story of this collection, Shīrīn, a judge's daughter who has joined a progressive revolutionary group, discloses the crimes, and judicial machinations of her father by sending him anonymous letters. The guilt-conscious father, having tried and condemned scores of alleged criminals during his lifetime, is now trying to judge his own past actions. The interest of the piece lies in his psychoanalytic self-trial.

"Ijāra-yi Khāna" ("House Rent") is a grim but telling tableau of the life of a poor family who are killed when the roof of their room falls on them. "Diz-āshūb" depicts the grief of a father who spends his last penny on the education of his only daughter in the hope of producing a midwife for their village. But on completing her training, the girl forgets all about the little village and chooses the more attractive life of the city. The sentimental little story "Yirinichikā" is touching, but rather like a piece of tender music or a romantic lyric that lacks clear meaning. In "Yak Zan-i Khushbakht" ("A Lucky Woman") and "Rusvā'ī" ("Scandal"), the consequences of compulsory marriages, dictated by parents, and the scandals of high society are exposed; while the last story, "Panj Daqīqa Pas as Davāzda" ("Five Minutes After Twelve") satirizes the Persian administrative bureaucracy.

Almost as soon as it was published, 'Alavī's novel *Chashm-hāyash* caused a great stir, particularly among left-wing intellectuals. The book has since been the subject of extravagant praise and equally strong condemnation. The strongest attack came from the author's political comrades and the critics within his own party. This attitude was also noticeable in the press and literary reviews of the Soviet Union, where the book's shortcomings are grossly magnified and its positive and artistic value underestimated. The theme of *Chashmhāyash* revolves around a portrait of an unknown woman painted by a famous artist, Mākān, who is also the organizer and key figure of the underground movement in Persia during Riẓā Shah's reign. The artist ends up in exile, and it is in the last days of his life that he paints his masterpiece and calls it "Chashmhāyash" ("Her Eyes"). What strikes one most in this painting is not the extraordinary beauty of the face, but the malice, mystery, and virulence that emanate from the eyes of the woman, and one cannot help feeling that these eyes have been a source of torment to the painter. The narrator, determined to unravel the secrets that surround the life of this distinguished man, does not rest until he finds the owner of the eyes.

Farangīs, the woman in the portrait, belongs to a wealthy aristocratic family. In her early youth she has the desire to become a painter, and, with this passion burning in her heart, she goes to Paris to study in the École des Beaux Arts. But to achieve distinction or to do anything worthwhile in this field is a laborious ordeal. Besides talent, it requires painstaking care and devotion. Born and bred in the luxury of a rich household, Farangīs was obviously not made for the task:

> They never taught me how to work. I didn't need to work for a living. There were always others who willingly did my work for me. My father had a maxim: Never bother yourself with work that others can do for you.

Having failed in art, she turns to the frivolities of Parisian life; her intelligence makes her cynical and she uses her bewitching beauty to tease and torment the young men around her:

> I had conceived a spite against these stupid lovers. I gained pleasure from tormenting them. I enjoyed teasing them. The crazier they got about me, the more harshly I handled them.

It is in this phase of her life that she meets a young, ailing painter who is devoting all his time and energy to political activities. Khudādād is a passionate revolutionary full of spite and pugnacity against his country's despotism. His heart is filled with hope, love, and an unshakeable faith in the destiny of his people and the ultimate victory of his cause. He is, moreover, engaged and does not show the slightest interest in Farangīs's physical attractions.

The charm and warmth of his life overpower the empty heart of the young girl, and at his inducement she decides to return home:

Go to Iran! The people of our country are so wretched and in need of help that you can be useful to them in a thousand different ways. To be an artist you must be human. You have no idea under what conditions your fellow-countrymen are living. Go to Iran and become human. Perhaps you'll find the way to success. Now that you have failed to depict on canvas the dragon which is devouring you, go and slay the dragon which is ravaging the social life of the people of Iran. There, a number of young people, who have studied in Europe, have underground movements. So far they haven't achieved anything. But one day they will render a great service to their country. They need the help of people like you. This very beauty of yours, which has become a burden to you may be helpful to them in carrying out their difficult tasks.

Back at home Farangīs meets Mākān, the distinguished artist, and under his direction she takes part in the clandestine activities of the revolutionary group. But her political fervour soon melts away ("I had no interest in the fate of the people of this country. Their afflictions didn't move me. I didn't share in their suffering and misfortune. Whatever happened my position was secure. What had I in common with the miserable wretches of whom this country was full?") and instead a passionate love for the artist seizes her. The rest of the story is taken up, on the one hand, by Farangīs's wiles to win the affections of the artist and, on the other, by Mākān's repressed and constrained response. Finally, when the artist is arrested, Farangīs accepts the long-standing proposal of the head of police, though she hates him as a man, and marries him. Her motive, she claims, is to save the life of the artist.

In relating the story of her life and her relations with Mākān, Farangīs tries to convince the narrator that those malicious eyes on the canvas are not hers and that the artist had misunderstood her. In the author's statement of her case there is not only abundant sympathy but every sign of his having "understood" her; and this is what gave rise to the violent criticism from the apostles of the left. To them, Farangīs represented a mere adventurous bourgeois girl who, tired of the trivialities and pleasures of her class and environment, turned to the revolutionary movement for the thrill and excitement it gave her. By her own confession, she had no interest in the fate of the people, nor any faith in the cause. The eyes given to her in the portrait were therefore very much hers. The artist was exact and realistic in his portrayal: it is the author who has gone astray in his final analysis.

In the work [wrote a Russian scholar] there are certain serious defects. The main hero, the leader of a democratic movement and a notable artist, Mākān, is portrayed weakly and in a hackneyed manner. All the attention of the author is directed to the flippant, light-minded aristocrat, Farangīs. The author from a subjective point of view, considers the love of Farangīs for Mākān sufficient basis for the justification of Farangīs's foolish and absurd actions.[1]

Speaking about tendencies towards realism and naturalism in modern Persian literature, another Russian critic, D. S. Komissarov, maintained:

A different kind of naturalism is to be found, for instance in Buzurg 'Alavī's creations. At times the author without striving for artistic completeness, merely copies from life, giving individual portraits instead of depicting types. It is probably for this reason that in the novel *Her Eyes* [*Chashmhāyash*] the figure of Farangīs is too eccentric, while the noble progressive painter Mākān is depicted as unjustifiably timid and even to some extent flaccid. By cluttering up the portrayal of the hero's character with inessential, unnecessary details, the author has rendered it vague, because an excess of realistic details often only leads to a distortion of the image.[2]

A more serious criticism that can be levelled against 'Alavī's novel is his indulgence in psychoanalysis and romantic introspection, which, especially when used as ends in themselves, interrupt the progress of the story and diminish the realism and objectivity of the portrayal. All the same, *Chashmhāyash* stands as a unique and moving work of art among the writings of modern Persia. There is nothing drab or dull in the entire story. The suffocating atmosphere of the dictatorial days, with which the book begins, is extremely well expressed. The description of the artist's pictures, such as "Khāna-hā-yi Ra'īyatī" ("Peasants' Houses") and "Kashf-i Ḥijāb" ("Unveiling of Women"), is in fact word-painting in which conditions of the time, and the miseries of ordinary men are vividly displayed. In his short appearance, the

[1] *Sovremenniy Iran*, edited by B. N. Zakhoder (Moscow, 1957).

[2] See *Kratkie Soobshcheniya Instituta Vostokovedeniye* (Akademiya Nauk SSSR), XXVII, 1958.

militant revolutionary Khudādād captures our affection and admiration. His portrayal and those of Rajab, the artist's faithful servant, and Colonel Ārām, the head of police, are masterly. The brief, tragic courtship of Farangīs by Donatello is described with extreme subtlety and dramatic effect.

Discussion of *Chashmhāyash* can hardly close without at least a short reference to its simple, economical, and at the same time exquisite language. Nor, as Professor Wickens remarks about another work of this author,

> without emphasising how remarkable an achievement in Persian is 'Alavī's use of this economical and unpretentious prose: unlike several others, he has not turned from artificial ornamentation and "correct" *clichés* merely to fall into banality, jargon, bizarre dialectal forms, exaggerated slang, or deliberate obscenity. His style is flexible, but in any given context it is absolutely normal and appropriate. It is more of a tribute than might at first appear to suggest that 'Alavī's writings offer admirable and virtually self-sufficient material on a practical manual of modern colloquial Persian!

A number of 'Alavī's works have been translated into German during recent years. An excellent translation of *Chashmhāyash* ("Ihre Augen") by Herbert Melzig was published in 1959 in Berlin; this novel has also been translated into Polish by Józef Bielowski. Rudolf Gelpke, the Swiss Persian scholar, has included a German rendering of "Raqṣ-i Marg" in his collection (*op. cit.*) of Contemporary Persian Writers. Another German collection, containing fifteen of 'Alavī's short stories, appeared in 1960: this book, *Die Weisse Mauer*, bears the title of a piece written in German by the author. Other stories in the collection are translated by Von Herbert and Manfred Lorenz.

'Alavī's wide acquaintance with foreign literature and his sound knowledge of several European languages have helped him to produce some excellent Persian translations of world literature. Among these are: Chekhov's *The Cherry Orchard* and Marshak's *Twelve Months*, from Russian; Bernard Shaw's *Mrs Warren's Profession* and J. B. Priestley's *An Inspector Calls* from English, and Schiller's *Jungfrau von Orleans* and Theodor Nöldeke's *Das Iranische Nationalepos* from German.

CHAPTER XIII

THE YOUNGER WRITERS

Jalāl Āl-i Aḥmad

AMONG the younger generation of Persian writers, Jalāl Āl-i Aḥmad deserves to be singled out for his versatility, a markedly individual style, and a deep conviction that runs through all his works. He was born and nurtured in a clerical household, with teaching as his profession and a background of Tūda Party affiliation in early youth. All that is truly Persian in the form and substance of Jamālzāda, 'Alavī and Hidāyat—modern Persia's three leading writers—becomes a happy blend in Āl-i Aḥmad's writing.

Āl-i Aḥmad's literary fame began in 1945, with the publication of a short story called "Zīyārat" ("Pilgrimage") in the journal *Sukhan*. This interesting piece and eleven others were collected under the title of *Dīd u Bāzdīd* ("The Exchange of Visits") and published later that year. The themes of these stories revolve round a criticism of superstition and of hypocritical clergy; denunciation of the unpleasant aspects of urban life, and an unremitting sympathy for the masses who suffer social and political disabilities. Except for a number of social and critical essays written for the press, Āl-i Aḥmad's attention during the early years of his career was chiefly devoted to short-story writing. Subsequently, four other collections of stories appeared: *Az Ranjī ka Mī-barīm* ("From Our Suffering") in 1947, *Sitār*[1] in 1948, *Zan-i Zīyādī* ("A Superfluous Woman") in 1952, and *Sarguẕasht-i Kandūhā* ("The Story of Beehives") in 1954. Then followed a period of stagnation—coinciding, significantly, with the downfall of Muṣaddiq and its political repercussions—during which, as if to relieve the frustration of his dormant genius, Āl-i Aḥmad turned to research into the customs, dialects, folklore, and other aspects of rural life in certain parts of Persia. Three studies have so far emerged from these researches: *Awrāzān* (1953); *Tāt Nishīnhā-yi Bulūk-i Zahrā* ("The Tat-settlers of Zahra District", 1958); and *Durr-i Yatīm-i Khalīj*,

[1] The name of a three-stringed musical instrument.

Jazīra-yi Khārg ("Kharg Island, the Gulf's Orphan Pearl", 1960). According to the specialists, and despite the author's modest disclaiming of serious scholarship, these studies have produced interesting data on the sociology, anthropology, and dialectology of three little-known areas.

In the field of fiction, Āl-i Aḥmad's latest works are a novelette, *Mudīr-i Madrisa* ("The Headmaster", 1958) and a long *qiṣṣa* (story), *Nūn Val-Qalam* ("Nūn and the Pen", 1961), told in the traditional manner of a Persian nursery tale. In *Mudīr-i Madrisa* the writer has realistically portrayed the life and preoccupations of a provincial schoolmaster and his teaching staff. Besides witnessing the humiliations and privations suffered by this group of minor officials, the reader is reminded of some of the defects and inadequacies in the country's educational system.

A distinctive feature in nearly all of Āl-i Aḥmad's fictional works is the abundant use of spoken forms, extending even to his descriptive passages; indeed, it is often hard to distinguish direct and indirect speech in his narrative. Further, he is a master of precision and economy of words: having very briefly sketched the outward appearances of his characters, he allows them to come to life through their own words. Cynicism and disillusionment that are always mingled with humour—a characteristic of Persian people—play a great part in his works. And in spite of his progressive, sometimes revolutionary, tendencies, Āl-i Aḥmad has remained an old-fashioned individual at heart. A fervent admirer of national traditions, especially of Persia's ancient canons of behaviour, he is indignant at the onrush of "modernization" and quasi-Western ways of life. In fact, the deterioration of ethics in the life of his countrymen has often driven him to extreme, fanatical judgements. An example can be found in his book about Kharg Island and more recently in the controversial booklet *Gharbzadigī* ("Westernization"), copies of which were confiscated from the bookstalls.

Apart from his scholarly and creative works, Āl-i Aḥmad has translated a number of books from French into Persian; well known among these are: Dostoevsky's *Igrok* ("The Gambler"); Albert Camus's *L'Etranger* and *Le Malentendu*; Jean-Paul Sartre's *Les Mains Sales*; and André Gide's *Retour de l'U.R.S.S.* and *Les Nourritures Terrestres.*

Ṣādiq Chūbak

Ṣādiq Chūbak was born in Bushihr in 1916. After his elementary education in Shiraz, he entered the American College of Tehran from which he graduated in 1937; at present he is working with the National Iranian Oil Company in Tehran. Chūbak came to the fore under the aegis of his friend Ṣādiq Hidāyat in the post-Riẓā Shah period, and he is now regarded as a highly gifted author of the younger generation, with two collections of short stories to his credit: *Khayma Shab-bāzī* ("The Puppet Show", 1945) and *Antar-ī ka Lūṭīyash Murda Būd* ("The Baboon Whose Buffoon was Dead", 1950).

But though originally encouraged by Hidāyat, Chūbak cannot be considered a mere imitator: his work is far too original. He is an obviously sincere and careful artist who imitates no one, though naturally he is influenced by a number of models. Besides Hidāyat, for whom he has a great admiration, the American short-story writers Hemingway, Faulkner and Henry James may be cited.

Chūbak has a firm sense of what the short story should be. Indeed, if he writes more, he has it in him to become one of the best short-story writers in modern Persia. His feeling for this form is illustrated by his economy of incident, and by the fact that each of his stories has a single theme developed on a small scale with a minimum of descriptive apparatus. His treatment of detail suggests the intricacy, combined with boldness of conception, of the Persian miniature painting. Chūbak keeps his picture balanced and spare; and yet a whole pattern of emotion and situation is revealed within it. The result is generally convincing and shows a moving insight into human nature.

The aim of the short story should be to develop a character through a series of incidents that all amplify one feature of that character. This can be done realistically and satisfactorily only if the utmost art is used in contriving the story, and if the author can convey a wealth of atmosphere by a few master-strokes of firm but controlled description. He has not the scope of the novelist, who can paint his portraits and scenes *in extenso*; nor has he the room to explain. In other words, his tale must have the quality of the perfect sketch, whose draughtsmanship is so firm, whose selection of detail so skilful, that the whole situation is indicated clearly without any need for explanation. This Chūbak succeeds in doing to a large extent.

These qualities are remarkably displayed in a number of stories in his *Khayma Shab-bāzī*, such as "Naftī" ("Kerosene Peddler"), "Zīr-i Chirāgh-i Qirmiz" ("Under the Red Light"), "Pīrāhan-i Zirishkī" ("Purple Dress"), "Mūsū Ilyās" ("Monsieur Ilyas") and "Mardī dar Qafas" ("A Man in a Cage"). The latter has been translated into German by Rudolf Gelpke and published under the title "Der Aristokrat und das Tier" (St Gallen, Tschudy-Verlag, 1961). Two other stories of this collection, "Yaḥyā" and "'Adl" ("Justice"), were translated into English.[1] Chūbak's second published collection, *Antar-ī ka Lūṭīyash Murda Būd*, contains three short stories: "Daryā Chirā Ṭūfānī Shuda Būd" ("Why the Sea had Grown Stormy"), "Qafas" ("The Cage") and the title piece; there is also a play called "Tūp-i Lāstīkī" ("The Rubber Ball"). Under the title of "Daryā" a film is now being made in Iran of the first story. "Antar-ī ka Lūṭīyash Murda Būd" has been translated into English by P. W. Avery and published in *New World Writing* (no. 11, May 1957).

In all these stories, as well as in the majority of his other works, Chūbak goes in search of his heroes in the lowest depths of society. But even there he is not content with the ordinary, commonplace sights, for his sharp, microscopic eyes catch only the ugliest and most repellent shades of life. Having found his characters, he captures their racy speech, but reproduces it almost excessively: he copies their abusive terms and obscene words with a fanatical zest, perceives their innermost feelings, and then exposes them with harsh realism. Writing about this trait, Věra Kubīčkovā (in J. Rypka, *History of Persian Literature*, Leipzig, 1959, p. 397) maintains that "Following Hidāyat's example Chūbak avails himself of the language of the people. However, we are apt to find exaggeration: for instance when he allows people to speak a vulgar language which in reality they would never use." Herbert W. Duda, an Austrian orientalist, commenting on the above statement in an article about Chūbak, expresses the curious idea that "Perhaps there is an intention [in Chūbak's use of vulgar language] to bring the younger generation around to new ways of thinking by means of shocking them 'pour épater le bourgeois'".[2]

[1] See *Life and Letters, op. cit.*

[2] *Bustan*, no. 3 (Vienna, 1962).

Another characteristic is a boundless naturalism, in which descriptive passages have an almost photographic precision. The disturbing piece "Qafas", in his second collection, is a good example. The symbolic palette and brush printed on the cover of this author's two published collections are indeed indicative of his gift of observation and his ability to paint scenes.

Ṣādiq Chūbak is an atheist. "Even as a child", says Professor Duda, "Islam and any connection to organized religion was an abomination." So it is not surprising to find a considerable amount of drollery aimed at Muslim clergy and their humbug superstitions, occasionally in the two story collections and more consistently in works he has in manuscript form being prepared for printing. These include a number of blank verses (*chakāmak*) written during recent years. The form of these stylistic pieces is new in Persian poetry, and the substance resembles the cries of anguish of a man under mental torture—hence the title he intends to give them: *Āh-i Insān* ("Human Grief"). Then, apart from a translation of Carlo Collodis's *Pinocchio* ("Ādamak-i Chūbī"), which he translated from English and published in 1955, he has a collection of fifteen short stories, to be called *Rūz-i Avval-i Qabr* ("The First Day in the Grave"), some of which have already appeared in Iranian Journals. There are also two novels: *Tangsīr* (the name given to the natives of Tangistān, a district in the province of Fars) and *Sang-i Ṣabūr* ("The Stone of Patience"). The first one is now in press.[1] The second is the tragic story of a misunderstood girl who, in her struggle to earn a living to support her small child, has resigned herself to temporary marriages (*ṣīgha*) arranged by a cunning *ākhund*. Besides the intricate texture of the narrative and a derisive language that bites and scorns throughout, Chūbak has used many new ideas in the style and characterization of his unusual tale and in the unfolding of its morbid plot. The composition is a mixture of fiction and drama, with illustrations here and there instead of words. Notwithstanding the author's relish for this work, on which he claims to have worked for fourteen years, it is hard to anticipate the reception it will have from Iranian critics. Yet whatever their judgement, there is little doubt that the modes of expression boldly employed in this book will open new horizons before Persian authors.

[1] This book was recently published and received enthusiastic reviews in the Iranian Press.

Chūbak's zeal for true craftsmanship and his conscientiousness are rare among modern Persian writers, whose approach is often more akin to that of the journalist than of the painstaking artist. He has the artist's readiness to observe and come to a proper understanding of his subject, as well as his capacity to identify himself in emotion and thought with his subject. It is this that gives Chūbak's stories such a fine quality.

Regrettably, we notice only very briefly the younger writers who have appeared on the literary scene during the past twenty years. With social and political problems as the predominant themes, their works are as a rule the sincere reflection of the turbulent years they have lived through. Some of the writers have shown real talent and originality. But few of these have yet achieved national recognition; and their works, having appeared mainly in journals and periodicals, are not easily accessible.

Bih-Āẕīn

Among the more prominent and promising writers of the new generation, mention should be made of Bih-Āẕīn (Muḥammad I'timādzāda), who owes his literary fame to the novelette *Dukhtar-i Ra'īyat* ("The Peasant's Daughter", 1951). His other published works, *Parākanda* ("Scattered Pieces", 1944/5), *Bi-Sūy-i Mardum* ("Towards People", 1948), and *Naqsh-i Parand* ("Silk Design", 1955),[1] are short stories and some stylistic sketches. The author shows considerable ability to introduce original themes and probe deep into sociological studies, but the treatment and development of his stories are somewhat perfunctory; his care and attention appear to be centred more on their form and style than on their purport. As a result, his prose works have an exemplary poetical lyricism. For their clarity, exactitude, and above all the choice of words, Bih-Āẕīn's compositions stand as a good example of how Persian can be written with simplicity, and at the same time with beauty and grace.

Bih-Āẕīn is also renowned as one of the most skilful and meticulous translators of modern Iran. The books he has rendered into Persian include such classics as: William Shakespeare, *Othello*;

[1] *Naqsh-i Parand* has been translated into Russian by L. S. Peisikov (Moscow, 1961).

Romain Rolland, *Jean-Christophe*, *Jean-Christophe à Paris* and *La Fin du Voyage*; and Honoré de Balzac, *Le Père Goriot*, *La Cousine Bette*, *Le Lys dans la Vallée* and *La Peau de Chagrin*.

Taqī Mudarrisī

Another young writer is Taqī Mudarrisī, who made his literary debut in 1956 with a short novel called *Yakulyā va Tanhā'ī-yi Aū* ("Yakulya and Her Loneliness") based on a biblical theme with the somewhat Miltonic design of discussing, if not seeking to justify, the ways of God. His novel was particularly important because it was one of the few original works of literature to appear in the later 'fifties, when most prose fiction took the form of translations of foreign works, and when Persian writers, possibly apprehensive of official censorship, seemed chary of writing. By selecting a biblical theme, Mudarrisī was able to give his story a remoteness that enabled him to write about fundamental human problems in a manner that carried no political import. What is surprising is the psychological insight shown by this young writer—a medical student only twenty-three when he wrote this book—who is so concerned with the problem of man's loneliness, his fears of the consequences of wrong-doing, and his proneness to follow a beguiling Satan rather than a benevolent Providence. The symbolism of his first novel is unusual and expertly handled. His prose style is not quite settled and his language not without faults. But whatever he may write in the future, this first work will always remain important.

'Alī Muḥammad Afghānī

No reference to the younger writers would be complete without mentioning 'Alī-Muḥammad Afghānī, whose colossal novel *Shuhar-i Āhū Khānum* ("Mrs Ahu's Husband") made an unusual stir among the intellectual and literary circles of Iran when it first appeared in 1961. The work took not only the reading public but also the critics by complete surprise. The latter, having wearily witnessed the outpouring of stereotyped writings and translations for almost a decade, were not expecting a substantial work of art to emerge under the prevailing circumstances, and especially from someone completely unknown to them. Thus their first reaction to the book was cool and non-committal. But largely because of the public's reception of the work, this initial scepticism soon died out, and with it the reticence of the critics. For months afterwards the remarkable talent of Afghānī and the impact of his book continued to be the talk of enlightened society in Tehran. Two of the most reputable critics described the work as the "greatest novel ever written in the Persian language", not hesitating in their great enthusiasm to compare it with the works of such masters as Balzac and Tolstoy.

The theme of *Shuhar-i Āhū Khānum* revolves around the lives and destinies of a generation of Iranians now gradually passing away. The book is encyclopaedic: the length and breadth of its story —spread over 863 pages—cannot be summarized in our present limited space. Yet some brief reference to the mainstream of the narrative will clarify our appraisal of the work.

The book opens in the nostalgic atmosphere of a Persian provincial town, the writer taking us at a gentle and deliberate pace back to the drowsy life of Kermanshah as it was thirty years ago. After a short tour of the town, we pause in front of a baker's shop and meet two of the main characters: Sayyid Mīrān, the kind, simple-hearted, elderly baker whose lifetime of honesty and moral rectitude have won him the respect of the townsfolk; and then Humā, a young and seductive wanton prepared to use every conceivable stratagem to capture the Sayyid's heart and so secure herself a shelter for life. The third and in many ways the principal character of the book, introduced to us when we later visit the baker's house, is his wife, Āhū Khānum. The interest of the story lies in the conflicts and interrelationships of the members of this triangle. The credulous baker, seduced by the lascivious young woman, slights all his moral and social obligations, brings her into the household under the guise of a concubine, and turns a blind eye to his devoted wife and their children. The peaceful and happy atmosphere of the baker's home soon becomes one of jealous rivalries, bitter quarrels, and vindictiveness—in a word, chaos. In this cat-and-dog life and throughout its incessant, scandalous bickerings, Āhū Khānum suffers a great many insults and humiliations, but she remains unshaken in her determination to defend her rights and win back her wayward husband. In the end she emerges victorious from the whole tragic embroilment.

As is apparent from this all-too-brief sketch, the dominant theme of *Shuhar-i Āhū Khānum* is the unfortunate plight of the Iranian woman. Readers of this study will recall that Persian novel-writing in the 'twenties and 'thirties was exclusively concerned with women and their predicament. But as explained earlier, the approach of nearly all of these writers was inane and superficial: though filled with the sufferings and "problems" of women in that society, every one of their books ingeniously dodged the crucial issues. Perhaps it was the conditions of the time, especially religious considerations, that discouraged them from laying bare the truth about women in twentieth-century Iranian society. Afghānī, on the contrary, has hit the nail right on the head. In his classic novel he exposes the slavery of the Iranian wife to her husband's caprices, the cruelty of the laws and customs imposed on women by men to bring about their submission, and the humiliations women have suffered in this patriarchal society, as well as their amazing forbearance, throughout history, in the face of such injustices—all with great mastery and in a manner unequalled in modern Persian prose.

One of the outstanding features of *Shuhar-i Āhū Khānum* is the wealth and variety of its characterization. The multitude of people appearing in the book are so real and true to life that hardly any Iranian reader could fail to recognize them among his family and friends. As one Persian critic put it, "Mrs Āhū can be found in every house of this land [Iran]. Her husband, Sayyid Mīrān, meets us in every street and bazaar. Their neighbours are just like our own". In other words, each of the characters has an individual as well as a universal appeal. By the same token, while the events of the story centre on everyday happenings in an ordinary, middle-class Persian household, they retain the intrinsic truth of the meaning of life to all men. The narration is woven of a marvellous blend of objectivity and inevitability, of a kind that marks nearly all classic fiction. The presentation is made through observation rather than analysis. For all the abundance of colour and vivid scenes, very little in the book could be ascribed to the writer's imagination. Everything is taken from life and portrayed with clarity of vision and daring.

Though our knowledge about the author is very limited (rumour in Iran has it that he was an army officer, spent some years in prison because of his leftist tendencies, and wrote his book there), nevertheless it is abundantly clear from his writing that Afghānī is endowed with the gifts of a sensitive and discerning artist, rather than with the erudition and acumen of a literary scholar. This has been both beneficial and detrimental to him as a novelist. On the one hand, his composition is refreshingly devoid of the kind of intellectual qualms that so often bedevil the professional *literati*. But ironically enough, he seems to have been worried by his lack of formal scholarship, and in his perhaps naïve efforts to gloss over this "handicap", he becomes ridiculously pedantic from time to time. The impression left on the reader is that of an author trying to stuff his characters, irrespective of their social background or intellect, with the sum total of his learning and worldly knowledge. Poor old Sayyid Mīrān, who cannot even sign his name, is made to quote Aristophanes, Pascal and Balzac, and to discourse on art, philosophy, and music, even on Rimsky-Korsakov's opera "The Golden Cockerel"! Humā, the illiterate village girl, cites Othello and Don Quixote in her arguments and is even knowledgeable about Cleopatra and Indian Sutteeism. Ḥusayn Khān, the brothel keeper, enters into earnest discussion of Confucius, Buddha, and the saintly Asita who predicted the latter's destiny. And towards the end of the book, the unfortunate Āhū Khānum suddenly turns into an eloquent lecturer analysing the most complex problems of society and human nature.

These faults and a few others—such as the excessive length of some of the dialogues, and the fairly frequent ramblings and disproportionate span of the author's descriptive passages—though regrettable in a novel of such high calibre, are none the less of little consequence beside the vast panorama of Persian life and society that the writer so skilfully depicts.

Shuhar-i Āhū Khānum has ample matter but suffers from inadequacies of style. The significance of the book, apart from its literary and artistic value, lies in the fact that it is a social history, belonging to a certain time and place, and containing a message. Whatever our criticism of Afghānī as a writer, there is no doubt that his novel is one of the very few contributions to modern Iranian fiction that clearly herald a promising future for Persian letters—a future compatible with a great literary heritage.

PART TWO

CHAPTER XIV

THE LEADING WRITER OF MODERN IRAN

Ṣādiq Hidāyat

TOWARDS the late 'twenties a young Persian student called Ṣādiq Hidāyat went to Europe on a government scholarship to study dentistry, which he shortly gave up for engineering. This field, too, he found little to his taste and decided to study the pre-Islamic languages and ancient culture of Iran. Contact with the literary and intellectual life of France stimulated him a great deal and gave him the habit of wide reading; but he did not take an academic degree because he realized that he was more of an artist than scholar. When he returned to Iran in 1930, the only ostensible fruits of study abroad he had to offer were his first attempts at authorship.

About twenty years later he went back to France. During this interval he had published thirty books and become recognized as Iran's foremost modern prose author. This second visit to France was more of an escape than a quest for new experience. Shortly after his arrival in Paris he committed suicide. This may have been his intention at the outset, for on a farewell card in Tehran he had written: "I left and broke your heart. See you on Doomsday. That's all." Perhaps he thought that in Paris he could commit suicide without staining the sacred soil of Iran, for he had fastidious, almost mystical, notions of the necessity for maintaining the purity of his own soil—notions fortified by his regard for Zoroastrian teaching. Or he may well have been motivated by a desire for privacy and anonymity, often denied in the conditions of Iranian society but easy to find in the capital of France. The only publicity his death at first elicited was a note on 10 April 1951 in a Paris newspaper: "An Iranian called Ṣādiq Hidāyat has committed suicide by opening the gas tap in his small flat in the Rue Championnet."

This Iranian was forty-eight years old. He had been born in

1903 in Tehran, where he grew up. He belonged to an aristocratic family that had furnished the Iranian Government with eminent officials since the Qajar Dynasty at the end of the eighteenth century. The Hidāyat family's roots were in the northern province of Mazandaran. Great landowners, they also owned estates in Fars, in the south, thus combining the roles of wealthy proprietors and influential bureaucrats. As such, they typified the class that came into prominence with the centralized government imposed on the country by the Qajar Dynasty. This bureaucratic development, a counterpoise to the separatist tendencies of powerful tribal leaders, was an urban-inspired pacification of the country after the decline of the Safavids and the Afghan invasion in 1721–2. Thus families like the Hidāyats were men of culture and peace. Prominent among them was Hidāyat's great-grandfather Riẓā-qulī Khān (1215/1800, 1288/1871–2), whose genealogy, according to his autobiography, goes back to Shaykh Kamāl of Khujand, a famous fourteenth-century poet. In the Qajar court Riẓā-qulī Khān occupied many important positions, such as treasurer, ambassador, poet laureate, tutor to the crown prince, and director of the *Dāru'l-Funūn*, Iran's first modern college. In addition he was celebrated as a man of letters, both poet and historian, and his *takhaluṣ* or pen-name, Hidāyat, became the family name. He compiled the detailed anthology and history of Persian poetry entitled the *Majma'u'l-Fuṣaḥā* ("The Concourse of the Eloquent") that served as one of the main sources for E. G. Browne's *Literary History of Persia.*

Riẓā-qulī Khān's descendants played a major part in the constitutional movement and helped to form Iran's modern institutions. Prominent were the *Mukhbiru's-Salṭana*, a member of the committee that drew up the draft of Iran's first electoral law, and his son the *Ṣanī'u'd-Dawla*, who was elected president of the first *Majlis*. Referring to their part in the constitutional movement, E. G. Browne speaks of the Hidāyats as:

> ...a large and influential family (comprising some forty living members), all of whom were well educated, and several of whom had studied in Europe....This family played a great *rôle* in the constitutional movement, especially the three brothers Ṣanī'u'd-Dawla, Mukhbiru's-Salṭana and Mukhbiru'l-Mulk, who lived together in a large house and had always refused to take office during the days of tyranny.

The following family tree shows where Ṣādiq Hidāyat belongs in this illustrious genealogy.

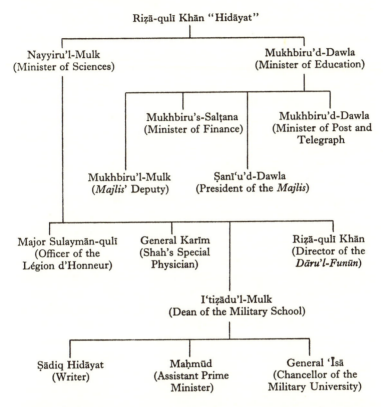

- Riẓā-qulī Khān "Hidāyat"
  - Nayyiru'l-Mulk (Minister of Sciences)
    - Major Sulaymān-qulī (Officer of the Légion d'Honneur)
    - General Karīm (Shah's Special Physician)
    - I'tiẓādu'l-Mulk (Dean of the Military School)
      - Ṣādiq Hidāyat (Writer)
      - Maḥmūd (Assistant Prime Minister)
      - General 'Īsā (Chancellor of the Military University)
    - Riẓā-qulī Khān (Director of the *Dāru'l-Funūn*)
  - Mukhbiru'd-Dawla (Minister of Education)
    - Mukhbiru'l-Mulk (*Majlis*' Deputy)
    - Mukhbiru's-Salṭana (Minister of Finance)
    - Ṣanī'u'd-Dawla (President of the *Majlis*)
    - Mukhbiru'd-Dawla (Minister of Post and Telegraph

Ṣādiq Hidāyat was three when the constitutional revolution broke out, and he lived his childhood through the disturbed years following the revolution. His literary activity began during Riẓā Shah's time, when the liberal outbursts of the early years of the century were being checked by a stern dictatorship, and when freedom of expression was also severely curtailed. Unfortunately, Hidāyat did not live long enough to see more moderate and hopeful times. "He is", maintains a Persian writer, "the child of the constitutional period and the writer of the dictatorial time."

To appreciate Hidāyat's life and work, and especially to understand his acute depressions and the possible cause of his suicide, these two factors must be borne in mind: first, the aristocratic surroundings he was born and bred in and, secondly, the disturbed state of his country.

Of Hidāyat as an individual little is known. He was modest, solitary, and retiring, therefore few had the privilege of intimacy with him. Even for those who knew him, it seems that the real man remained obscure. In his works, however, certain aspects of his character can be detected. First, his love for Persia and his consuming interest in its people, its traditions, culture, and past glories can be seen in almost every thing he wrote; at times it even drove him to a kind of fanatical chauvinism. Honesty was another prominent trait, and this constantly brought him into sharp conflict with many of his country's institutions. His sympathies were with the humble and downtrodden; he despised the privileged. Although he had every opportunity to do so, he never held any high government positions; and he avoided the upstart "aristocracy" of Pahlavi times, with which his own genuinely aristocratic family came to terms.

The idea of suicide seems to have obsessed him ever since his early youth. During his first stay in France, it appears that he tried to drown himself in the river Marne, from which he was rescued. He believed, at least for the greater part of his life, in predestination. Thus he cherished the conviction that "nobody decides to commit suicide, it is *with* some people, it is in their nature, they cannot get away from it. It is Fate which commands". In his writings as well as in his actual life Hidāyat gives the impression of being irresistibly attracted to Death, and he often praises it as a poet might praise his beloved:

> Death...the best asylum for pains and sorrows and troubles and the injustices of life....If there were no dying everybody would aspire to it, the screams of despair would rise to the heavens, everybody would curse nature. How disgusting, how horrible it would be if life were not a transient thing.

In the same revealing piece of self-expression is this significant complaint: "I have never shared others' happiness." Death, loneliness, despair, and disgust are the dominant themes of his writings:

> We are all alone, we should not be deceived. Life is a prison....Some people paint shapes on prison walls and amuse themselves thus. Some

try to escape: they wound their hands uselessly. Others mourn. But the main thing is to deceive ourselves...yet there comes a time when one even gets tired of deceiving oneself.

It is not surprising, therefore, to find that many of Hidāyat's characters die, either naturally or by murder or suicide. But this must not be taken to imply a streak of cruelty in his creations: on the contrary, their keynote is compassion. Death is included because, as Hidāyat sees it, it is the inevitable shadow over all human affairs. And his power as a writer comes through his ability to make this tragic attitude, not only perfectly natural, but incontrovertible.

Hidāyat himself was so involved in this fatalistic attitude that his power to describe the involvement comes almost unexpectedly. The objectivity of the artist is powerfully juxtaposed to a subjective situation that eventually dominated it. His personal pessimism is expressed in the following, though he rarely spoke this directly of his own feelings: "If it is true that everybody has a star in the sky, mine must be very remote, dark and obscure. Perhaps I have no star at all!"

Hidāyat's literary life can be divided into five distinct periods:

(1) *The early period* (1923–30): from the publication of his first book until he returned from Europe.

(2) *The creative period* (1930–7): the period immediately after his return to Iran until his visit to India.

(3) *The barren period* (1937–41): after his journey to India until the abdication of Riẓā Shah.

(4) *The period of high hopes* (1941–7): from the Allies' occupation of Iran to the Azerbaijan crisis.

(5) *The aftermath* (1947–51): the last four years of Hidāyat's life until his death in Paris.

CHAPTER XV

THE EARLY PERIOD (1923–30)

BEFORE his first visit to France, Hidāyat had published two books: *Rubā'īyāt-i Ḥakīm 'Umar Khayyām* ("Omar Khayyām's Quatrains", 1923)[1] and *Insān u Ḥayvān* ("Man and Animal", 1924). Neither of these is a work of any literary weight. The first is simply a new edition of the celebrated quatrains, with an introduction that is principally a rendering of E. G. Browne's study of Khayyām. The style, however, is an interesting example of Hidāyat's early prose: the stilted, conventional prose of any educated Iranian youth of the time doing an exercise for old-fashioned teachers. It contains no sign of the lucid simplicity of Hidāyat's later writing, which was to be a major influence on modern Persian prose. But his mature style does show signs of his conservative beginning, for it is that of a man who had mastered the old techniques before making innovations. Perhaps in these early days, if Hidāyat had any literary ambition at all, it was to become an eminent scholar. At any rate, this booklet indicates his interest in Khayyām, who remained a source of inspiration to him all through his literary career.

The second book, *Insān u Ḥayvān*, is simply a curiosity. A small pamphlet of eighty-five pages, very like a schoolboy's composition, it consists of a criticism of human beings' cruel treatment of animals and a defence of animals' rights to live; it concludes by advocating vegetarianism. Clearly, substantial research has gone into the book, but the composition is extremely clumsy. The text is slipshod, full of grammatical mistakes and long, awkward, frequently unclear sentences. Occasional cribs and the literal translation of French phrases are easily discernible; and the author's conclusions, coupled with his sentimentalism, sound naïve and fantastic. But students of the later Hidāyat will find the book important for several reasons. Stylistically it shows him beginning to leave the conventional, polished upper-school form exercise—

[1] Not to be confused with his well-known study and classification of the quatrains (see below, pp. 149–50).

hence the unevenness and awkward writing, as Hidāyat gropes in a new technique for which the only prototype was to be his own. In subject-matter the book brings out Hidāyat's humanity and compassion. It also, incidentally, shows his belief at this time in an Almighty God.

After he had become more matured in his craft, Hidāyat must have noticed the shortcomings of his first two books. For, perfectionist that he was, three years after the publication of *Insān u Ḥayvān*, while in Paris, he published *Favāyid-i Gīyāh-khārī* ("The Advantages of Vegetarianism", 1927), which is a wider and more thorough treatment of the same subject; and in 1934 came a second book on Khayyām, which elucidates his views on the famous *Rubā'īyāt*.

Hidāyat's early works also include a short play, or rather a puppet show, which he wrote while in Paris. *Afsāna-yi Āfarīnish* ("The Legend of Creation") was the author's first attempt in the realm of fancy and extravaganza, and the first sign of the young writer's gift for satire. The scenario is based on unscientific theories about the creation of man, the universe, and the whole nature of existence. The names of the characters represent various nationalities: Khāliq-uff, Gabriel-Pāshā, Michael-afandī, Israel-beg, Monsieur Satan, Bābā-Adam and Nana-Eve. The piece as a whole resembles a burlesque *fantocci'ni*; and it contains some extremely funny sequences, which, from the religious point of view, are derogatory and profane. The play was written in 1931 but not published until December 1946 by "Adrien Maisonneuve", Paris, in an edition limited to 105 copies that were not for sale.

A German translation of *Afsāna-yi Āfarīnish* and of two other stories by Hidāyat, with no mention of the name of the translator, appeared in Berlin in 1960. The book is illustrated and has an introduction by Buzurg 'Alavī about the writer's recollections of Hidāyat.[1]

[1] *Die Legende von der Schöpfung*, mit farbigen Federzeichnungen von Bert Heller (Rütten and Loening, Berlin, 1960).

CHAPTER XVI

THE CREATIVE PERIOD (1930–7)

On returning from Europe, Hidāyat published his first collection of short stories, *Zinda Bi-gūr* ("Buried Alive", 1930). The following six years were the most fruitful of his literary life. He became the centre of a group of progressive intellectuals known as "extremists" by conservative literary circles, whose bombastic writings were still the fashion. Hidāyat and his friends—young writers, artists, and musicians—started a new movement in art and letters. This gathering was most exciting to Hidāyat; he was the hub and the guiding star of the group, stimulating and encouraging them by his personal contribution. *Sāya-hi Mughul* ("Mongol Shadow", 1931);[1] the historical drama *Māzīyār* (1933),[2] and *Vagh Vagh Sāhāb* ("Mister Bow Wow", 1933)[3] are the fruits of these days.

At the same time, two other collections of his short stories were being published, first *Sa Qaṭra Khūn* ("Three Drops of Blood", 1932) and then *Sāya Rushan* ("Chiaroscuro", 1933). A collection of popular songs, *Usāna* (1931); a book on traditions, superstitions, and ancient beliefs, called *Nayrangistān* (1933); two travelogues, *Iṣfahān Niṣf-i Jahān* ("Isfahan: Half the World", 1932) and *Rū-yi Jāda-yi Namnāk* ("On the Wet Road", 1935);[4] *'Alavīya Khānum* ("Madame 'Alaviya", 1933); *Tarāna-hā-yi Khayyām* ("The Melodies of Khayyām", 1934); and *Būf-i Kūr* ("The Recluse", 1937) were all written during this period.

Despite his prolificness, Hidāyat was a disappointed man during this period, because he was unable to accustom himself to his environment. Many other intellectuals were facing a similar dilemma, but most of them had made their choice. Some had submitted to the stern threats of tyranny, joined the ranks of

[1] Published in a collection entitled *Anīrān* ("Non-Iranian") in collaboration with Buzurg 'Alavī and Shīn-i Partaw.

[2] In collaboration with M. Mīnuvī, who wrote the introductory remarks to the play.

[3] In collaboration with Mas'ūd Farzād.

[4] Unpublished; the manuscript is believed to be lost.

flatterers, obtained high positions, and thus could enjoy a leisurely life. Others had revolted against the ruling system, and with their very small organization and limited means were trying to extend underground activities against the autocracy that was gaining rapid control of the country. A third group of sensitive men, who could neither co-operate with the régime nor find the courage to fight it, chose to retire and put aside their talents, forgetting surrounding conditions with the help of drugs and alcohol.

The young Hidāyat could not ally himself with any of these groups. For the first one he was too honest and too proud to truckle to a despotic régime supported by minions. For the second group he was clearly not the right type: a lonely and retiring man who had always kept aloof from society, he was not made for political skirmishes, nor could he associate himself with a bold revolutionary struggle. Finally, with his vitality and love for artistic creation, he was unable, at least for the time being, to tread the path of the third group. Therefore he devoted himself to his art and tried to seek consolation in study. Scrutiny of Hidāyat's writings during this period (1930–7) reveals five distinct themes, of which three are discussed in this chapter; the remaining two merit separate chapters.

Folklore and traditional beliefs

Hidāyat is considered the first Iranian writer to recognize the importance of folklore and popular songs in the nation's culture. He was certainly the first to begin serious and methodical research in this field. *Usāna*, a collection of popular local songs, was published in 1931 in a very limited edition. But though copies of it were very rare, it was fortunately reprinted in a collection of Hidāyat's miscellaneous writings called *Nivishta-hā-yi Parākanda-yi Ṣādiq Hidāyat* ("Miscellaneous Writings of Sadiq Hidayat", 1955). *Nayrangistān*, the sequel to *Usāna*, is a valuable source-book on the beliefs, superstitions, religious ideas and other traditions of ancient Iran. The name is derived from the title of an old *Pahlavi* code of laws. In the Introduction Hidāyat points out that there were several books left from Sassanian times that clearly showed the existence of some of these old Persian traditions and beliefs. He mentions the *Artāy Vīrāz Nāmak*,

Shāyast Na-Shāyast, *Dīnkert* and the great *Bundahishn* and *Nayrangistān*. The latter he describes as "a book resembling the ordinary books of prayer, which attributes special effects to some prayers".

Professor Henri Massé, an eminent scholar in Persian folklore, speaks very highly of Hidāyat's rendering of *Nayrangistān*.[1] Hidāyat himself attached great significance to this book, and after its first publication compiled additional notes and data which, it is hoped, will be added to the original text when the new edition comes out. The first edition of the book was unfortunately banned in Persia, and it is very difficult to find copies of it now.

Excursion into the past

Hidāyat's second concern during this period was to revive Iran's historical glories. He concentrated especially on the various revolts and uprisings conducted by Iranians against the Arab and Mongol invaders. *Sāya-hi Mughul*; two historical dramas, *Parvīn Dukhtar-i Sāsān* ("Parvin, the Sasan Daughter", 1930) and *Māzīyār*; part of *Iṣfahān Niṣf-i Jahān*; and the two short stories "Ātash Parast" ("The Fire-worshipper") and "Ākharīn Labkhand" ("The Last Smile") are all based on this familiar theme, which remained one of the pre-occupations of his entire literary career.

Sāya-hi Mughul (1931) is the story of a young Iranian, Shāhrukh, who, faithful to the cause of his country, is fighting against the alien influences of Arabs and Mongols in Iran. During this time the Mongols kill his fiancée, Gulshād, in a most savage manner, and Shāhrukh takes an oath to avenge her. He becomes the leader of a band of half a dozen riders who lie in ambush in a forest and attack the passing Mongols. A number of the Mongols are killed, but during the fight Shāhrukh is injured in the arm. His horse shies and gallops away, two yelling enemy riders on his tail. Shāhrukh faints, and when he regains consciousness he finds himself in the branches of a tree; his arm, which is still bleeding, reminds him of the fight with the Mongols and he smiles with a sense of victory. For five days he drags himself through woods and swamps, then weak and helpless he takes shelter in the hollow trunk of a tree. He feels the blood gradually clotting and freezing in his arteries.

[1] See *Croyances et Coutumes Persanes* (1938), I, 14.

His body is insensitive now, but his mind remains active. He recalls happy memories of his fiancée; then he remembers her body being torn into pieces by the Mongols.

Next spring two peasants passing through the forest notice the complete skeleton of a man, seated in the hollow of a tree trunk; his head, stuck in the gap, seems to be hideously laughing. The old peasant pulls the young one away and says: "Come, come, let us go, this is the shadow of the Mongol!"

In *Iṣfahān Niṣf-i Jahān*,[1] Hidāyat tours the historical monuments of a city that is "a symbol of the Sassanids' prosperity", and as a keen and observant sightseer he describes the marvellous mosaics and tileworks of the mosques, and the grandeur of the historical buildings. Fascinated by the city's beauty, he muses: "So much greatness, so much beauty! In their presence wisdom is dumbfounded." But even here, in "the unique city of the world... the city of industry, glory, wine, painting, tile-work, architecture and agriculture, with domes, minarets and the cerulean tiles...", his nostalgia rests upon the ruins of a Sassanid fire-temple built on top of a hill. And when the old farmer who irrigates land at the foot of the hill, with his "black and white beard and blue buckram caftan", squats beside him and relates the fables connected with the fire-temple, Hidāyat asks himself: "Is this all true? Is this man a clever story-teller, or does he represent the people of the period when this mountain, *Ātashgāh*, was populous?...How great, ancient and mysterious is Persia!" And on his departure: "Now that I want to go back, I feel as if I have lost something, as if something has fallen from me. What that thing is I know not, perhaps some part of my being is left there, in that fire-temple."

In "Ākharīn Labkhand" the reader witnesses an historical meeting whose glory and majesty revive "destroyed Sassanid aristocratic life". The scene is a secret meeting among high officials, army leaders, and dignitaries of the Barmecides, to arrange a plot against the Caliph, Hārūnu'l-Rashīd. The Barmecides served as ministers to the Abbasids; and according to Hidāyat,

> Barmak and his sons came into agreement with the Caliph and adopted their [the Abbasids'] religion in order to influence their ideas and

[1] This and thirteen other writings and stories of Hidāyat have been translated into Russian by A. Rozenfeld and published in a collection called *An Anthology of Ṣādiq Hidāyat's Work* (Moscow, 1957).

achievements, to weaken and, little by little, to destroy their religion, rebuild the *Noubahār* temple, invite the people to Buddhism and provoke them against the Caliph. It was to this end that they tried to win the confidence of the Arabs.

Hidāyat's deep love for Iran often provokes most bitter attacks against the Arabs, who invaded Persia and destroyed the old Iranian civilization. Sometimes his indignation drives him to extremes of sentimentality:

It is our fault that we taught the Arabs civil administration, prepared a grammar for their language, made up a philosophy for their religion, crossed swords and sacrified our youths for them and tendered with both hands our ideas and souls and industry and science and literature to them, so that we might tame and civilize their wild and restive spirits. But alas! there is such a vast difference between their race, their thoughts and ours, and it ought to be so. These brutal faces, burnt complexions and dirty hands are made for highway robberies. Thoughts developed among the urine and dung of camels can be no better.

This concept is also revealed in parts of one of his best short stories, "Ṭalab-i Āmurzish" ("Asking Absolution"). Another short story, "Ātash Parast" ("The Fire-worshipper"), based on the memoirs of Eugèn Flanden, the French painter who travelled to Persia in 1841, has the same theme: love of ancient Iran, its religion, traditions, manners, and grandeur. One day while excavating at Persepolis, Flanden sees two old Zoroastrians praying at the *Naqsh-i-Rustam*. Standing there watching them, he becomes so fascinated by the holiness and purity of the scene that when the two praying men are gone, he loses his self-control, kneels before the smoking fire, and worships it. "I do not believe in anything", he says to a friend later, "but all through my life I have only once worshipped God without dissimulation, in all my honesty and fidelity, and that was in Persia, near that fire-temple."

A touch of this reverence for old days and departed glories can also be sensed in some of Hidāyat's other writings of this period, especially in "Gujasta Dizh" ("The Cursed Castle"),[1] "Āfarīnigān" ("The Requiem"), and, as we shall see in detail, in *Būf-i Kūr*.

[1] Translated into French by F. Raẓavī, see below, p. 154 n.

Omar Khayyām and his philosophy

His works show that throughout his life Hidāyat was attracted by Khayyām and his philosophy; but it is especially during this phase of his life that he was most under the spell of the great philosopher-poet. In his book *Tarāna-hā-yi Khayyām*, which is a vehicle for many of his own ideas, Hidāyat classifies the famous quatrains under eight main heads:

The Secret of Creation
The Torment of Life
Written Since Eternity (Preordained Fate)
The Vicissitude of Time
The Rotating Atoms
Come What May
Nothingness
Appreciate the Present Moment (*Carpe Diem*)

But it is in the Introduction to this book that he includes his interpretation of Khayyām's philosophy:

> The philosophy of Khayyām will never lose its freshness. The reason is that these songs, scanty in appearance but full of meaning, discuss all the important, dark philosophical problems which have puzzled man throughout the ages, discuss the ideas inflicted on him forcibly and the secrets which remain unsolved to him. Khayyām becomes the interpreter of these spiritual torments. His cries are the reflection of tortures, worries, fears, hopes and despairs that have successively racked the thoughts of millions of human beings.

Continuing, Hidāyat admits that,

> In order to distinguish the way of thinking and the philosophy of the man who has written the quatrains we have to pick out his ideas and philosophy as understood from his quatrains. For we have no other means: his personal and public life, people whom he associated with, his environment, way of life, the inherited influences, the philosophy he followed and his scientific and philosophical education, are all unknown to us.

Furthermore, the general, mystic nature of the quatrains make them subject to various contrasting interpretations.

Thus if we ever hesitate about the exactness of his portrait of

Khayyām, the materialist philosopher, we can hardly doubt its resemblance to Hidāyat, the pessimistic author. In fact their ideas about life, religion, society, etc., often sound so identical that it is hard to separate the poet who presents us with "exciting nightingales" and "sweet roses" from the writer who gives "the blind owl" and "scentless water-lilies".

Let us consider some characteristics of this portrait:

> Only a desire, an inclination, or sympathy and regret for past Iran are left in Khayyām (p. 39).
>
> Khayyām wanted to destroy this ridiculous, sordid, gloomy and funny world and build a more logical one on its ruins (p. 42).
>
> Khayyām was weary and disgusted with the people of his time, condemned their morals, thoughts and customs with bitter sarcasm and had not accepted at all the instructions of the society (p. 38).
>
> Khayyām is the representative of the suffocated talent, tormented soul, the interpreter of the laments and revolt of a great, dignified, prosperous and ancient Iran which little by little was being poisoned and destroyed under the oppression of harsh Semitic thoughts and Arab domination (p. 63).

Yet one significant difference between the two men ought not to be overlooked. Despite his later flights into realism, Hidāyat is fundamentally a romanticist, irresistibly drawn to death and glories of the past; whereas Khayyām is a relatively sober-headed realist whose feet are firmly planted on the sure soil of here and now. In fact it is chiefly his refreshing no-nonsense depiction of life that has made Khayyām so widely and fondly accepted in the Western world.

CHAPTER XVII

THE LIFE OF HIS COUNTRYMEN

CONSCIOUS of the fact that the writer, as Fielding maintained, is "the historian of private life", Hidāyat took a keen interest in the life of his countrymen, particularly the small man and the underdog. He penetrated into their monotonous lives, searched the dark corners of their souls, and with an amazing insight revealed their petty aspirations, anxieties, and sorrows. It is in the story of these people—farmers, workers, tradesmen, and the like—that we find not only Hidāyat's masterpieces, but also some of the most beautiful passages of contemporary Persian literature. No other writer in modern Persia has illustrated and analysed with such mastery the life of the hungry peasant, the unfortunate beggar, hypocritical preacher, and greedy bazaar trader.. Characters like Dāvūd, Ābjī Khānum, Dāsh Ākul, Mīrzā Ḥusayn-'Alī, Mīrzā Yadullā, Gul Babū, Zarīn Kulā, 'Alavīya Khānum, Āqā Mūchūl, 'Iṣmat-Sādāt, Hājjī Āqā, and a host of others are so true to life that they are met again and again in any Persian town. Explaining the secret of Hidāyat's power to depict his characters so skilfully, Henry D. G. Law writes:

Firstly his sincerity. After that the magic of his prose...Hidāyat does not write objectively; with his "reckless soaring genius" he infuses into each of his tales his own personality, his own mood of pity, indignation, or tenderness: so that you may enter fully into the mind and thoughts of his characters, whoever they may be—seeing them as he sees them. They live and they haunt you long after you have closed the book.[1]

This is exactly the case when we read, for instance, "Dāvūd-i Kūzh-Pusht" ("David, the Hunchback"), the story of a poor miserable creature who through no fault of his own is born a cripple. Everybody avoids him, people ridicule him and make fun of his love and sentiments:

...from his earliest childhood up to now he had always been an object either of ridicule or of pity to others. He recalled how his teacher in a

[1] *Life and Letters*, *op. cit.* p. 253.

history class had said that the Spartans used to kill children who were born deformed or crippled. All the children had turned and looked at him, a strange feeling had taken hold of him then. But now he was wishing that that rule had been enforced everywhere in the world, or at least that as in most other places sick and unsound persons had been prevented from marrying, for he was well aware that all this was the fault of his father. He pictured his father...the old man, branded with syphilis, who had married a young wife and begot blind and palsied children, for that is what they had all been. One of his brothers had survived, but even he had been an idiot and dumb, till he died two years ago. He wondered if they had not been the lucky ones....Some years ago he had twice made an offer of marriage, but both times the women had laughed at him.

So continues the story of Dāvūd until the moving climax where he seeks the companionship of an outcast vagrant dog, but is denied even that consolation:

He dragged himself along till he sat down beside the dog....He pressed its head against his bulging chest. But the dog was dead.[1]

At the end of the story the reader is no more an outsider, an impartial observer: he feels Dāvūd's physical and mental sufferings as if they were his own.

This engagement in the characters' despair occurs with a great number of Hidāyat's short stories, especially "Ābjī Khānum" ("The Elder Sister"), "Dāsh Ākul" and "Zanī-ka Mardash rā Gum Kard" ("The Woman who lost her Man"), three masterpieces of modern Persian short-story writing.

"Ābjī Khānum" is the story of a girl who, in contrast to her younger sister, Māhrukh, is unattractive. From her childhood she was always beaten and reproached by her mother. "Oh what can I do with this peck of troubles?", her mother used to complain. "Who will marry a girl so ugly?" These humiliating remarks led the unfortunate girl to despair. She forgot all about marriage and devoted herself to worship and prayers. "But her sister did not pay any attention to such things...and when she was fifteen she went away and became a housemaid. Ābjī Khānum was twenty-two but still at home." One day Māhrukh came home and whispered for some time to her mother; in the evening when the father

[1] An English translation of this story by Henry D. G. Law is published in the special number of *Life and Letters*, *op. cit.*, which is devoted to Persian writers.

returned from his job, the mother informed him that 'Abbās, a servant in the house where Māhrukh worked, had proposed to her. The father nodded and said: "Very well, it is all right", without wondering, showing any exultation, or making any comment.

But Ābjī Khānum was furious and raged with jealousy. "She rose up unconsciously and pretending that she was going for prayers, she went downstairs...looked in the small mirror she had and found herself old and broken down. As though the few past minutes had made her several years older." While the preparations for the wedding were in progress, she would sit in a corner silent and gloomy, her mother constantly nagging at her. This went on until the night of the wedding. That night Ābjī Khānum went out; it was late when she returned home, but the wedding ceremonies were still on; she walked straight into a room and lifted a corner of the curtain: there she saw her sister spruced up and seated beside the groom, who looked a young man of twenty. "The groom had his arm around Māhrukh's waist whispering something in her ear. Very likely they had noticed her. Perhaps her sister recognized her. But in order to vex her they both laughed and kissed each other....A feeling of hatred and envy captured Ābjī Khānum. She dropped the curtain."

At midnight, a splashing sound woke up the people in the house. They looked everywhere but there was nothing unusual. Suddenly they found Ābjī Khānum's slippers near the water storage tank; when the lamp was brought closer, they saw a dead body on the water. It was Ābjī Khānum. "She had gone to heaven!"

The hero in "Dāsh Ākul" is a champion wrestler who gets involved in a series of clashes with another champion, Kākā Rustam. Of the two champions Dāsh Ākul is the stronger and nobler. He always manages to defeat his stammering rival and has the game well in his own hands, until he falls in love with a girl who is under his guardianship. Despite all his virtues and noble character, Dāsh Ākul is in anguish in his love, because "he had an ugly appearance. His face repelled one at first sight". And there are other doubts: "Perhaps she does not love me! Perhaps she will find a young handsome husband....No, it is monstrous. [as] She is only fourteen while I am forty....But what can I do?" For seven years Dāsh Ākul suffers from this unrequited passion, doing all in his power to take care of the girl and the family whose guardian he had become rather against his own will. At last there comes a suitor for the girl, "older and uglier than Dāsh Ākul". On the night of the wedding, after fulfilling his duties as guardian, he goes out and gets drunk. On his way home he encounters Kākā Rustam. After some bragging and showing off, the two rivals pick a fight; but Kākā Rustam plays a cowardly trick from which Dāsh Ākul receives a fatal injury and dies the following day.[1]

The last of these three stories, "Zanī-ka Mardash rā Gum Kard", is a description of country life, a rustic love affair, and the excitements of a simple country girl who has innate masochistic tendencies. The story is very elaborately told, and the scenes of fruit-picking girls, their songs, views of Mazanderan, and, moving amid them, Zarīn Kulā and her naïve love, all have such captivating magic that it would be an injustice to recast the story in any abridged form. Nietzsche's famous saying, "Thou goes to women? Do not forget thy whip. Thus spake Zarathustra", is quoted as the epigraph; and the story ends after the ruthless husband deserts Zarīn Kulā and she follows another donkey-driver, hoping: "Perhaps this lad is also used to using the whip and his body smells of donkeys and stables?..."

So far, writing about the people of his country, Hidāyat may have impressed us as a sympathetic writer with an amiable, even a mild, disposition. But all trace of mildness disappears when he handles themes like corruption, superstition, and especially religious hypocrisy. "Ṭalab-i Āmurzish"[2] is an interesting description of the old-fashioned, long, and exhausting pilgrimages on camels and mules to holy shrines; it also shows the character of the pilgrims and their appalling conditions; but most of all, it is the sinister confession of a woman who, out of jealousy, murdered the rival wife (*havū*) and her children and has now come to Karbala to ask forgiveness and absolution from the *Imām*. 'Azīz Āghā had been happily married but turned out to be barren. So with her consent the husband brought a second wife, a *Ṣīgha* (a wife by temporary marriage), into the house. But as soon as the new wife became pregnant everything changed: "My husband paid all his

[1] This and six other stories by Hidāyat were translated into French by F. Raẓavī and published in a collection called *Trois Gouttes de Sang et Six Autres Nouvelles* (Tehran, 1959). "Dāsh Ākul" is also translated into German: see R. Gelpke, *op. cit.*

[2] Translated into French, by F. Raẓavī, *ibid.*

attention to her.... I had become a ruined, unfortunate wife!... Then I realized what a mistake I had made." The child was finally born, and "one day when she [the second wife] went out to the public bath and the house was quiet, I went to the baby's cradle, drew out the pin I had below my neck, turned my head aside and pressed it to the end into the child's fontanel.... For two days and nights the child did not stop crying... and died on the second night". She also murdered the second child and finally the mother.

When she confided her secrets to other pilgrims, they simply laughed and assured her that they had committed similar crimes. After all, "What do you think we have come here for?", asked Mashdī Ramaẓān-'Alī, shaking the ashes out of his clay pipe:

Three years ago I was a coachman on Khorasan road. The coach broke on the way. I had two rich passengers. One of them died. I strangled the other and took out one thousand and fifty Tumans from his pocket. Growing old, this year, it came to my mind that that money was illegitimate so I came to Karbala to legitimize it. Today I gave it to one of the '*Ulamā* [religious authorities] and he made a thousand Tumans of it lawful to me. The whole ceremony did not take more than two hours. Now this money is more legitimate to me than my mother's milk.

After hearing the cynical confessions of other fellow pilgrims, 'Azīz Āghā starts rejoicing and says: "Then... then, you too?..." The other lady traveller pronounces: "Did you not hear from the pulpit that as soon as the pilgrims specify their intention and set out, they become chaste and purified even if the number of their sins is as many as the leaves of a tree?"

"Murda-Khurhā" ("The Ghouls", or literally, "Eaters of the Dead") is another story that exposes his countrymen's moral depravity. A critical account of the false sympathy and mourning shown by the relatives of a "dead man", it describes how the rival wives and relatives mourn over a man they suppose to be dead, while they are in fact engaged in a bitter conflict over the inheritance. In the midst of this the corpse recovers from what was only a stroke and suddenly appears in his shroud. The women all scream. One of the wives hurriedly removes a purse from around her neck and throws it, together with a bunch of keys and a bracelet, before Mashadī: "No, no, do not come near me!... Take your bunch of keys, the hundred Tumans I took from your chest are in the purse." Her rival takes out something from the corner of her shawl and flings it before him crying, "And these are your false teeth...". The story ends with the first wife's complaint of the negligence and delay of the *Shaykh* who left the body unburied for three hours so that Mashadī managed to regain consciousness. "And this...well done! This is how Āshaykh 'Alī works! He left the body on the ground for three hours!"

Another excellent piece in this vein is "Mardī-ka Nafsash rā Kusht" ("The Man who killed his Passion"), a psychological study of the life and character of a studious young schoolteacher, Mīrzā Ḥusayn-'Alī, who wanted to lead an ascetic life like a Sufi. To attain his spiritual aspirations, all he needed was a guide whose example he could follow: this he found in the person of Shaykh Abulfaẓl, an older colleague of his, and the advice the guide gave him was "Kill your passion!". For several years Mīrzā Ḥusayn-'Alī shut himself in seclusion, studied the classical texts of well-known Sufis, and subjected himself to rigorous self-discipline. But the more he tortured his body and denied himself physical pleasures, the more his frustrated passions became enflamed. Once again he decided to go and seek his guide's advice. When he arrived at Shaykh Abulfaẓl's place he saw an angry man standing outside, shouting: "Tell Āshaykh, tomorrow I will take you to the court. ...You brought my daughter here as a maid-servant and did all kind of mischief to her. You infected her, and made free with her money...." After some waiting, Mīrzā Ḥusayn-'Alī was ushered into the Shaykh's presence, to find him dining: "A handkerchief was spread before him, in it some dried bread with an onion." But suddenly there came an uproar of noise and tumult, a cat sprang into the middle of the room, a cooked partridge in its mouth, and a crying woman on its tail.

Bitterly disappointed, Mīrzā Ḥusayn-'Alī left his guide's house. On his way home he went into a tavern, got drunk, and then stepped out staggering, his arm around the neck of a prostitute. Two days later it was reported in the newspapers: "A serious young teacher called Āqā-yi Mīrzā Ḥusayn-'Alī has, for unknown reasons, committed suicide."

The point of this story is clearly the hypocrisy of the Sufi guide. Sufism had been a refuge of the Iranian people when they had found the formalism of the established Muslim religion unsatisfactory, or when Muslims had betrayed the democratic and egalitarian preaching of Islam. Even as his young schoolteacher had attempted to do, Hidāyat might have sought spiritual solace in the Sufi path; but the tragedy manifest in his story is that not even this solace exists in modern Iran: he is describing the debasement, not only of formal religion, but of what might have been a satisfactory substitute for it.

In another short story, "Muḥallil" ("The Legalizer"),[1] a comical situation arises from the application of a shameful, ridiculous and antiquated religious law concerning matrimony: "And if he hath divorced her (the third time), then she is not lawful unto him thereafter until she hath wedded another husband. Then if he (the other husband) divorce her it is no sin for both of them that they come together again..." (*Koran*, Sura 11, verse 230).

After thrice announcing the divorce formula to his wife, Mīrzā Yadullā cannot remarry her unless he finds a man, a "legalizer", who will marry and then divorce her. He succeeds in finding a husband for his ex- (and would-be) wife, but after the marriage takes place the man in question refuses to divorce his new wife. This second marriage is not successful either. The story opens years later, when the two rivals, without recognizing each other, meet in a coffee-house and complain to one another about their ill-luck and wicked "wives".

Sympathetic or wicked, mostly from the lower strata of society, these are the kinds of characters we have so far met in Hidāyat's stories. They are not the only types that appear in his works. In fact, as we shall see in his later works, Hidāyat wrote about people from almost every walk of life. However, in this period of his life there does emerge another important type of character: the eccentric. Usually belonging to the middle class, the *petite bourgeoisie*, he is very often trying to imitate the European way of life; but, as usually happens in a changing society, he can neither hold on to his own cultural heritage nor grasp European ideas properly. It is the confusion, desperation, and pessimism of these people that form the subject matter of short stories such as "Zinda Bi-gūr" ("Buried Alive"), "Sa Qaṭra Khūn" ("Three Drops of Blood"),[2] "Girdāb" ("The Whirlpool"), "Ṣūratak-hā" ("The Masks"),

[1] Translated into French by F. Raẓavī, *op. cit.*
[2] Translated into French by F. Raẓavī, *op. cit.*

"'Arūsak-i Pusht-i Parda"[1] ("The Puppet Behind the Curtain") and "Shab-hā-yi Varāmīn" ("The Nights of Varamin"). In all these stories the abnormalities of the characters are striking. They are the deformities produced by a deformed society, and it is therefore not surprising that Hidāyat should make them all either die violently, by committing suicide perhaps, or end up in a lunatic asylum. The hero of "Zinda Bi-gūr", for example, is a suicidal maniac who tries a variety of methods of self-destruction, but none is effective: "Yes, I have become invulnerable....Nothing effects me. Took cyanide didn't affect me. Tried opium but I'm still alive. If a dragon bites me, it's the dragon that will die." And the eccentric man in "Sa Qaṭra Khūn" who is detained in a madhouse wants to have the authority of the asylum doctor, for: "If I were in his position [the doctor's] I would poison the food one night and feed them all with it. Then in the morning I would stand in the garden, hands on my waist, and watch the dead bodies being carried away."

Or there is the sentimental lover in "Ṣūratak-hā", who, suspecting the faithlessness of his girl friend, leaves her and decides to take his revenge; and in an impressive way:

> He would make a reconciliation with Khujasta [the girl friend] and exchange this life, which his parents had one night given him in bed, for another. Khujasta would be there, they would take poison and die in each others' arms. This idea sounded beautiful and poetical to him.

The lugubrious nature of this writing is best seen against the background of social conditions in modern Iran, where traditional patterns of life have been violently disrupted and the superficial aspects of alien patterns acquired. Thus besides creating great literature, Hidāyat has provided a commentary on the mental condition of sensitive people in a period of rapid transition. It is in this role of commentator on the tragedy of twentieth-century Iranian society, notably its urban society, that Hidāyat is at his best. Where he attempted a different type of writing—in stories like "Asīr-i Farānsavī" ("The French Prisoner of War"), "Mādlīn" ("Madeleine") and "Āyina-yi Shikasta" ("The Broken Mirror"), concerned mostly with characters and events outside Iran—he proved himself much less effective.

[1] Translated into German by R. Gelpke, *op. cit.*

The language of Hidāyat's characters deserves some attention. We have noted how Jamālzāda, and before him Dihkhudā, the author of the travelogue of *Ibrāhīm Beg*, the translator of *Hajji Baba*, and others introduced into modern Persian the use of popular idioms, proverbial allusions, and echoes of famous lines from the poetry of the classical period. We have also seen how later writers carried on this new tradition, writing Persian as it is spoken. In Hidāyat the tradition became not only an established but a *natural* mode of literary expression. In Jamālzāda, for instance, it was never quite natural: those notes he admits he always makes on reading Persian are too apparent in his display of popular phraseology, and one is left with the feeling that he has lived abroad but still relishes the idiom of his people. Hidāyat, however, not only presented living characters "in the round", but also made them talk with perfect verisimilitude. Rather than creations from recollected experience, his dialogues sound like conversations just heard and immediately recorded. Thus besides vividly picturing his countrymen, of all classes, in their own surroundings, he puts into their mouths the speech of their city, their district, even their quarter. There is no overstatement: no use of idiom and proverb just to prove how conversant the author is with the infinite varieties of Persian speech. Idioms and those telling popular phrases are used to just the extent that they occur in natural speech—an innovation that Hidāyat mastered with exactitude and grace.

And his interest in everything Persian, coupled with a dislike of the Arab impact on Persia, led Hidāyat to avoid an excessive use of Arabic words and constructions, though he never took the extreme course of some other Persian writers.

We can sum up this phase of Hidāyat's writing by saying that he unfolded a panorama of the habits, traditions, and dialects of various groups of Persian people. And yet, having known Hidāyat as a lonely figure, as a man who constantly held himself aloof from people and public life, and bearing in mind that he grew up in the restricted circle of an aristocratic and extremely conventional family, it is puzzling how he captured such a gallery of "typical" characters from various walks of life; how he reproduced their language and described their habits and preoccupations with such precision. That he had the artist's gift of exact observation helps to solve the puzzle. Sensitive to other people's feelings, he identified with their suffering and could therefore comprehend, share, and re-create their plight and tragedy. He also possessed, as his careful annotations of his own and other people's books prove, the scholar's fastidious love of exactitude. He thus observed things as they are, not as he thought they should be. He watched his fellow-creatures, or, as he would put it, his fellow-sufferers, with the painstaking attention of a scientist looking down his microscope. Inform this power of observation with an extraordinary feeling of sympathetic anguish for the plight of men on earth, and perhaps we have the answer to how Hidāyat managed to record experience so accurately and with such universal validity.

CHAPTER XVIII

THE SARDONIC GRINS

SATIRE is one of the prevailing traits in Hidāyat's art. Not only in his completely facetious works but in most of his other writings one can trace a melancholy derision.

Satirical criticism has been frequently used in Persian literature, usually when political circumstances have prevented the writer from approaching his readers directly. Dihkhudā, we recall, was the first modern Persian writer to make use of this weapon for social criticism; this was in the post-Constitutional period, when Muḥammad 'Alī Shah's autocracy was opposing the rights granted by the Constitution. A similar tyranny, though far better established and in many respects much more effective, existed during the second decade of Riẓā Shah's reign. Here, Hidāyat's gift for satire, mockery, and lampooning grew and flourished. And he employed this technique in an entirely new way.

Apart from one earlier attempt (*Afsāna-yi Āfarīnish*)[1] his main achievements in this field are: the novelette *'Alavīya Khānum* ("Madame 'Alaviya", 1933), followed by a miscellany of rather bizarre pieces called *Vagh Vagh Sāhāb* ("Mister Bow Wow", 1933) and, later in his life, *Vilingārī* ("Tittle-tattle", 1944) and finally *Tūp-i Murvārī* ("The Pearl Cannon", 1947). At present, however, we are concerned with only two of these: *'Alavīya Khānum* and *Vagh Vagh Sāhāb*. Both books are criticisms of the old customs, deep-rooted superstitions, and social and cultural conditions of modern Iran. In them the solemn and sometimes apparently nonchalant Hidāyat becomes a sarcastic critic who gives not an inch to hacks and humbugs, and who ridicules the naïve beliefs and reactionary mental habits of the masses.

'Alavīya Khānum is about a woman's pilgrimage to the shrine of *Imām* Riẓā at Meshed, one of the most important Iranian centres of pilgrimage. Stage by stage, from Tehran to Meshed, we follow the route of four carts (*gārī*) loaded with simple men, women, and children. The hopes and fears, the intrigues, quarrels, and shocking

[1] See above, p. 143.

accusations of these people form the backbone of the story; and not only the story's amusing incidents but every word, phrase, and passage carries the odour of Persia and the high sense of tragedy that is a feature of the life of the masses. It is, however, 'Alavīya Khānum—an outwardly pious but inwardly vicious woman—who dominates the story and whose speech, consisting mostly of abuse, affords one of the most unusual pieces of modern Persian writing. Hidāyat makes the submerged masses come to life by reproducing their speech in all its vividness. Yet while he does this with consummate skill, his disgust for the ignorance and degradation of these characters is not concealed.

A German translation of *'Alavīya Khānum* and eleven other short stories by Hidāyat was published in Berlin in 1960; the collection also contains an introduction to Hidāyat's work and life, written by Buzurg 'Alavī, and has a thirteen-page appendix giving the definition of slang words and expressions used in the book.[1]

Vagh Vagh Sāhāb[2] is of an entirely different pattern. It is a rather tart criticism of conditions during Riẓā Shah's reign, especially in art and culture. It also served, at the time it was written, as a riposte to the pampered scholars of that "golden era". During this period of Hidāyat's life, triviality was not only the stimulus for fashionable art and letters but also a dominating factor in the whole pattern of Persian life. Poetry was the strictly guarded domain of a handful of "high-minded dignitaries" whose essential merit was to copy the great classics. Cinemas presented the public with every piece of rubbish Hollywood produced, and the theatre was the scene of cock-and-bull stories mainly about clumsy love-making. In the literary field, apart from a few "established" scholars, two groups of upstart novelists and translators had emerged: the first group produced with breathless haste genial stories for the popular papers. The second group, the translators, faithfully followed the direction Hidāyat had ironically pointed out to them:

After you have been to a school for a few months and have learnt a few of the foreigners' words so that you can read just the name of the author

[1] *Die Prophetentochter*, aus den persischen ubertragen von Eckhardt Fichtner und Werner Sundermann, Herausgegeben von Bozorg Alavi, Rüttenund Leoning (Berlin, 1960).

[2] Written in collaboration with Mas'ūd Farzād.

or the title of an article, you are in a position to push yourself among the distinguished translators. Then try to know who has written the book and what it is about. Having done that, write whatever nonsense comes to your pen and publish it under the name of the well-known original writer.

Vagh Vagh Sāhāb consists of thirty-four narratives, called "cases", which are in fact case-histories of the most prevalent forms of corruption of the day. These are written chiefly in the form of mock verse, *Knittelvers*, in which all the rules of Persian poetry are deliberately perverted, so that the form as well as the content of the book reflects the authors' contempt for the issues they are criticizing:

...Our present literature is almost the monopoly of a handful of biographers of a few nonentities, it is the property of some ex-theologians, of annotators, of imitative-poets who exchange mutual flatteries and are continuously engaged in petty pilfering from here and there.

As an example, this is the authors' approach to melodramatic theatrical productions and bad playwrights, in their "Ghazīya-hi Tūfān-i 'Ishq-i Khūn Ālūd" ("The Case of the Storm of the Blood-stained Love"):

The play was by an unrivalled distinguished writer who had belittled Shakespeare, Goethe and Molière. Dramatic, tragic, comic, moralistic, social, historical, entertaining and scholarly, comic-opera besides being great drama, a theatre, altogether, quite unique.

Their criticism of the cinema and of its impact on the simple man in the street is appropriately contained in "Ghazīya-hi Kīng Kung" ("The Case of King Kong").

In a number of other narratives, such as "Ghazīya-hi Jāyiza-yi Nubil" ("The Case of the Nobel Prize"), "Ghazīya-hi Āqā-yi Mātampūr" ("The Case of Mr Matampur"), "Ghazīya-hi Dāstān-i Bāstānī yā Rumān-i Tārīkhī" ("The Case of the Early History or the Historical Novel") and "Ghazīya-hi Ikhtilāṭ-i Nūmcha" ("The Case of the Confused Names"),[1] the writers

[1] A few pages of the last *Qaẓīya* are reproduced in Professor A. J. Arberry's *Modern Persian Reader* (Cambridge, 1944), pp. 53–8. The accompanying note reads: "The book from which this dialogue is taken is a satirical miscellany commenting on literary fashions in modern Persia. Note throughout the rhymes parodying the elegant style of classical Persian prose" (p. 76).

ridicule vainglorious authors, high-flown poets, and flamboyant scholars; they also give a "recipe" for those who wish to become "prominent" scholars, historians, translators, or philosophers, and they reveal their indignation at anything false, sordid, and inhuman around them.

When *Vagh Vagh Sāhāb* first appeared in 1933 it was denounced as a wicked piece of nonsense by the established men of letters, but of course welcomed by the younger intelligentsia as a superb exposure of the lack of taste and the false criteria of the men who were supposed to be their teachers. Yet at the time the full significance of the work was missed, because many took it to be concerned with follies that would soon be corrected; they thought Hidāyat and Farzād quixotic in their profound pessimism. Time has shown that now, more than three decades after this book was written, its criticisms remain valid.

CHAPTER XIX

HYSTERICAL SELF-ANALYSIS

"*Būf-i Kūr*"

HIDĀYAT turned from the evils of society to self-analysis in one book. *Būf-i Kūr* ("The Recluse") means literally "blind owl"; and its significance lies in Persian folk-lore:

The owl is commonly regarded as a sinister and lonesome bird and an omen of ill-luck. Normally lives in ruined and desolate places away from cities and people. The bird is supposed to be afraid of light, hiding in dark crevices or thick trees in day time. When the sun sets, it emerges from its seclusion in search of prey. The owl has a dismal and hideous appearance, with peculiar screams turning to hisses and snarls at night. The belief in the inauspiciousness of this bird in Iranian tradition and folklore goes back to the advent of Islam and the Arab influence. Damīrī, in *Ḥayātu'l Ḥayvān* ("The life of Animals"), relates that according to Arab fables when a man dies, or is killed, he sees himself metamorphosed into an owl sitting on his own grave and moaning his bodily death. And in the *History of Ibn-i Najjār* we read that Chosroes ordered his functionary to hunt for the worst bird, whereupon he caught an owl. Stories and references of this kind pertaining to the obnoxiousness of the owl are also found in abundance in the classical prose and poetry of Persia.

To quote from the opening sentences of the book, Hidāyat's *Blind Owl* is the story of "the wounds that eat into the soul like cancer and grind it down little by little in seclusion". But before we plunge into the miasma of *Būf-i Kūr*, let us look back and review briefly Hidāyat's work after his return from France. This may give us an insight into the forces that made him write and indeed become a "Būf-i Kūr" himself.

As already indicated, when Hidāyat returned home he found little to content him. Some of the Iranian intellectuals had arrived at a *modus vivendi*, but for Hidāyat this was impossible. He decided to ignore the unpleasantness around him and devote himself to his art. The first theme we traced in his work during this period was folklore and traditional beliefs. After exhausting this subject, he turned to history and revived the memory of his gallant ancestors who stood up against force and aggression and gave their lives for their country. But neither of these studies satisfied him. He then took refuge in Omar Khayyām and his philosophy of wine and forgetfulness, informed with a hard scepticism. As Hidāyat himself put it,

...in the quatrains wine is to dispel the sorrows of life. Khayyām takes refuge in goblets of wine. He tries to attain mental peace and forgetfulness by means of red wine. Let us be merry, enjoy and forget this silly life, above all forget, for our orgies are haunted by a horrible shadow, the shadow of death.

But even Khayyām failed to give him comfort. The odd point was that, while the root of his perplexity lay right beside him, in the life of his countrymen, indeed in his own life and in the general conditions around him, he was searching in dark corners of history, in old traditions, and in Khayyām's philosophy for salvation; trying to escape the chaos by refusing to look at it.

Yet now and then came moments of intensity when a glimpse of purpose, sympathy, or anger made him focus his attention on his immediate environment. These observations produced two conflicting results. On the one hand they left for us an immense wealth of realistic writings, mainly in the form of short stories, which, as already suggested, should serve as a handbook of reference and instruction to every modern Persian writer or student of Iran. But on the other hand, as the morbid realities of life unravelled before him, a sense of *weltschmerz*, a sort of nausea at anything real, earthly and alive grew in him little by little. He mistook effects for causes: instead of attacking the political system, the social and economic conditions that had made simple people so blind and unfortunate, he condemned the people—condemned his own self. That is where his "sardonic grins" began to appear, leading him gradually to the black pessimism of *Būf-i Kūr*.

In sum, he exerted all his faculties in finding a way out of his impasse, but each time became more and more enmeshed in his own complexities. As his friend Dr Khānlarī said:

He starts from the early stages of the life of mankind, the beginning of creation (*Afsāna-yi Āfarīnish*), describes the story of the monkeys which were man's ancestors. He climbs the stairs of history...he drops in on the world of spirits and from all these journeys returns sad and hopeless. Is this gloom the effect of the social conditions of his time? Perhaps, and perhaps in another environment, under different social conditions, he would have appeared more optimistic.

To understand and analyse the repellent, unpeopled life of Būf-i Kūr, it is necessary to remember the writer's life and environment. And besides reading carefully one should also keep one's head clear and steer a straight course through this strange book. For the reader, despite all his awareness, is constantly driven into an hypnotic dream-state. He starts reading with a determined critical approach, but gradually an atmosphere of obscurity creeps in; the thread of events becomes blurred, and in the end an attitude of uncritical acceptance prevails. The critic of *Būf-i Kūr* is like a surgeon who becomes affected by the anaesthetic every time he starts to operate. Like Kafka, Hidāyat deliberately applies a "dream technique" to evoke this sense of unreality.

Told deliberately in the first person singular—an unusual style for Hidāyat—*Būf-i Kūr* is certainly his most self-revealing work. It is an assertion of his self-doubts, and it expresses his intricate self-perception in a highly wrought yet laconic style. Its hero leads two lives. His real life is one of misery, poverty, and a self-imposed denial of needs. To find escape he has become addicted to opium and alcohol, and under their influence his other life begins, his dream life. Then, however, it becomes almost impossible to draw a clear line between the two; ugly scenes of his real life overlap the boundaries of the dream life, his visions becoming coloured by illusions. In order to get to know himself better, he has cut himself off from other human beings—*rajjāla-hā* (the riff-raff), as he calls them. He says he writes because he has decided to introduce himself to his shadow. He does not care in the least whether others believe him, or even read his story. He is only worried in case "he dies tomorrow without having got to know himself". He lives in a room "just like a grave" pervaded with the smell of everything that had ever been there:

The smell of the body's sweat, the smell of ancient sicknesses, the smell of bad breath, smell of feet, strong smell of urine, smell of stale fat, rotten mats, burned omelet, fried onions, medicinal herbs, clotted milk and babies' dirt; the smell of the room of a boy who had just reached puberty....

Būf-i Kūr is an artist who paints the small designs on pen-cases, but the subject of his paintings is always the same: A cypress tree, under which an old man squats, clad in an *'abā*, a turban around his head like an Indian yogi, his left forefinger on his lips as a sign of astonishment. In front of him a young girl in a long black dress, leaning over a stream offering a lotus to the old man.

Būf-i Kūr has no proper sense of time, place, or identity: "To what place does this piece of sky over my head or these few spans of land under me belong, to Nishapur, Balkh or Benares? I do not know. I am not sure of anything." He is not even sure of his own identity: "I looked in the mirror but I did not recognize myself, no, that former 'I' is dead, has decomposed...." Būf-i Kūr is, to borrow a sentence from Keats, "leading a posthumous existence";[1] he is a living corpse caged in timeless moments. "Days, months, what are they? To me they have no meaning. To a man who is buried, time is meaningless."

We turn the pages of the book, read the tales of his parents' past, learn about his own childhood, his upbringing, all without having the vaguest idea what could have made this creature as he is. At length, we reach the middle of the book and discover to our surprise that Būf-i Kūr is married and desperately in love with his wife. Yet he has never slept with her nor even kissed her. The reason?

On the night of our marriage when we were left alone in the room, for all that I begged and implored her she did not turn an eye....She switched the light off and went to sleep in the other corner of the room. ...Nobody will believe it—well it is incredible, but she did not let me take a kiss from her lips. The second night I slept where I had slept the night before, on the floor, and the same happened on the following nights....

Then he discovers that his wife has numerous admirers and even shows signs of pregnancy. Afraid of losing her, he goes to the length of accepting her lovers. He flatters them, even takes them to her. "I wanted to learn the behaviour, manner and the art of seduction from my wife's lovers! But I was a miserable pimp." No doubt something is amiss with Būf-i Kūr, and he himself

[1] From a letter to Charles Brown: "I have an habitual feeling of my real life having passed, and that I am leading a posthumous existence" (*The Letters of John Keats*, p. 529).

realizes it: "I am sure one of us [he or his wife] has a defect." And then even more frankly: "...In all these, I sought what I was deprived of, something which was private to me and which I had been denied."

Later on, when we are made to realize that this "something" is "the state of despairing lust below his belly", we have an important clue to the mystery of Būf-i Kūr and his suffering. He is a highly sensitive man who is unable to share normal physical pleasure. He therefore begrudges the life of normal people and becomes a misanthrope, calling others silly and vulgar because they are healthy and sane: "Why should I think of *rajjāla-hā*, the imbeciles who are healthy, eat well, sleep well, copulate well and have never felt a bit of my agonies?"

Or: "I passed aimlessly amongst *rajjāla-hā* who all had a greedy look and were running after lust and money. I had no need to look at them, for one represented the rest: one and all were a mouth tailed by a handful of hanging bowels which ended in their genital organs."

But that is not all. There are other elements of discord in his life, most of them stemming from his physical defect. There is, for instance, his spiritual isolation. Būf-i Kūr is not an ordinary, well-adjusted social being: he is an outsider, a misfit whose dreams and ideals are alien to the grotesque realities he finds in the universe. He wants to change his fate, to escape from himself, but finds himself always trapped in the blind alley of his own identity. He is a complete stranger even to himself. "I had become an unknown race among *rajjāla-hā*....The frightening thing was the feeling that I was neither quite alive nor quite dead. I was just a living corpse who had no relation with the world of the living, and could not benefit from the oblivion and peace of death." His room is a coffin for him, his bed colder and darker than the grave. People look hostile and ugly. Their life repels him.

I had not yet got used to the world I was living in....I had a feeling that this world was not made for me. It was for a handful of impudent, cheeky, beggarly, pedantic, mumping and stingy people.

To top all these complexities he has one constant hidden dread: he expects to be caught and crushed by the police: "For a long time I have been waiting to be caught....Who knows, perhaps this very moment, perhaps an hour later, a group of drunken patrolmen will come and arrest me." This fear of police and detention runs throughout the book. The succession of events (wherever one can trace any), the dreams as well as the realities are every now and then interrupted by a group of drunken patrolmen who pass by in the street, shouting abuse at one another and singing a vulgar song at the tops of their voices. This fear of police conveys, though rather implicitly, the universal state of mind of socially maladjusted people (the homosexual for instance); and in a patriarchal society such psychosexual reactions to male symbols of authority are quite common.

Beauty, purity, and noble ideas are what Būf-i Kūr seeks in his world; but a stumbling block, "a heavy wall, a damp barrier without any breathing-holes and as heavy as lead", always obstructs his way. He spends his days wandering in search of a vale, a bit of blue sky: some solace; but every time he confronts the impenetrable stubborn facts around him.

Every day at dusk I used to go out for a walk. I do not know why I wanted to and was so persistent in looking for the stream, the cypress-tree and the lotus bush...if only I could find the place, if only I could sit under that cypress-tree I would undoubtedly have peace in my life. But alas there was nothing except dust, hot sand, horses' rib-bones and a dog sniffing among the rubbish.

The most disturbing fact about Būf-i Kūr is that he is so fully self-conscious and aware of his miseries: "I have been lying in a black coffin all my life", he says. Convinced that he can do nothing positive about his condition, he has found his *real* life in the opium-induced scenes of his imaginary world. "A man", says André Maurois, "experiences the need to create a poetic, an imaginary world, because the world of reality has denied him happiness."[1] But even Būf-i Kūr's imaginary world is gloomy and funereal. The angel of his dreams first appears to him through a hole in his room, "like a mirage in an opium haze". She is not like ordinary people. She is an ethereal creature with magical eyes and a heavenly body, very much like the girl he paints on his pen-cases. She is leaning over a stream offering a lotus flower to an old man who is squatting under a cypress-tree, chewing the nail of his

[1] Introduction to *Letters of Byron* (London, 1933), p. v.

forefinger. Upon seeing this scene, Būf-i Kūr falls into a trance. When he regains consciousness he cannot see any hole in the wall. He rushes out but there is no cypress-tree, no running water, no girl or old man. He starts searching but finds no trace of her. Finally, coming back home one evening he finds the angelic creature waiting for him at the door of his house. He opens the door, she walks in "like a sleepwalker" and lies down on the bed. But " it was as if there was a crystal wall between us", and "I had no desire to touch her at all".

There is a bottle of old wine mixed with naja's poison that his parents had left him as his inheritance. He fetches the bottle, pours out a glass, and forces it down the throat of the sleeping girl. And then he rejoices. "For the first time in my life I felt a sudden peace....As though the cancer which tormented me and the claws of the nightmare that wrenched my inside had found repose." This sudden peace is the result of her death: it is because those "eyes with the scornful expression" can watch him no more. Now he unhesitatingly undresses and gets into bed. "I wanted to warm her with the warmth of my own body, I wanted to give her the warmth of my body and take from her the coldness of death....I failed in all my attempts. I got out of bed and dressed again."

Then, conceiving a desire to preserve the memory of his beloved, he sits all night trying to paint her. After many failures he finally manages to paint her face, catching the real expression of her eyes, and then he feels a sense of relief: "The main thing was her face—nay, her eyes. And now I had them. I had the essence of her eyes on paper. Her body was of no use to me any longer."

The next problem was what to do with the girl's body. Should he bury it in his room or in a well surrounded by dark blue lotuses? Of one thing he is quite sure: he will not allow any ordinary man's eyes to look at her. To prevent this he decides to cut the body up into pieces and carry it away in his suitcase:

> This time I did not hesitate any longer. I brought the ivory-handled knife I kept in the cellar and carefully tore open, first the thin transparent dark dress which had imprisoned her like a spider's web....She looked taller than usual to me, as though she had grown in height. Then I severed her head—drops of cold clotted blood oozed out from her throat. I cut her arms and her legs and placed all her body with its

limbs tidily in the suitcase and covered it with her own black dress. I locked the suitcase and put its key in my pocket. As I finished I breathed more freely....

In an attempt to analyse *Būf-i Kūr*, the Iranian writer Jalāl Āl-i Aḥmad has said:

What does one read in *Būf-i Kūr*? What is its underlying idea? *Būf-i Kūr* is a miscellany and a mixture of the ancient Aryan scepticism, of Buddha's Nirvana, of Persian gnosticism, of the yogi-like seclusion of an oriental, of the escape which a Persian, an oriental, with all his mental background, tries to achieve within himself. *Būf-i Kūr* is a refuge from the disappointments, repulsions, sighs, sorrows and hopes of the writer. It is an attempt to comprehend the eternity of beauty. It is the vengeance of the mortal, short-lived man against this life, against this atmosphere. It is the revenge of the mortal being against mortality and triviality.... *Būf-i Kūr* is the cry of vengeance, the cry of revenge which arises only within and causes a tumult only beneath the cloister of the mind, and descends like a whip on the back of the memories. *Būf-i Kūr* is the image of all the hatred that the weak feel for the "strong", it has all the spite that can arise from frustration.

The influence of Buddha can be easily detected in the book. Buddha seems to have been Hidāyat's last refuge during this period, and, as we shall see in the next chapter, Buddhism and Hinduism remained his main preoccupation all through the later period of his life. In *Būf-i Kūr* Buddhist ideas are mostly infused with Hidāyat's own pessimistic views. The whole story revolves round Buddha's *inward contemplation and meditation*, i.e. the command to "look within". The ideas of past lives, oneness of existence, contempt for earthly life, rebirth, and "ceasing to be of the not-self" are plainly discernible.

At the beginning of the story, as Būf-i Kūr's eyes fall on the ethereal girl, he says,

It was as though I had heard her name before. The gleam in her eyes, her colour, her scent, her every movement, were all familiar to me. It was as if in an earlier life, in the World of Vision, my soul had been close to hers, as though our souls had been of the same origin and substance...and that I was to be near her in this life.

The Buddhist philosophy of death and suffering dominates the whole book. Buddha believed that:

Birth is suffering, decay is suffering, disease is suffering, association with unpleasant is suffering, separation from pleasing is suffering, not to get what one wants is suffering.... Buddhism is, therefore, to some extent a philosophy of suffering. If life is filled with suffering, and if suffering is the means by which we learn to put an end to suffering, is it not foolish to attempt to run away from school?[1]

In this light Būf-i Kūr proves to be an ardent student.

On the crucial question of death—Hidāyat's obsession throughout his life—Būf-i Kūr sounds somewhat uncertain. Expressing his disbelief in religion and in the existence of an almighty god, he observes: "All my teachings on the reward and punishment of the soul and the Day of Resurrection had become an insipid deceit and the prayers they had taught me were of no value against *the fear of death.*"[2]

A few pages later he contradicts himself:

I had so often thought of death and the decay of the particles of my body, that *this thought frightened me no more.* Quite the opposite, *I sincerely aspired to non-existence.*[3]

Buddhism regards death as "a gateway to a different form of life", whereas the idea of rebirth and a second life is sometimes unbearable for Būf-i Kūr: "My only consolation was the hope of nothingness after death. The thought of a second life exhausted and terrified me." And yet there are passages in the book where he praises and identifies himself completely with the Buddhist conception of death and Nirvana. Take for instance these impassioned sentences:

It is death alone which does not lie! The presence of death destroys all illusions. We are all the children of death and death is our salvation from the deceptions of life, and it is death which stands at the bottom of life, calling and beckoning us.

Buddha's compassion for animals and the Buddhist prohibition against killing animals for food are also vividly reflected in *Būf-i Kūr*. The butcher whose shop is across the street from Būf-i Kūr's house is portrayed as the symbol of cruelty and evil. (Hidāyat himself was a vegetarian.)

[1] Christmas Humphreys, *Buddhism*, p. 84.
[2] Italics are mine.
[3] Italics are mine.

The whole plot, and especially the climax of the story, seems to derive from Buddhist ideas. While Lakkāta (the name he has given his wife) represents a vile creature at everyone's disposal, the ethereal girl is the image of grace and innocent virtue beyond the reach of the *rajjāla-hā*: the unearthly counterpart of Lakkāta. Būf-i Kūr kills Lakkāta at the end of the book; and despite all his love and admiration for her counterpart, she must also be killed. "Death", say the Buddhists, "is the death of the body and its invisible counterpart."[1]

Besides Buddhism and other oriental ideas, the book carries the mark of certain Western writers, particularly Poe, Dostoevsky and Kafka. Its hero also has much in common with some Western characters who have a contemptuous attitude towards life. There is Barbusse's hero in *L'Enfer*, for example, "who shuts himself away from the world in his hotel bedroom and lives vicariously by spying through a hole in the wall". Or Shelley's Alastor, "who pines away and dies because he can find no earthly counterpart of the beautiful girl who had embraced him once in a dream". There is also Dostoevsky's Raskolnikov, who confines himself alone in a room, morose, self-conscious, panic-stricken at the thought of arrest, hating the human condition and human weakness. Even more striking is Būf-i Kūr's resemblance to another of Dostoevsky's characters, the peculiar creature portrayed in *Notes From Under the Floorboards*. Both men are under the strain of unsatisfied desires, both indulge in suffering, loathe human beings, shun society, and take shelter in seclusion. One is pictured as a beetle-man, the other as a blind owl.

There is also a similarity between the dreams of Būf-i Kūr under the influence of drugs and the states described in the *Confessions of an English Opium Eater*. De Quincy speaks of his feelings of having lived seventy or one hundred years in one night:

> I seemed every night to descend, not metaphorically but literally, to descend into chasms and sunless abysses, depth below depth, from which it seemed hopeless that I could ever re-ascend (p. 224).

This can be compared to Būf-i Kūr's:

> Little by little a drowsy feeling of numbness overtook me, like a pleasant tiredness, caressing waves leaked out through my body. Then I felt that

[1] Humphreys, *op. cit.* p. 105.

my life was retrogressing. Gradually I could see the events and feelings of the past, the erased and forgotten memories of my childhood parading before my eyes. Not only could I see them but I had part in them, I could even feel them. With every moment I grew smaller and more of a child. Then suddenly my thoughts grew dim and began to disappear, it seemed to me that all my being was hanging from a slender hook and I was dangling at the bottom of a dark, deep well. Then I was let loose from the hook, slipping and going farther without encountering any obstacle. It was as though I was let loose in a bottomless abyss, in an everlasting night.

Būf-i Kūr was written when Riẓā Shah's rule was at its most severe. It could not be published then. In 1937 when the writer went to India he took the manuscript with him and published it there. A small book of sixty pages, stamped "Not for sale or publication in Iran", it was printed in Bombay in a limited mimeographed edition. It has been suggested that the object of Hidāyat's journey to India was merely to publish *Būf-i Kūr*, an idea supported even by some of his friends. But as we shall see in the next chapter, there seem to have been much deeper reasons behind this journey. At any rate, for several years after it appeared only Hidāyat's closest friends knew about the book. In 1941, with the abdication of Riẓā Shah and the dawning of a new political era, *Būf-i Kūr* appeared in Tehran for the first time.[1] Its impact was instantaneous and forceful; and the controversy that ensued was not confined to literary circles: it embraced almost the entire reading public.

Despite the unusual nature of the book, the style is simple. To quote Jalāl Āl-i Aḥmad again:

Būf-i Kūr is an example of the fact that Persian (simple Persian) is capable of describing the most novel sensual expressions of a writer; that it is possible to employ this language for introspection. Even in the surrealistic interpretations (of *Būf-i Kūr*) this simple language is preserved: "Suddenly I found myself in the alleys of an unknown town which had wondrous and strange houses in the form of geometrical symbols: prisms, cones, cubes with low dark windows; the doors and walls were covered with lotuses. I was strolling freely and breathing peacefully, but the inhabitants of this town had died a curious death. All had dried up where they were, two drops of blood had fallen

[1] First as a serial in the daily *Iran*.

from their mouths to reach their clothes. The head of everyone I touched was plucked and tumbled down...." This nightmare [continues the critic], which reminds the reader of the strange paintings of Salvador Dali and is a result of profound research into a sensual experience, is unprecedented in our literary heritage.

The exactitude of its language, the mode of expression, and the writer's extraordinary versatility are sufficient to make *Būf-i Kūr* one of the most remarkable books in Persian literature. In some passages the composition and music of words are unique: for example, the opening sentences of the book, the picturesque descriptions of India, and the scenes where Būgām Dāsy (Būf-i Kūr's mother) dances. The following is a translation of a popular passage describing daybreak.

Stealthily, stealthily the night was creeping on; maybe it had shed enough of its weariness. Soft, distant sounds were sensed, perhaps a bird on the wing dreaming, perhaps the whisper of the grasses growing?

The pale stars were now fading behind the massed clouds in the sky. I felt on my face the gentle breath of the dawn and in the same instant heard from far off the clamant crowing of a cock [translated by Henry D. G. Law].

Būf-i Kūr consists of two parts. In the first part the reader is taken into the hero's imaginary world. By the time the second part, the story of Būf-i Kūr's real life, opens, the pathos and trance-like emotions of the first part have such a grip on us that, as in a fairy tale, even the grim realities carry an air of absorbing fantasy. Thus in order to form a clear perception of the book, the second part should perhaps be read first! Having learned about Būf-i Kūr's background and upbringing, the reader can then turn to the hero's dream life.

An important feature of *Būf-i Kūr* is the similarity, even identicalness, of the characters. Besides the ethereal girl who represents the counterpart of Lakkāta and thus resembles her, nearly all the characters, whether in Būf-i Kūr's dream episodes or in his real life, are alike. There is a shabby old man, hunchbacked, with a woollen scarf wrapped round his head. He is the symbol of wickedness, an ever-present devil disturbing Būf-i Kūr's peace. In the first chapter we meet him in the guise of the old man beside the stream, then as the grave digger. Būf-i Kūr's uncle, his father, his father-in-law, and the old rag-and-bone man, his wife's seducer, all have his features. He also appears on Būf-i Kūr's pen-cases; even on the curtain in his room. And finally, as Būf-i Kūr kills his wife and looks in the mirror, he sees himself transformed into the old man. This reappearance of the same character in different situations, the recurrence of events and scenes, and the frequent return to familiar motifs—lotuses, the cypress-tree, geometrical houses, "golden bee-flies",[1] drunken patrols and the song they sing—are all designed to convey the hero's delirium.

"Būf-i Kūr" in the eyes of the Western critics

During the Second World War Roger Lescot[2] translated *Būf-i Kūr* into French but did not succeed in publishing it until 1953; his translation, *La Chouette Aveugle* (published by "Librairie José Corti"), is said to have been seen and approved by Hidāyat, and the unusual form and substance of the book made a great impact on French literary circles. The most informative and comprehensive French criticism is perhaps that of Pasteur Vallery Radot, a member of the French Academy, published in the monthly *Hommes et Monde* for March 1954. After comparing Hidāyat with Gerard de Nerval, Dr Radot describes Hidāyat's life and his works and ideas, quotes some interesting passages from his writings, and identifies *Būf-i Kūr*'s world with Sartre's portrayal of hell in *Huis Clos*. He reminds his readers that Hidāyat's philosophy reflected that of another Persian pessimist, Khayyām, and he concludes by emphasizing Hidāyat's high position in contemporary world literature.

Another article, published in *Les Lettres Française* (no. 503), is by Gilbert Lazard,[3] who, unlike other French critics, first gives a brief account of social and political conditions in Persia during the time Hidāyat wrote his books. The rest of the article is devoted mainly to some general aspects of Hidāyat's works, his characters and his themes. There is little comment on *Būf-i Kūr*, though M. Lazard regards the book as "the highest degree of Hidāyat's despair" and ends his article with these remarks: "The

[1] *Zanbūrhā-yi magas ṭalā -'ī.*

[2] The French orientalist whose speciality is Kurdish dialects.

[3] According to Vincent Monteil (*Sâdeq Hedâyat*, p. 53) Lazard has translated *Ḥājjī Āqā*, one of Hidāyat's famous books (see below, pp. 192–7), into French.

new Persian realism is in the height of its progress, and Ṣādiq Hidāyat will always be honoured as the creative leader and real teacher of this movement."

Under the title "Hidāyat and his Masterpiece", the famous French critic André Rousseaux has published an article in the weekly *Le Figaro Littéraire* (18 July 1953). Apart from some introductory words about the life and background of Hidāyat, Rousseaux's article is a close study and interpretation of *Būf-i Kūr*. His judgement on the book is one of unreserved praise:

In my opinion the inspiring effect of *Būf-i Kūr*, Hidāyat's masterpiece, is sufficient to place him, at first contact, among the most eloquent and expressive writers of the present time....I think this novel has left a special impression on the literary history of our century.

The leading French surrealist André Breton, writing in *Le Médium* (July 1953), says of *Būf-i Kūr*: "If there is any such thing as a masterpiece, this is it." He then draws a parallel between *Būf-i Kūr* and works like *Aurelia* by G. de Nerval, *Gradiva* by Jensen, and *Les Mystères* by Knut Hamsun.

Another contribution, published in *Journal de Genève* for 6 September 1953, is by P. Souppault, a French writer who had met Hidāyat in Tehran. His article is of a more journalistic nature and his verdict on *Būf-i Kūr* looks somewhat overcoloured: "This novel is the masterpiece of imaginative literature in the twentieth century." His reference to *Būf-i Kūr* has a touch of poetical euphony: "I know quite well that this incontestible novel cannot be 'summarized' for the book itself is a 'summary' of man's fate."

A more cautious approach is maintained by R. Lalou in *Les Nouvelles Littéraires* (20 August 1953): "Is this book a masterpiece?", he asks, "I am rather inclined to call it an exceptional and exciting work."

In an article published in *La Table Ronde*, August 1953, the writer states that: "Because of the words used in it, the sudden change it causes in the train of thought, and the events which take place beyond any reason, this book remains a strange, magical and astonishing work." And in the first issue of a new magazine called *Bizarre* (which carries a translation of "Ṭalab-i Āmurzish", one of Hidāyat's short stories),[1] the brief, introductory article

[1] See above, pp. 154–5.

entitled "Une Révélation, Sādeq Hedāyat, 'la Chouette Aveugle' et le Cinéma" discusses the expressionistic setting and symbols of *Būf-i Kūr*. Trying to ascertain how some European expressionists, especially German films like *The Cabinet of Dr Caligari*, have influenced the book, the writer states:

Būf-i Kūr can in its visual scope be related to German expressionist films which Hidāyat had seen during his stay in France—bodies covered in blood with worms swarming upon them as heralds of decay, coffins, the journey in "the broken-down old hearse drawn by a pair of black nags little more than bags of bones", the old coachman, face hidden behind a great muffler, perched on the seat, a long whip in his hand, and the carriage which crosses hills, plains, rivers mysteriously, swiftly, silently—all these might be out of Marnau's *Nosferatu*. The background against which this story is enacted is that of *Caligari* and other expressionist works. Consider this: "One could see the jagged serrated edge of the mountain tops, strange stunted wretched trees; through them could be seen grey triangular prismatic houses, dark windows lacking any glass; low streets, high streets but always in a geometrical conical form or like parts of a cone with narrow, stunting, dark neglected windows." Hidāyat also makes use of a recurrent image in Oriental tales, namely the heroine's two black eyes, enlivened by a tenacious life, even on ancient vases on which they were painted centuries ago. It corresponds to the mouth of "Blood of a Poet" which Cocteau himself took from folk tradition.

One last article worth mentioning among the French reviews is G. Ribemont Dessaigne's "Things that the Blind Owl Sees", published in *Arts et Spectacles*. This writer, after mocking Western "culture and civilization", regrets that *Būf-i Kūr* has not had its fair share of literary prizes and then tries to compare the hero's universe with Einstein's conception of space-time in his Theory of Relativity!

In Germany, in keeping with the divided status of the country, two translations of *Būf-i Kūr* have appeared, one from each side of the "border". The first one, by Heschmat Moayyed, Otto H. Hegel, and Ulrich Riemerschmidt, was rendered from Persian and appeared in 1960.[1] The second one, published in East Germany, is translated by Gerd Henniger from the French version and has an informative epilogue on Hidāyat by his friend Buzurg

[1] *Die Blinde Eule* (verlag Helmut Kossodo, Genf und Hamburg, 1960).

'Alavī; it is here that we learn about Hidāyat's addiction to opium.[1]

Reviewing this second translation in "A Gloomy Song from Persia" (*Buecher Kommentare*, no. 3, 1961), Karl Begner remarked:

This terrible visionary world [*Būf-i Kūr*'s] is only comprehensible if one considers it as a work created under the spell of opium rather than by an artist's imagination. For the maze and density of the hallucinations and their terrifying inferences are beyond what imagination can achieve. It is merely the author's introspective experiences which have been realised and settled down in the guise of "Būf-i Kūr". Psychologists and those wishing to do research into the bounds of sciences will find the book interesting.[2]

D. P. Costello's English translation of *Būf-i Kūr* appeared in 1958.[3] It is a rather literal translation—even the Persian expressions and idiomatic phrases are often rendered literally—with a misleading blurb (for which the translator was not responsible) calling Hidāyat "a Persian disciple of Sartre". The book had less success in England than in France and perhaps in Germany. For instance the *Sunday Times*'s short verdict was: "This narrative is a rambling, inchoate mass, a sort of verbal bouillabaisse. A western nightmare is a small marvel of lucidity beside this eastern fable. Mescalin before reading might help, but don't try."[4] The critic of *Time and Tide* regarded the book as "a mixture of opium dream and fatalism", where the phrases "repeat like the coils of a serpent, and with each repetition they tell us more of the story of the past, the present and the future....Reading the hallucinations and fears is like sipping from a bottle of poisoned wine."[5] Hidāyat may not be everyone's cup of tea, he continued, but the book was recommended to those who wish to vary their literary diet and as a "stimulating exercise for poetical muscles".

About the prose style of the English version *The Twentieth Century* wrote: "The rather garish and turbid prose of the English

[1] *Die Blinde Eule* (Karl H. Henssel verlag, Berlin, 1961).

[2] The data on French and German reviews are drawn mainly from Persian sources. It was, unfortunately, not possible to find the originals to check the accuracy of the Persian translations.

[3] *The Blind Owl* (published by Calder).

[4] Michael Crampton, 16 Feb. 1958 (no. 7031).

[5] Oswell Blakeston, 22 Feb. 1958 (vol. XXXIX, no. 8).

version exposes a very painful inner condition, but one which it is difficult to relate to the literature of normal human experience."[1]

Judged by the only review accessible at the time of writing, the American edition of this translation appears to have achieved more success while attracting considerable attention and speculation. William Kay Archer of Hunter College, writing in the *Saturday Review* (27 December 1958), begins his interesting article about *Būf-i Kūr* with a shrewd surmise: "Possibly some understanding of the forces of change at work in Asia might be gained from reading 'The Blind Owl'." He considers the book a "moving work of art" and fears that it might be threatened with the type of outrage inflicted on *Dr Zhivago*. Elaborating his point further, he says:

There are dangers in store for "The Blind Owl". It is susceptible to adoption by the coterie readers: tired of Vivaldi, fearing Beckett optimistic, wearying of Zen, they may easily find their newest *frisson* in this macabre Iranian sensibility, heightened by the author's romantic suicide....In the morbid, exhausted, depressing, anguished, frightful story itself, they may be over-powered by the oil lamp smell of Poe and Baudelaire, and in the filigree, arabesque, and inlay of the prose, a Scheherazade orientalism.

Mr Archer's subtle remark about Hidāyat is also worth mentioning: "...He was aware of a great infinitude behind him. It was part of his gift that he had, with all the defects of its virtues, that terrible Persian awareness of time, of the past, of the direct burden of a great and unique culture."

We may fittingly conclude this chapter on *Būf-i Kūr* with Mr Archer's closing observation:

No reader, I think, will be bored by "The Blind Owl" nor left unhorrified at its end, though his literary judgment may be more reserved than mine. But the imperative to read it is other than literary. It is to confirm for us, once again, the affirmation contained in a gentle couplet of Hidāyat's seventeenth century compatriot, Sa'ib of Isphahan: "All this chatter about religion and infidels at the last leads to one place. Only the interpretations differ, the dream is the same dream".

[1] Eileen Fraser, May 1958 (vol. CLXIII, no. 975, p. 490).

CHAPTER XX

THE BARREN PERIOD (1937–41)

...I want to go far, very far, to a place where I can forget myself, be forgotten, lost and vanished. I want to escape from myself and go very remote...to India, for instance, under the burning sun, in the dense forests, to go amongst strange and wondrous people, somewhere where no one would recognize me, no one would understand my language, I want to feel everything in my own self....

SEVEN years after these lines were written Hidāyat's dream of going to India materialized. Various motives have been suggested for this journey, but it seems to have been primarily an escape. For many years he, like most Iranian intellectuals, had borne the social and political frustrations of Riẓā Shah's reign. Now, in the closing years of that reign, i.e. the late 1930's, Hidāyat could tolerate political suppression no longer; his exhausted patience drove him into voluntary exile.

His stay in India, mainly in Bombay, did not last more than a year. There he published *Būf-i Kūr* and studied *Pahlavi* under a Parsee scholar. As a result of the latter he translated some ancient *Pahlavi* texts, which were gradually published in Iran in the later years. Famous among these are: *Kārnāmak-ī Artasīr-ī Pāpakān* (1939), *Gujasteh Abālīs* (1939),[1] *Skand Gumānīk Vicar* (1943), *Ayātkār-ī Zāmāspīk* (1943), *Zand-ī Vohuman Yast* (1944) and *Sahr* (*estān*) *īhā-ī Ērān* (1944). During his sojourn he also wrote two short stories in French, "Lunatique" and "Sampingue", which have been translated and published in Persia. Both show a marked influence of Buddhism and Hinduism; and both have some of the familiar themes of *Būf-i Kūr*: in "Lunatique", for instance, Felicia's strange affection for the shabby old Indian cobbler reminds us of Lakkāta and the old rag-and-bone man. Even in the course of his Indian journey, and years after he had written *Būf-i Kūr*, Hidāyat was still haunted by the spirit and impact of the book.

[1] The title of this work is now given as *Gujastak Abdallah* by Jean-Pierre de Menasce (see *Le Dēnkart*, Paris, 1958, p. 11, n. 2).

On his return from India, Hidāyat found the political condition of the country, and also his own social environment, more intolerable than before. The harshness of the reign had increased. A strict censorship was kept on newspapers and all other publications. Speaking of these days to the First Congress of Iranian Writers, Dr Khānlarī has said:

These difficulties and restrictions gradually extinguished in Iran the enthusiasm for art.... For a three to four year period until after the events of Shahrīvar 1320 [August 1941] there existed no literary magazine throughout Persia, except the official magazine *Īrān-i Imrūz* whose editor was held in trust by the police, and which had taken the place of all the former, vigorous magazines....

The clique formed by Hidāyat and his intimate friends had by now broken up; one was in prison as a communist, another had gone abroad, and the others were burdened with the problems of their own lives. It is during this phase of his life that Hidāyat took increasingly to drink and drugs. His entire literary activity during this period consists of a few newspaper articles and the *Pahlavi* translations already mentioned. In point of fact, between the year *Būf-i Kūr* was first published (1937) and the abdication of Riẓā Shah (1941), Hidāyat had nothing to say.

CHAPTER XXI

THE PERIOD OF HIGH HOPES (1941–7)

THE last decade of Hidāyat's life coincided with an exceptionally eventful period in the history of Persia, and most of his works during this period are a reflection of that period.

Following the abdication of Riẓā Shah and the beginning of the new era, Hidāyat, after years of silence and resignation, brought out a new collection of short stories, *Sag-i Vilgard* ("The Stray Dog", 1942). Most of these eight stories were apparently written during the earlier years, for they carry the familiar gloom and melancholy so characteristic of Hidāyat's earlier works. Two of the pieces, "Sag-i Vilgard"[1] and "Bun Bast"[2] ("The Dead End") rank among Hidāyat's best short stories.

"Sag-i Vilgard" is the story of a dog who loses his master and, in contrast to the comfort and compassion he formerly enjoyed, becomes the victim of brutality. To a Westerner, and especially to an English reader brought up to love and care for animals, the story might sound somewhat unrealistic and overdramatized; but if we remember that dogs are considered unclean in the Islamic world, then the sad story of Pat, the unfortunate Scottish terrier, is given its true perspective.

The story opens with a neat description of the square of the locality where the dog lost his master, and it closes with the moving scene of his death. A very simple story on the whole, but the writer's tender and humane treatment, the way he touches upon the emotions of the stricken animal, describing his look, character, and feelings as though he were a fellow-creature, turn the story into an impressive episode:

> Two clever eyes, like those of a man, were sparkling in his woolly snout. There was a human soul in the depth of his eyes.... There was not only a resemblance but a kind of equivalence between his eyes and those of a human being.

[1] Translated into French (see F. Raẓavī, *op. cit.*) and German (see R. Gelpke, *op. cit.*).

[2] Translated into French by V. Monteil (Franco-Iranian Institute), 1952.

Or,

What tortured Pat more than anything else was his need for affection. He was like a child who has always been beaten and abused, but his tender feelings had not yet been extinguished. Especially in his new life, branded with pain and torment, he needed endearment more than ever before. His eyes were begging for such blessings; he was prepared to give his life if only a man would show interest in him, caressing him on the head. There was an urge in him to render his love and devotion to somebody, to express his feeling of worship and faithfulness to someone, but nobody cared for his emotions, nobody helped him; he looked into every eye but saw nothing but spite and wickedness in them, and every move he made to attract the attention of these people merely seemed to excite their rage and bitterness.

Prefacing the Russian translation of the story, published several years ago in Moscow,[1] E. Bertels suggests that under the disguise of a dog Hidāyat has depicted the life of a simple person in Persia—in fact his own life; and this disguise was necessary, he says, because of the cruel censorship and political repression of the time. He goes on: "In the author's own words the tale 'Sag-i Vilgard' was inspired by Chekhov's story 'Kashtanka'. The dog described by Hidāyat is the author himself and he carefully depicts how, all in vain, he looked for sympathy in those oppressing him and his like. Like the author, the dog too is finally driven to take his own life." But the progress of the story is not always so simple. In one fascinating passage, for instance, the dog is caught between two conflicting emotions: whether to remain faithful to his duty and obligations, i.e. follow his master; or whether to pay heed to the ruthless call of his passions and stay with his mate. He finally goes "the way of all flesh".

The story is written with a close-knit texture; it leaves the reader with a feeling of distress and irritation as he broods over the nostalgic sentiments of the dog and comes to the creature's pathetic end.

Distress, irritation, nostalgia, and a pathetic end also form the substance of the second story, "Bun Bast", one of the grimmest of Hidāyat's grim stories. Here, as in so many other stories, he reaffirms his belief in destiny as an inexorable, foreordained fate.

After twenty-two years of vagrant life, Sharīf has come back to

[1] *Stories by Persian Writers*, "Sag-i Vilgard" translated by N. Osmanov.

his native town; old and broken, with his opium brazier and his bottle of *arrack*, without any zest or enthusiasm, he wants to spend the rest of his days in peace and quiet. All his life Sharīf has had to contend with three disadvantages: his innate decency and kindliness, his uncomely appearance, and the fact that he was not a shrewd, impudent rascal like the rest of his fellow-workers. Just as he could never mix with these people, so he cannot now indulge in the life of his home town, for:

After his return everything looked petty to Sharīf, narrow, cramped and superficial. Everybody looked worn-out. They seemed to have lost their youth, to have lost their glamour. But they had managed to dig their claws more deeply into life, they were more fearful, more superstitious, more selfish than before. Some of them had more or less succeeded in achieving their petty desires—their bellies now prominent, their lusts transferred from the lower part of their bodies to their jaws; and in the rough and tumble of their life they had applied their wits to swindling, robbing their tenants, collecting cotton, opium, wheat; and to the linen of their babies or their own chronic gout.

In Sharīf's uneventful life there had been one inspiring memory: his youthful friendship with Muḥsin. Muḥsin, it seems, was the only person who was ever unconscious of Sharīf's unsightly appearance; moreover, he had appreciated his virtues and showed a genuine regard towards him. For his part, Sharīf had cherished a kind of fraternal love and devotion for him, so that "the presence of Muḥsin gave rise to a feeling of beauty-worship in him". Yet this dear friend suddenly vanished before Sharīf's eyes, drowned in the sea; and ever since, doomed and embittered, the fateful words "It had to happen" have become the blind axiom of Sharīf's life.

One day in his office Sharīf receives a young man just arrived to join the department. No sooner has he set eyes on the newcomer than he is struck with astonishment and alarm: "Sharīf knew the young man well, of course. He had been at school with him, when he was of the same age. In outward appearance, he was his old school friend Muḥsin: not only that, but his voice, every movement, his puzzled expression, the way he cleared his throat—in everything he was the living image of his unfortunate friend." The newcomer is Muḥsin's son. The old devotion and memories revived, Sharīf decides to take the young man under his wing as his own son, and invites him to live in his house. Once more a ray of hope, a meaning, has appeared in Sharīf's life, and he becomes a new man: friendly, sociable, and alive, "he had regained his lost life".

But the new life does not last more than "two magical weeks"; the wheel turns again, and one day in his office the news of Majīd's death is brought to him—he has drowned in the pool in the garden behind the house. Sharīf rushes home and beholds Majīd's body, lying on the veranda. "A dark curtain descended over Sharīf's eyes; with slow, heavy steps he returned by the way he had come. He pressed his arms against his back, went out of the house in the rain. He experienced the same feelings he had had at the time of Muḥsin's death....He kept repeating to himself: 'This had to happen'."[1]

The reader of the story may not care much for fate and predestination; he may even favour Gertrude Bell's view that "oriental fatalism, which sounds fine in theory, breaks down woefully in practice. It is mainly based upon the hopelessness of a people to whom it has never occurred to take hold of life with vigorous hands";[2] yet having reached the end of "Bun Bast", he cannot but sympathize with Sharīf. This, indeed, is one of Hidāyat's outstanding gifts: the ability to make the fate of his characters seem inevitable. His stories may repel us, but our repulsion is not directed against the characters, for no matter what their dispositions may be, they always have the disarming force of conviction.

None the less, Hidāyat has been severely criticized, both at home and abroad, for the negativity and sullen temperament of his characters, the unhappy finale of his stories, the black pessimism, boredom, and affliction that permeate most of his works. These *are* the prevailing traits in his writings, but to charge them against him is to isolate his work from the social conditions that nurtured it. Similarly, one could forget the philosophical pessimism that existed in Europe between the two world wars: "...everywhere there arose thinkers who deepened this pessimism and who built up their *weltanschauung* on some philosophical generalization of despair".[3] Hidāyat, too, susceptible to the conditions in his

[1] A partial translation of this story into English by Henry D. G. Law is published in the already cited number of *Life and Letters*, pp. 260–70.

[2] *Persian Pictures* (London, 1928), p. 47.

[3] George Lukàcs, *Studies in European Realism* (London, 1950), pp. 1–2.

country, built up his *weltanschauung* thus; and, as we shall see in the forthcoming pages, when these conditions changed, Hidāyat's world outlook also changed—though, alas, temporarily.

Other stories in the *Sag-i Vilgard* collection include: "Tajallī" ("Apparition"), the compassionate treatment of an episode in the life of a violinist; and "Takht-i Abū-Naṣr" ("The Throne of Abu-Nasr"), an imaginary tale based on the discovery, by an American archaeological mission, of the mummified body of Simuya Marzban, the Sassanid king, near Persepolis. Despite its fanciful theme (including the reanimation of the body through necromancy), the plot of the story is carefully fashioned, and the minutiae show Hidāyat's deep interest in the rites and witchcraft of old Iran.[1] "Kātīyā" is a loose account of a casual café conversation between the narrator and an Austrian prisoner of war in Russia. And "Dun Zhūvān-i Karaj" ("The Don Juan of Karaj")[2] is a light treatment of the life of gigolos and gigolettes in modern Iran.

But the last story of this volume, "Mīhan-Parast" ("The Patriot"), was a landmark in Hidāyat's career, for it heralded a phase that was to embrace all but the last of his future creations. Once again, however, the change can be understood only against the background of social and political changes that took place in Persia during the post-war years. For when the régime changed, a new, democratic era was heralded. In the following years there was a good deal of demonstration, oratory, and political manoeuvring everywhere in the country; and on the surface it looked as though the history of Iran had been given an abrupt twist.

The younger generation was naturally very impressed by these developments. This group included many who were fully aware of the needs and defects of their country. They knew, for instance, that during the past century and a half the country had been "a pawn of international diplomacy";[3] that "the life of peasants has changed little in the past thousand years";[4] and that "it was not difficult for a foreign legation to 'buy' a newspaper, an editorial

[1] During his first stay in France, Hidāyat had published an article on this subject entitled "Le Magic en Perse", in *Voil d'Asis*, no. 79, 1928.

[2] Translated into French by F. Raẓavī, *op. cit.*

[3] George Lenczowski, *Russia and the West in Iran*, p. 1.

[4] Richard N. Frye, *Iran* (New York, 1953), p. 7.

writer or an underpaid employee in one of the administrations".[1] They not only knew of these flagrant evils, but for many years they had cherished the desire to rid the country of them. Now their chance had come. After long years of silence, resignation, and frustration, they were suddenly free: free to express their opinions and release their pent-up desires. Here the role of intellectuals was of special significance: in fact, they stimulated the whole movement of political reform. For two decades they had been denied freedom of expression, but now that they had it they could not use it judiciously, and their first outpourings were, naturally, directed against the atrocities of the former régime.

Hidāyat could not stay out of this conflict. Under the old régime he had endured enough suffering to make him raise his voice against it now; and before he realized it, he was swimming with the currents of the time. "Mīhan-Parast"[2] was his first contribution to this new theme. It is an ironical account of the sea voyage of Sayyid Naṣrullā, one of the die-hard connoisseurs of the ministry of education who is sent on a commission to India to unfold the "dazzling cultural progress" in Iran during the "golden era". The plot is commonplace, but the wit, the sharp irony, and violent humour make the story memorable. The reader, especially if he is Persian, can hardly help savouring the portrayal of the conceited, ludicrous Sayyid Naṣrullā, for he is so utterly typical of his species. He claims to be erudite in French, Arabic, and Persian literature, in oriental as well as occidental philosophy, in gnosticism, and in the ancient and modern sciences; he regards himself as "the pride of mankind", and he delivers such pronouncements as: "English is in fact French, only they have spoiled the spelling and pronunciation." The story also contains bitter attacks on the Farhangistān (The Iranian Academy) and its "ludicrous, nonsensical coinages",[3] as well as some derisive criticism of the general plight of culture and education during the reign of Riẓā

[1] Lenczowski, *op. cit.* p. 179.

[2] Translated into Russian by V. Abrahimian (see *Stories by Persian Writers, op. cit.*).

[3] "Farhangistān" was founded in 1936 by the government. Its primary purpose was to purify the Persian language of Arabic and European elements. Hidāyat was a formidable opponent of this institution; he also wrote an amusing etymological epigram, called "Farhang-i Farhangistān" ("The Dictionary of the Academy") published in the collection *Vilingārī* (1944).

Shah and of the way in which ministers and high officials achieved promotion.

Though full of hope, humour, and spirit, Hidāyat's writings during this period often lack the depth, the grace, and pathos of his earlier works. His fastidious economy of words is abandoned, and in its place are an unsparing sense of humour, a great deal of journalese, and (as with the work of all the intellectuals during these critical years) an unrestrained liking for babbling and bitter sarcasm. These habits dominate "Qaẓīya-hi Namak-i Turkī" ("The Case of the Rock-salt") published in the collection *Vilingārī* ("Tittle-tattle", 1944): forty pages of sardonic gibing and medley. It is useless to look for any specific purport, relevance, or consistency: he just goes on and on, playing the fool, writing whatever comes to his mind; and yet every line, every word is a sharp prick at the ironies of human life—like Lucky's tirade in Beckett's *Waiting for Godot*. Of the same pattern, though with more substance, are two other pieces in this collection: "Murgh-i Rūḥ" ("The Soul-Bird") and "Zīr-i Buta" ("In the Wild"), the first a witty piece teasing a friend and the second a somewhat obscure allegory against the racial theories of Fascists. In the same volume there is also "Dast-i Bar Qaẓā" ("It happened that"), written in the style of the celebrated *Vagh Vagh Sāhāb*, a masterly juxtaposition of words, with lots of drollery and little sense.

An exception among the pieces in this miscellany is "Qaẓīya-hi Khar Dajjāl" ("The Case of the Antichrist's Donkey"), a very refined, clever, and suggestive allegory about the politics and general state of affairs in Persia from the early days of Riẓā Shah's rise to power until the period when the work was written. In its characterizations the piece resembles George Orwell's satire, *Animal Farm*.

The language used in this collection, as in the rest of his works during this period, is that of the ordinary man. Hidāyat, we remarked, took pride in bringing the songs, idioms, and slang of the common people into literature. But this innovation, which won the admiration of the new generation, never pleased the so-called classical scholars; that is why, in the words of Professor Arberry, Hidāyat was regarded in Persia as "the villain of the conservatives and the hero of the progressives in the conflict of contemporary Persian criticism".[1] The conservative elements argued that to use

[1] *Life and Letters*, *op. cit.* p. 236.

the common language in writing is to break away from traditional literature and thus to level down and debase the classical language. To enhance their point, they recited some obvious grammatical mistakes made by Hidāyat and his followers. The first of these charges did not win much support for the "upholders" of the classical heritage. With their exemplary contributions to modern prose, Hidāyat and his ardent pupils showed that introducing the language and folklore of the simple man into literature is by no means a departure from tradition: on the contrary, it is an enrichment of the language and the development of a new tradition. The second charge, that of grammatical mistakes, was directed mainly against colloquial usages; and though valid from a purely scholarly viewpoint, it does not carry sufficient weight when applied to short stories, where usage is the criterion of language. As Henry Sweet states: "Whatever is in general use in a language is for that reason grammatically correct."

This literary battle was not settled until the new era began, for with the appearance of many new periodicals and publications and the political propaganda of the various parties, a new reading public was born. And the young writers, anxious to enlighten and elevate the masses, tried to write in their language. This was how Hidāyat's language and style became the popular medium of literary expression. Once more Hidāyat was the guiding star; his position as the leading literary figure was established throughout the country, and he began writing with great vigour for the common people and their cause. For the first time his books were published not in limited editions but in abundance, for the thousands of new readers who were showing an interest in literature. And the host of young writers who claimed to be Hidāyat's disciples all tried to imitate him and follow the track he had beaten for years. Hidāyat himself seems to have been fully aware of his role and responsibilities, knowing quite well whom his art was meant for. And so his works—without any exception all through this period—are not only written in the simple language of the people, but are topical as well. Indeed, they mirror the complexities of Persian society during post-war years.

The legendary tale *Āb-i Zindigī* ("The Elixir of Life"), which appeared at this time, is a good example of these qualities. The unadorned beauty and ease of style, the flow of words and the simplicity of the story are probably unprecedented in Persian prose. The story is based on an old nursery tale, and Hidāyat, faithful to the original, envelopes it in a fairy tale atmosphere. Hence on the surface *Āb-i Zindigī* appears to be a children's story, while underneath, some of the most fundamental sociological problems are being dealt with. One immediately notices that a new Hidāyat has been born, with hardly a trace of despair or gloom left in him. We now see a social crusader who shows amazing insight, clairvoyance and understanding of a society in transformation. He portrays the emancipating class struggle and ends his attractive story with the victory of knowledge and humanity over the black forces of ignorance, tyranny and enslavement to gold.

Analysing *Āb-i Zindigī* in detail,[1] Dr Věra Kubīčkovā, a Czech orientalist, has emphasized its dominant philosophical tone and has argued that Hidāyat begins the story as a fairy tale but abandons this form as the action develops—a view hardly acceptable to Persian readers, who are bred in the bone with these fairy tales. But she rightly affirms that Hidāyat's version brings the action up to date, giving it more force and directness. About the purport of the story, Dr Kubīčkovā stresses Hidāyat's condemnation of dictatorships, of governments in general, and of aggressive wars. He is also opposed to the purposeless accumulation of money and riches. But he espouses freedom for the individual and the brotherhood of nations.

For all that, Hidāyat's most representative writing of this period was yet to come: *Ḥājjī Āqā* (1945), a one-character novelette, was the culmination of his optimism and the perfection of his new themes and style. Abandoning depth, pathos, and different kinds of mysticism, he shows a tendency for babbling and journalistic invective: these are the dominant tones in this masterpiece of sarcasm and denunciation. Ḥājjī Āqā himself is a monstrous phenomenon whose prototype might be found nowhere except in Persian society of the time. The son of a tobacconist, with little education and no solid background, Ḥājjī Āqā has managed, through fraud, pretension and political charlatanism, to acquire a vast fortune as well as considerable social status. A prominent figure in the country, he now owns estates, factories, and houses, has a business in

[1] "Un Eclair de Sourire sur un visage Tragique", *Charisteria Orientalia* (Praha, 1956).

the bazaar, trades in opium, hoards medicine and foodstuffs, and contrives various kinds of smuggling through his connections with ambassadors abroad. At the same time he is stingy and frugal to excess: "I counted the plums", he says when interrogating his old servant, "then the stones: four were missing."

His father having been completely unknown in his lifetime, Ḥājjī Āqā has invented a title for him "Ḥājj Muqtadir Khalvat". Ḥājjī, the son, enters the higher society and gains influence in various ministries and the civil administration. He spies for the police, extorts land from helpless people, has underhand dealings with high officials, and even facilitates the appointment of ministers and *Majlis* deputies. Ḥājjī Āqā's audience-chamber, where he receives all his clients from the prime minister down to the notorious procurer of the town, is the vestibule of his house. This "office" serves a double purpose: first, he is not obliged to show hospitality to his guests and, secondly, from there he can keep an eye on the movement of his wives. Nearing ninety, Ḥājjī Āqā has a brilliant matrimonial record—"six divorced and four passed away"—and he still keeps a flourishing harem—"seven still living". However, he still carries on, taking medicine for his impotence and showing a curious suspicion of his wives. Ḥājjī Āqā's eldest son has been spoiled by European education, and so he has disinherited him. Resolving to make a "man of the world" out of his younger son, he lectures him on the kernel of his life-philosophy, which is the fruit of his own experiences:

There are two classes of people in the world: the exploiters and the exploited. If you don't want to be exploited try to exploit others. You do not need much education, it is a handicap in life, makes you soft in the head....Be impudent, don't let yourself be forgotten. Boast and show off as much as you can....Do not be afraid of abuse, humiliation or slander....When kicked out from one door enter with a smile from another....Be impudent, insolent and stupid, for it is sometimes necessary to pretend stupidity—it helps. This is the type of man our country requires today....Faith, morals, religion and the rest are mere hypocrisy, though faith is essential for the common man: it serves as a muzzle, and without it society turns into a nest of vipers; everywhere you put your hand it stings....Be an opportunist. Try to establish connections with the holders of high offices. Agree with everybody, no matter what his opinion is, so that you may attract his utmost favour. I want you to grow up as a man of the world independent of people. Books, lectures, and things of this sort are not worth a penny. Imagine you are living in a den of thieves, turn your eyes away and you are robbed. All you need to learn are a few foreign words, a few pompous expressions and you can sit back and take it easy! I give lessons to all these ministers and deputies. What is important is to show them that you are a smart crook, that you can't be caught easily and that you are one of them, willing to negotiate.... But most important of all is money. If you happen to have money in this world then you will also have pride, credit, honesty, virtue and everything else. People adore you, you will be considered intelligent and patriotic, they will flatter you, they will do everything for you.... The educated engineer takes pride in operating your machine, the architect truckles to you to build your house, the poet licks the dust and writes your eulogy, the painter who has starved all his life paints your portrait, the journalists, deputies, ministers will all stand ready to do your bidding.... These scoundrels are all slaves to money. Do you know why knowledge and education are of no use in life? Because when you have got them you still have to serve the rich people....

Ḥājjī himself follows these counsels wholeheartedly. When he is in the company of the younger generation he puts forth progressive ideas, endorses all their fervent aspirations and ideals. When with Bahais he sounds most unbiased, speaks of his quarrels with *mullahs*. When among the constitutionalists he becomes the vanguard of the liberation forces, makes up stories about his participation in the revolution. And when he meets the supporters of autocracy he starts dreaming of the good old days; proclaims that the constitution was imposed by foreigners and that the secret police and the iron heel are indispensable to tame the people and keep them down.

A strong admirer of Riẓā Shah and Hitler, Ḥājjī has a striking knowledge of international politics. He believes, for instance, that the Second World War broke out because the Russians were covetous of his fortune, whereas the Germans were out to support him. In his view Hitler was a Muslim and had tattooed on his arm the Muslim device لا اللّه الا اللّه ("There is no God save Him"). One of Ḥājjī's fabrications to prove his importance is that "the Maharajah of Deccan twice requested me to take up his foreign ministry, but I refused".

When the Allied forces occupy Iran, Ḥājjī Āqā flees to Isfahan, but after some time he notices that "all the thieves, traitors, spies, criminals and his colleagues who had travelled with him returned to Tehran triumphantly". He, too, goes back and becomes a devotee of the new régime and a bigoted opponent of Riẓā Shah, "this morose leader who extorted whatever the country owned, stole the crown jewels and took away the antiques with him...". The man who, upon Riẓā Shah's seizure of his lands in Mazanderan, had said, "I laid them at the feet of His Majesty", now becomes bravely outspoken: "In those days there was no security for people's lives and property. They exchanged my lands in Mazanderan for nothing and compelled me to go and lay the purchase-deed at Riẓā Khān's feet. Nobody dared to utter a word!"

Under the auspices of the new government, Ḥājjī declares his candidacy for the *Majlis* and decides to "compose" a poem for his campaign: that is, he asks a modest young poet to write the poem for him. But the poet refuses, and the argument that follows is the real climax of the book. It is the conflict between new and old, between good and evil, between the vindicator of right and the wrongdoer. The poet is in fact Hidāyat himself, voicing the spirit of the new generation: the spirit of anger and abhorrence of the reactionary rulers and their corrupt, oppressive rule:

You are right [says the young poet]. In this despicable environment where fools, vermin and the dregs of society are cherished, and you are its prominent public figure, busy building up life in accordance with your avarice, ignominy and imbecility—in such society, supported by and made for the life of your type, I cannot be of any consequence. My existence is useless. You are right to abuse, humiliate and above all rob this nation. If they had courage they would destroy the lot of you.... For seventy years you have robbed, deceived and made a laughing stock of the people....Do you think you will carry this on generation after generation?...You are wrong. If the fate of this people remains for one more generation in your hands they will vanish. The world, even if you build up the wall of China around you, is rapidly changing. Supposing that we fail to demonstrate to you our right to live, others will speedily replace us. Then it is farewell to Ḥājjī Āqā and his world....

It is only natural that you do not know what poetry means, it would be strange if you did. You have never had or seen beauty in your life and if you come across any you fail to appreciate it. You have never been moved by a charming view, by a beautiful face, or an enchanting piece of music, a rhythmical word; a noble thought has never touched your heart. You are nothing but the slave of your belly and your nether parts. ...Now you can rest assured! I have divorced the craft of poetry. Henceforth the greatest and the loftiest poem in my life will be the destruction of you and your kind....

Ḥājjī Āqā is not a close-knit story but a rather extended commentary; a bitter exposure of moral decline and social crimes. To suggest the pattern and the kernel of the story it was thought necessary to quote at some length, for there are, in fact, no incidents, not even a central plot, in the book. But despite all its rancour, none of Hidāyat's books is so full of humour as this one. There are passages that will make even the most unsympathetic reader laugh. One of the novelties in the book is that, although primarily a one-character work, it *introduces* the reader to thirty different characters without actually letting him meet them. This Hidāyat achieves by his genius for coining names. People like Falākhunu'd-Dawla, Sarhang Buland Parvāz, Banda-yi Dargāh, Muntakhab Darbār, Ḥizqil Mash'al, and many others never appear in the story, but their names immediately illustrate and colour their characters for us.[1]

Ḥājjī Āqā was by far Hidāyat's most popular work, especially among the general public. At the same time it met with disapproval by the establishment and by carping, highbrow scholars. The latter suggested that it was not a work of art; that the character of Ḥājjī Āqā is a mere caricature, more exaggerated than typical. None of these charges is based on a real critical judgement. For, in the first place, Hidāyat never intended *Ḥājjī Āqā* to be a work of art; his aim, like that of most young writers of the period, was to appeal to the taste of the time, and to open his fellow-countrymen's eyes to the blemishes and scandals in their society. Secondly, given that Ḥājjī Āqā *is* a caricature, he can also be a literary creation provided he remains forceful and vigorous. To go even further, "Where there is no character there can be no caricature. Caricature is an artistic excess of character".[2] And lastly, the question of type versus individual is, in fact, the old argument in literature:

[1] Although translation deprives such names of their full allusive flavour, a rough English version might aid the non-Persian reader. Hence the above five mean: "The state's catapult", "Colonel climb-high", "The slave of your threshold", "The Court's nominee" and the last a Jewish name, to imply greed and usury.

[2] George Sampson, *The Concise Cambridge History of Literature* (1953), p. 764.

whether the character should be the photographic reflection of an ordinary man in everyday life, with all his average qualities; or an artistically magnified creation, with all his human impulses there, but presented in the extreme. In *Ḥājjī Āqā*, Hidāyat has employed the latter conception.

What makes a type a type [says G. Lukàcs] is not its average quality, not its mere individual being, however profoundly conceived; what makes it a type is that in it all the humanly and socially essential determinants are present on their highest level of development, in the ultimate unfolding of the possibilities latent in them, in extreme presentation of their extremes, rendering concrete the peaks and limits of men and epochs.[1]

However, one criticism may be launched against the book as an illustrative narration: besides being superficially stretched, it ends in an anti-climax, leaving the fate of Ḥājjī Āqā in the air. The book reaches its real culmination when the young poet addresses his last words to Ḥājjī: "Henceforth the greatest and the loftiest poem in my life will be the destruction of you and your kind who have condemned hundreds of thousands of men to death and misery and still carry on swaggering. You dishonest grave-diggers!" One would rather have the book end there.

With copies of *Ḥājjī Āqā* widespread all over the country, Hidāyat was at the peak of his popularity. The attention of the younger people, the intelligentsia, and particularly the extreme-left group was focused on the man and his works. Hidāyat himself, by contributing an occasional article or publishing a new story in the periodicals of the latter group, showed an interest in their activities; and the apostles of the left, trying to draw him nearer to the movement, missed no opportunity to praise him. On his way home from the U.S.S.R., the famous French novelist and playwright Jean Richard Bloch visited Tehran and sent this complimentary message to Hidāyat through his friends: "Tell him, 'your withdrawal is not a noble deed'. Tell him, 'the world needs you'." Meanwhile there came an invitation from Moscow, and Hidāyat travelled to the Soviet Union and stayed for some time in Tashkent. Later Professor Joliot-Curie wrote to him, asking him to take part in the First Congress of Peace, which was meeting in

[1] *Studies in European Realism*, *op. cit.* p. 6.

Paris. Unable to travel abroad at the time, Hidāyat approved its agenda by proxy. In his reply to Joliot-Curie he wrote: "The imperialists have turned our country into one great prison. To express one's opinion and to think rightly is a crime here. I admire your views on the defence of peace...."

Not only did Hidāyat associate himself with new ideas, but he began atoning for many of his old beliefs. Exceptionally striking to the reader is his renunciation of fate and predestination, which had formed the substance of so many of his earlier works. Going through *Vilingārī* and *Ḥājjī Āqā* we often come across passages like this one: "...thus they [the advanced countries] had not become fatalists, flabby and snivelling. They did not worship the dead and so achieved ever-increasing progress in science, industry, art, exploration and stupendous inventions" (*Vilingārī*, p. 153). And among Ḥājjī's cynical advice to his son we read: "People must obey and believe in fate so that we can make sure of enslaving them."

Other works during this period show that Hidāyat has become more and more a militant humanist, conscious of the class struggle in society; while trying to disgrace the people's enemies, he fights vigorously for the rights of the downtrodden. For instance, the short story "Fardā" ("To-morrow", 1946),[1] which appeared after *Ḥājjī Āqā*, is purely proletarian in nature. It sketches the turbulent dreams of two workmen, who, in their insomnia, picture for us the inner lives of a group of workers in a printing-shop: their political wranglings and petty tiffs, their hopes, anxieties, and comradeship. The story is in two complementary parts. In the first, one of the workers, who has to leave his job and go hunting for another in a distant town, tells us of his fears and perplexities; in the second part he has been killed in a strike, and a fellow-worker meditates on the life and character of his deceased friend. Both parts merge into the workers' worried glance at the future, with the word "to-morrow" rippling on their lips.

[1] Translated into French by V. Monteil, *op. cit.*

CHAPTER XXII

THE AFTERMATH (1947–51)

THE morrow was to hold no roses for the workers, nor for Hidāyat himself. Just as Sharīf, the doomed character of "Bun Bast" lived "two magical weeks" before the wheel of his life turned back again, so the period between 1941 and 1947 contained the magical years of Hidāyat's life—and then he sank, this time forever, to the bottomless abyss of *Būf-i Kūr*'s despondency. Once more the cause is to be sought in the person of Hidāyat, in his social surroundings, and in the political currents of his country.

About these we have already spoken at some length, stressing the hopes and expectations of the younger people and intellectuals; what remains to be added is that none of their wishes was fulfilled in those years. Despite all its flying colours, the new democracy soon proved to be a solemn mockery of itself. As far as the ruling clique and their decayed régime were concerned, nothing had in fact changed, "only" (to quote Hidāyat) "the word democracy had replaced the word dictatorship". Unpopular with the masses, the reactionary circles failed to form a large, solid, political organization of any significance. Nevertheless, with the decisive power of the army behind them, they managed to hold their grip on the key positions of the administration. The seats in the *Majlis*, cabinet posts, and higher offices remained the exclusive property of the upper class, who were naturally loath to allow any radical change in the social structure.

In fact the new system [as G. Lenczowski maintained] resembled more an oligarchy of a thousand wealthy families than a democracy in the Western sense. The Majlis was representative, with a few exceptions, of the rich landowning and merchant class, and as such it reflected conservative and essentially *status quo* trends. What the country needed was sweeping reform, but parliament could hardly be expected to serve as an instrument of any radical changes. Under such circumstances, there was a marked revival of disturbing political extremism both on the left and on the right.[1]

[1] *The Middle East in World Affairs*, p. 176.

In 1947, following the tragic events in Azerbaijan, the right-wing elements gained a large measure of success, and as a result they stifled leftist organizations and imprisoned many of their political opponents. Disillusioned and tantalized by all these discrepancies, and hearing again the footfalls of the iron-heel, Hidāyat and a number of other intellectuals bade farewell to their high hopes and retired once more to their sombre seclusion.

The interlude of gaiety was over. Hidāyat, at this stage of his life, had been the Atlas on whom the weight of Iran's history and sense of destiny were pressing. Between 1947 and 1951, the year of his suicide, he wrote two books: *Tūp-i Murvārī* ("The Pearl Cannon", 1947) and *Piyām-i Kāfkā* ("The Message of Kafka", 1948). The first is an indiscreet narrative, probably his shrug of the shoulder at what was happening in his country. The book is not yet published, and its profane and maledictory language will most likely prevent its publication in the near future. Some fragments, taken from the unrevised manuscript of the book, were published in the Persian translation of Vincent Monteil's *Sâdeq Hedâyat* (pp. 102–27), but it is unfair to judge the book on this mutilated selection.

Piyām-i Kāfkā is both a brilliant introduction to the Persian translation of Kafka's *The Penal Colony* and a description of Hidāyat's own pessimism. A mature work both in thought and style, it is the complete expression of a philosophy of despair.

> Before the last World War [he states] there still existed a vague hope of freedom and respect for the rights of mankind. The supporters of dictatorship had not yet openly replaced freedom by slavery, the rights of humanity by the atomic bomb and justice by injustice. The masses of the people had not yet been transformed by politicians and robbers into cattle, and living men into half-dead creatures.

Hidāyat's grim philosophy is recited in *Piyām-i Kāfkā* with a mastery and confidence that denote the great artist at the height of his powers. But having reached this height, Hidāyat had also made up his mind on a problem that had engaged him all his mature life: the problem of whether or not the highly sensitive and idealistic individual could sustain the experience of mortal life; that is of a solitary life where all pain is perceived and loneliness suffered, which becomes all the more complete for its being so largely incommunicable. This was the predicament of an artist whose temperament was made for pessimism and for whom neither religion nor philosophy held any consolation. For Hidāyat, life could not be borne; he had to shed it.

This he did with a characteristic concern for others. His refusal to say goodbye to his aged and dignified parents at the airfield at Mehrabad was not malice; his courage failed him, that is all. He chose a remote city in which to die, and thought of his friends—the creatures who knew so little of his agony—to the very last. He even attempted to leave them with a gay word and a joke—his farewell note, "See you on Doomsday". A rather macabre one, but a joke and a jaunty gesture all the same.

The "blind owl" could not stand the ugliness that his psychology and brand of introspection revealed to him in the harsh light of day. This was a failure, of course. But the final giving up must not blind us to his importance in continuing the greatest that is in Iran's literary heritage. Hidāyat above all others has proved the endurance of Iran's literary genius. No reference to this genius will ever again be possible without his name.

APPENDIX

LIST OF ṢĀDIQ HIDĀYAT'S WORKS

Dates inside brackets represent the Persian solar calendar.

Entries bearing asterisks are republished in the collection, *Majmū'a-yi Nivishta-hā-yi Parākanda-yi Ṣādiq Hidāyat* ("The collection of Sadiq Hidayat's miscellaneous writings") (Tehran, 1334/1955), 645 pp.

I. FICTION

1930 (1309) *Zinda Bi-gūr* (*Buried Alive*), Tehran, 80 pp. A collection of 8 short stories.

1. "Zinda Bi-gūr" ("Buried Alive").
2. "Ḥājjī Murād".
3. "Asīr-i Farānsavī" ("The French Prisoner of War").
4. "Dāvūd-i Kūzh-Pusht" ("David, the Hunchback").
5. "Mādlīn" ("Madeleine").
6. "Ātash-Parast" ("The Fire-worshipper").
7. "Ābjī-Khānum" ("The Elder Sister").
8. "Murda-Khurhā" ("The Ghouls").

Second edition, including *Āb-i Zindigī* (Tehran, 1331/1952), 131 pp.

*1931 (1310) *Sāya-hi Mughul* (*Mongol Shadow*), Tehran, 14 pp. First published in a collection of 3 short stories called *Anīrān* (*Non-Iranian*) in collaboration with Buzurg 'Alavī and Shīn-i Partaw. Second edition, *Nivishta-hā-yi Parākanda*, pp. 102–18.

1932 (1311) *Sa Qaṭra Khūn* (*Three Drops of Blood*), Tehran, 102 pp. A collection of 11 short stories.

1. "Sa Qaṭra Khūn" ("Three Drops of Blood").
2. "Girdāb" ("The Whirlpool").
3. "Dāsh Ākul".
4. "Āyina-yi Shikasta" ("The Broken Mirror").
5. "Ṭalab-i Āmurzish" ("Asking Absolution").
6. "Lāla".
7. "Ṣūratak-hā" ("The Masks").
8. "Changāl" ("The Claw").
9. "Mardī-ka Nafsash rā Kusht" ("The Man who killed his Passion").

10. "Muḥallil" ("The Legalizer").
11. "Gujasta Dizh" ("The Cursed Castle").

Third edition (Tehran, 1333/1954), 181 pp.

1933 (1312) *Sāya Rushan* (*Chiaroscuro*), Tehran, 155 pp. A collection of 7 short stories.

1. "S.G.L.L." ("The Serum of Sterility").
2. "Zanī-ka Mardash rā Gum Kard" ("The Woman who lost her Man").
3. "'Arūsak-i Pusht-i Parda" ("The Puppet Behind the Curtain").
4. "Āfarīnigān" ("The Requiem").
5. "Shab-hā-yi Varāmīn" ("The Nights of Varamin").
6. "Ākharīn Labkhand" ("The Last Smile").
7. "Pidarān-i Ādam" ("The Man's Ancestors").

Second edition (Tehran, 1331/1952), 179 pp.

1933 (1312) *'Alavīya Khānum* (*Madame 'Alaviya*), Tehran, 66 pp. Second edition published together with *Vilingārī* (Tehran, 1333/1954), pp. 1–49.

1933 (1312) *Vagh Vagh Sāhāb* (*Mister Bow Wow*), Tehran, 190 pp. A collection of 35 *Qaẓīya* (narratives) written in collaboration with M. Farzād. Second edition (Tehran, 1334/1955), 183 pp.

1937 (1315) *Būf-i Kūr* (*The Recluse*), Bombay, 144 pp. First edition, in limited stencilled copies. Second edition, as a *feuilleton*, in the daily *Īrān*, 1320/1941. Third edition (Tehran, 1320/1941), 60 pp. Fourth edition (Tehran, 1331/1952), 128 pp.

1942 (1321) *Sag-i Vilgard* (*The Stray Dog*), Tehran, 180 pp. A collection of 8 short stories.

1. "Sag-i Vilgard" ("The Stray Dog").
2. "Dun Zhūvān-i Karaj" ("The Don Juan of Karaj").
3. "Bun Bast" ("The Dead End").
4. "Kātīyā".
5. "Takht-i Abū-Naṣr" ("The Throne of Abu-Nasr").
6. "Tajallī" ("Apparition").
7. "Tārīk-Khāna" ("The Dark House").
8. "Mīhan-Parast" ("The Patriot").

Second edition (Tehran, 1330/1951). Third edition (Tehran, 1332/1953), 170 pp.

1944 (1323) *Vilingārī* (*Tittle-tattle*), Tehran, 75 pp. A collection of 6 narratives (*Qaẓīya*).

1. "Murgh-i Rūḥ" ("The Soul-Bird").

2. "Zīr-i Buta" ("In the Wilds").
3. "Farhang-i Farhangistān" ("The Dictionary of the Academy").
4. "Dast-i Bar Qaẓā" ("It happened that").
5. "Khar Dajjāl" ("The Antichrist's Donkey").
6. "Namak-i Turkī" ("The Rock-salt").

Second edition, with *'Alavīya Khānum* (Tehran, 1333/1954), pp. 52–163.

*1944 (1323) *Āb-i Zindigī* (*The Elixir of Life*), Tehran, 19 pp. First published as a *feuilleton* in the daily *Mardum*. Second edition, collection *Zinda Bi-gūr* (Tehran, 1331/1952), pp. 103–31. Third edition, *Nivishta-hā-yi Parākanda*, pp. 220–48.

1945 (1324) *Ḥājjī Āqā*, Tehran, 105 pp. Second edition (Tehran, 1330/1952), 143 pp.

*1946 (1325) "Fardā" ("To-morrow") Tehran, 10 pp. First published in the monthly *Piyām-i Naw* (Khurdad-Tir, 1325/1946). Second edition, with "Bun Bast" (with French translation of both stories by V. Monteil) published by the Franco-Iranian Institute (Tehran, 1331/1952), pp. 25–40. Third edition, *Nivishta-hā-yi Parākanda*, pp. 188–206.

Tūp-i Murvārī (*The Pearl Cannon*), unpublished, written in 1326/1947.

II. DRAMA

1930 (1309) *Parvīn Dukhtar-i Sāsān* (*Parvin, the Sasan Daughter*), Tehran, 48 pp. A historical drama in 3 acts. Second edition, together with a number of other stories (Tehran, 1333/1954), pp. 9–55.

1933 (1312) *Māzīyār*, Tehran, 57 pp. A historical drama in 3 acts written in collaboration with M. Mīnuvī. Second edition (Tehran, 1333/1954), 140 pp.

1946 (1325) *Afsāna-yi Āfarīnish* (*The Legend of Creation*), Paris (Adrien Maisonneuve), 32 pp., a satire for marionettes in 3 acts.

III. TRAVELOGUES

1932 (1311) *Iṣfahān Niṣf-i Jāhān* (*Isfahan: Half the World*), Tehran, 51 pp. Second edition, collection *Parvīn Dukhtar-i Sāsān*, pp. 57–118.

Rū-yi Jāda-yi Namnāk (*On the Wet Road*), unpublished, written in 1314/1935.

IV. STUDIES, CRITICISM AND MISCELLANEA

*1923 (1302) *Rubā'īyāt-i Ḥakīm 'Umar-i Khayyām* (*Khayyām's Quatrains*), Tehran, 97 pp. A new edition of the Quatrains with some introductory remarks. Second edition (the introduction alone), *Nivishta-hā-yi Parākanda*, pp. 252–61.

*1924 (1303) *Insān u Ḥayvān* (*Man and Animal*), Tehran, 85 pp. Second edition, *Nivishta-hā-yi Parākanda*, pp. 264–90.

*1927 (1305) "Marg" ("Death"), Berlin (Iranshahr), 2 pp. Second edition, collection *Parvīn Dukhtar-i Sāsān*, pp. 120–2. Third edition, *Nivishta-hā-yi Parākanda*, pp. 292–3.

1927 (1306) *Favāyid-i Gīyāh-Khārī* (*The Advantages of Vegetarianism*), Berlin (Iranshahr), 80 pp. Second edition (Tehran, 1336/1957), 106 pp.

*1932 (1310) "Ḥikāyat-i bā Natīja" ("The Story with a Moral"), Tehran (magazine *Afsāna*, no. 31). Second edition, *Nivishtihā-yi Parākanda*, pp. 54–5.

1934 (1313) *Tarāna-hā-yi Khayyām* (*The Melodies of Khayyām*), Tehran, 116 pp. Second edition (Tehran, 1334/1955), 111 pp.

*1940 (1319) "Chāykuvskī" ("Tchaikovsky"), Tehran (magazine *Mūsīqī*, no. 3). Second edition, *Nivishta-hā-yi Parākanda*, pp. 366–72. An article written on the centenary of Tchaikovsky's birth.

*1940 (1319) "Dar Pīrāmūn-i Lughat-i Furs-i Asadī" ("About Asadi's Persian Dictionary"), Tehran (magazine *Mūsīqī*, no. 8). Second edition, *Nivishta-hā-yi Parākanda*, pp. 374–80.

*1940 (1319) "Shīva-yi Nuvīn dar Taḥqīq-i Adabī" ("A New Method of Literary Research"), Tehran (magazine *Mūsīqī*, nos. 11–12). Second edition, *Nivishta-hā-yi Parākanda*, pp. 382–91.

*1941 (1320) "Dāstān-i Nāz" ("The Story of Nāz"), Tehran (magazine *Mūsīqī*, no. 2). Second edition, *Nivishta-hā-yi Parākanda*, pp. 394–401.

*1941 (1320) "Shīva-hā-yi Nuvīn dar Shi'r-i Fārsī" ("New Trends in Persian Poetry"), Tehran (magazine *Mūsīqī*, no. 3). Second edition, *Nivishta-hā-yi Parākanda*, pp. 404–9.

1944 (1323) A Review on the Film "Mullā Naṣru'd-Dīn", Tehran (magazine *Piyām-i Naw*, no. 1).

1944 (1323) A literary criticism on the Persian translation of Gogol's *The Government Inspector* (*Piyām-i Naw*, no. 1).

*1945 (1324) "Chand Nukta dar Bāra-yi Vīs u Rāmīn" ("Some notes on Vis and Ramin"), Tehran (*Piyām-i Naw*, nos. 9–10). Second edition, *Nivishta-hā-yi Parākanda*, pp. 486–523.

1948 (1327) *Piyām-i Kāfkā* (*The Message of Kafka*), an introduction to the Persian translation of Kafka's *The Penal Colony* (*Gurūh-i Maḥkūmīn*), by Ḥ. Qā'imīyān, pp. 5–48.

Al-Bi'thatu'l-Islāmīya Illal-Bilād'l-Afranjī-ya (*An Islamic Mission in the European Lands*), undated and unpublished.

V. STUDIES IN FOLKLORE

*1931 (1310) *Usāna*, Tehran (Ariyan Kuda), 36 pp. A collection of folklore songs. Second edition, *Nivishta-hā-yi Parākanda*, pp. 296–327.

1933 (1312) *Nayrangistān* (*Persian Folklore*), Tehran, 164 pp. Second edition (Tehran, 1334/1956), 202 pp.

*1939 (1318) "Tarāna-hā-yi 'Āmīyāna" ("The Popular Songs"), Tehran (magazine *Mūsīqī*, nos. 6–7). Second edition, *Nivishta-hā-yi Parākanda*, pp. 344–64.

*1939 (1318) "Matal-hā-yi Fārsī" ("Persian Tales"), Tehran (magazine *Mūsīqī*, no. 8). An introduction with two examples of Persian tales ("Āqā Mūsha" and "Shangūl Mangūl"). Second edition, *Nivishta-hā-yi Parākanda*, pp. 120–6.

*1940 (1319) "Lachak-i Kūchūlū-yi Qirmiz" ("The Small Red Shawl"), Tehran (magazine *Mūsīqī*, no. 2). Second edition, *Nivishta-hā-yi Parākanda*, pp. 127–30.

*1941 (1320) "Sang-i Ṣabūr" ("The Patient Stone"), Tehran (magazine *Mūsīqī*, nos. 6–7). Second edition, *Nivishta-hā-yi Parākanda*, pp. 131–8.

*1944 (1323) "Fulklur yā Farhang-i Tūda" ("Folklore, the Culture of the Masses"), Tehran (journal *Sukhan*, nos. 3–6). Second edition, *Nivishta-hā-yi Parākanda*, pp. 448–83.

"Ṭās-i Chil Kilīd" ("A Bowl with Forty Keys"), undated and unpublished.

VI. STUDIES ON PAHLAVI TEXTS

1939 (1318) *Kārnāma-yi Ardashīr Pāpakān* (*The Book of the Deeds of Ardashir Papakan*), Tehran (magazine *Mūsīqī*), 36 pp. Second edition, with *Zand-i Vuhūman yasn* (Tehran, 1332/1953), pp. 161–212.

*1939 (1318) *Gujasta Abālīsh*, Tehran, 12 pp. Second edition, *Nivishta-hā-yi Parākanda*, pp. 330–42.

*1942 (1321) *Shahristānhā-yi Īrān* (*The Provincial Capitals of Iran*), Tehran (magazine *Mihr*, nos. 1–3). Second edition, Bombay (Iran League). Third edition, *Nivishta-hā-yi Parākanda*, pp. 412–33.

1942 (1322) *Guzārish-i Gumān-shikan* (*The Doubt-dispelling Treatise*), Tehran, 97 pp.

*1944 (1323) *Yādigār-i Jāmāsp* (*The Memories of Jamasp*), Tehran (journal *Sukhan*, nos. 3–5). Second edition, *Nivishta-hā-yi Parākanda*, pp. 436–45.

1944 (1323) *Zand-i Vuhūman Yasn* (*Commentary of the Vohuman Hymn*), Tehran, 128 pp. Second edition, with *Kārnāma-yi Ardashīr-i Pāpakān* (Tehran, 1332/1953), pp. 9–158.

1945 (1324) *Āmadan-i Shāh Bahrām-i Varjāvand* (*The Arrival of Shah Bahram Varjavand*), Tehran (journal *Sukhan*, no. 7).

*1945 (1324) "Khaṭṭ-i Pahlavī va Alifbā-yi Ṣutī" ("Pahlavi Script and Phonetic Alphabet"), Tehran (journal *Sukhan*, nos. 8–9). Second edition, *Nivishta-hā-yi Parākanda*, pp. 526–41.

*1946 (1325) "Hunar-i Sāsānī dar Ghurfa-yi Midālhā" ("Sassanid Art in the Gallery of Medals"), Tehran (journal *Sukhan*, no. 5). Translation of an article by L. Morgenstern, originally published in *Esthétiques d'Orient et d'Occident* (Paris, 1937), p. 112. Second edition, *Nivishta-hā-yi Parākanda*, pp. 544–8.

VII. TRANSLATIONS (FROM FRENCH)

*1932 (1310) "Kūr u Barādarash" ("The Blindman and his Brother"), by Arthur Schnitzler, Tehran (magazine *Afsāna*, nos. 4–5). Second edition, *Nivishta-hā-yi Parākanda*, pp. 58–100.

*1932 (1310) "Kalāgh-i Pīr" ("The Old Crow"), by Alexandre Lange, Tehran (magazine *Afsāna*, no. 11). Second edition, *Nivishta-hā-yi Parākanda*, pp. 17–23.

*1932 (1310) "Tamishk-i Tīgh-dār" ("The Gooseberry-Bush"), by Anton Chekhov, Tehran (magazine *Afsāna*, no. 23). Second edition, *Nivishta-hā-yi Parākanda*, pp. 26–43.

*1932 (1310) "Murdāb-i Ḥabasha" ("The Abyssinian Lagoon"), by Gaston Cherau, Tehran (magazine *Afsāna*, no. 28). Second edition, *Nivishta-hā-yi Parākanda*, pp. 46–51.

*1943 (1322) "Jilu-yi Qānūn" ("Before the Law"), by Franz Kafka, Tehran (journal *Sukhan*, nos. 11–12). Second edition, *Nivishta-hā-yi Parākanda*, pp. 140–1.

1943 (1332) *Maskh* (*The Metamorphosis*), by Franz Kafka, Tehran (journal *Sukhan*, nos. 1–9). Second edition, published with some other stories by Kafka (Tehran, 1329/1950).

*1944 (1325) "Urāshīmā" ("A Japanese Fable"), Tehran (journal *Sukhan*, no. 1). Second edition, *Nivishta-hā-yi Parākanda*, pp. 250–6.

*1945 (1324) "Shughāl u Arab" ("Jackals and Arabs"), by Franz Kafka, Tehran (journal *Sukhan*, no. 5). Second edition, *Nivishta-hā-yi Parākanda*, pp. 144–50.

*1945 (1324) "Dīvār" ("Le Mur"), by Jean-Paul Sartre, Tehran (journal *Sukhan*, nos. 11–12). Second edition, *Nivishta-hā-yi Parākanda*, pp. 152–85.

*1946 (1325) "Qiṣṣa-yi Kadū" ("Conte de la Courge"), by Roger Lescot (A Khurdish story translated from *Textes Kurdes*, vol. 1, p. 3), Tehran (journal *Sukhan*, no. 4). Second edition, *Nivishta-hā-yi Parākanda*, pp. 208–18.

1946 (1325) "Girākūs-i Shikārchī" ("The Hunter Gracchus"), by Franz Kafka, Tehran (journal *Sukhan*, no. 1). Second edition, published together with *Maskh* (Tehran, 1329/1950).

VIII. WRITTEN IN FRENCH

*1926 (1305) "Le Magic en Perse" ("Jādūgarī dar Īrān"), Paris (*Le voile d'Isis*, no. 79). Second edition, *Nivishta-hā-yi Parākanda*, pp. 625–40. (A partial Persian translation of this study was published in the monthly *Jahān-i Naw*, no. 1, second year.)

*1945 (1324) "Sampingue" ("Sāmpīnga"), Tehran (*Samedi*). Second edition, together with Persian translation, collection *Parvīn Dukhtar-i Sāsān*, pp. 123–48. Third edition, with Persian translation, *Nivishta-hā-yi Parākanda*, pp. 552–78.

*1945 (1324) "Lunatique" ("Havasbāz"), Tehran (*Samedi*). Second edition, with Persian translation, collection *Parvīn Dukhtar-i Sāsān*, pp. 149–83. Third edition, with Persian translation, *Nivishta-hā-yi Parākanda*, pp. 580–625.

BIBLIOGRAPHY

I. GENERAL AND HISTORICAL

(*a*) *Persian sources*

AMĪR-KHĪZĪ, ISMĀ'ĪL. *Qīyām-i Āzarbāyijān va Sattār Khān* (*Sattar Khan and the Uprising of Azerbaijan*). Tabriz, 1960.

BAHĀR, MUḤAMMAD TAQĪ (the *Maliku'shu'arā*). *Tārīkh-i Mukhtaṣar-i Āḥzāb-i sīyāsī-yi Īrān: Inqirāẓ-i Qājārī-ya* (*A Short History of Political Parties in Iran: The Fall of the Qajars*). Tehran, 1942.

DAWLAT-ĀBĀDĪ, YAḤYĀ. *Ḥayāt-i Yaḥyā* (*The Life of Yahya: Autobiography*). Tehran, 1949.

KASRAVĪ, AḤMAD. *Tārīkh-i Mashrūṭa-yi Īrān* (*The History of Persian Constitution*). Tehran, 1937.

KASRAVĪ, AḤMAD. *Mashrūṭa va Āzādigān* (*The Constitution and the Free-thinkers*). (Collection of Speeches.) Tehran, 1945.

KASRAVĪ, AḤMAD. *Tārīkh-i Hījdah Sāla-yi Āzarbāyijān yā Dāstān-i Mashrūṭa-yi Īrān* (*Eighteen Years of Azerbaijan's History or the Story of the Iranian Constitution*). 6 vols. Tehran, 1939–41.

KHĀJA-NŪRĪ, IBRĀHĪM. *Bāzīgarān-i 'Aṣr-i Ṭalā'ī* (*The Heroes of the Golden Age*). 2 vols. Tehran, 1941–2.

KHAL'ATBARĪ, ARSALĀN. *Arīstukrāsī-yi Īrān* (*Iranian Aristocracy*). Tehran, 1945.

KĪYĀNŪRĪ, N. *Mubārizāt-i Ṭabaqātī* (*Class Struggle*). Tehran, 1948.

MAḤMŪD, MAḤMŪD. *Tārīkh-i Ravābiṭ-i Sīyāsī-yi Īrān va Ingilīs dar Qarn-i Nūzdahum* (*History of the Anglo-Iranian Diplomatic Relations in the Nineteenth Century*). 3 vols. Tehran, 1950.

MAKKĪ, ḤUSAYN. *Kitāb-i Sīyāh* (*The Black Book*). Tehran, 1951.

MAKKĪ, ḤUSAYN. *Tārīkh-i Bīst Sāla-yi Īrān* (*Twenty Years of Iranian History*). 3 vols. Tehran, 1946.

MALIKZĀDA, MIHDĪ. *Tārīkh-i Inqilāb-i Mashrūṭīyat-i Īrān* (*A History of the Iranian Constitutional Revolution*). 7 vols. Tehran, 1951.

MUSTAWFĪ, 'ABDULLĀ. *Sharḥ-i Zindigānī-yi Man yā Tārīkh-i Ijtimā'ī va Idārī-yi Dawra-yi Qājārīya* (*My Life, or a Social and Administrative History of the Qajar Period*). 4 vols. Tehran, 1945.

NĀẒIMU'L-ISLĀM, M. *Tārīkh-i Bīdārī-yi Īrānīyān* (*A History of the Awakening of Persians*). Tehran, 1909.

SAKHĀ'Ī, MAḤMŪD. *Muṣaddiq va Rastākhīz-i Millat* (*Musaddiq and the Awakening of the Nation*). Tehran, 1952.

SIPIHR (the *Muvarikhu'd-Dawla*). *Īrān dar Jang-i Buzurg, 1914–1918* (*Iran in the World War, 1914–1918*). Tehran, 1957.

ṬABARĪ, IḤSĀN. "Dar bāra-yi Mashrūṭīyat-i Īrān" ("On Persian Constitution") in *Mardum*, II, no. 12, 1–8.

TAQĪZĀDA, ḤASAN. "Tahīya-hi Muqadamāt-i Mashrūṭīyat dar Āzarbāyijān" ("The Preliminary Preparations of the Constitution in Azerbaijan"), in *Nashrīya-hi Kitābkhāna-yi Millī-yi Tabrīz*, I, no. 1, 18–25.

TAQĪZĀDA, ḤASAN. *Tārīkh-i Avāyil-li Inqilāb-i Mashrūṭīyat-i Īrān* (*The History of the Early Years of Iran's Constitutional Revolution*). Tehran, 1959.

(*b*) *Foreign sources*

AFSCHAR, MAHMOUD. *La politique européenne en perse*. Berlin, 1921.

ALAVI, BOZORG. *Kämpfendes Iran*. Berlin, 1955.

AMIRIAN, A. M. *Condition politique, sociale et juridique de la femme en iran*. Paris, 1938.

BANANI, AMIN. *The Modernization of Iran, 1921–1941*. Stanford, 1961.

BOR-RAMENSKY, E. "Kvoprosu o roli bol'shevikov zakavkaz' ya v iranskoi revolyutsii 1905–1911 godov", in *Istorik Marksist*, II (1940), 89–99.

BROWNE, EDWARD GRANVILLE. *A Brief Narrative of Recent Events in Persia*. (With an appendix on the Persian Constitution.) London, 1909.

BROWNE, EDWARD GRANVILLE. *The Persian Revolution of 1905–1909*. Cambridge, 1910.

BROWNE, EDWARD GRANVILLE. *The Reign of Terror at Tabriz, England's Responsibility*. Manchester, 1912.

BROWNE, EDWARD GRANVILLE. *The Persian Crisis of December 1911: How It Arose and Whither It May Lead Us*. Cambridge, 1912.

BROWNE, EDWARD GRANVILLE. *A Year Among the Persians*. Cambridge, 1927.

BROWNE, EDWARD GRANVILLE. *The Persian View of the Anglo-Russian Agreement*. Suffolk, undated.

COURTOIS, V. "The Tudeh Party", in *Indo-Iranica*, 7ii (1954), 14–22.

ELWELL-SUTTON, L. P. *Modern Iran*. London, 1941.

ELWELL-SUTTON, L. P. "Political Parties in Iran: 1941–1948", in *Middle East Journal*, no. 3 (1949), 45–62.

ELWELL-SUTTON, L. P. *A Guide to Iranian Area Study*. Ann Arbor, Michigan, 1952.

ELWELL-SUTTON, L. P. *Persian Oil: A Study in Power Politics*. London, 1955.

ELWELL-SUTTON, L. P. "Nationalism and Neutralism in Iran", in *Middle East Journal*, no. 12 (1958), 20–32.

Encyclopaedia of Islam, The. 5 vols. London, 1938.

FARMANFARMAIAN, HAFEZ. *The Fall of the Qajar Dynasty*. (Unpublished doctoral dissertation.) Georgetown University, 1957.

FATEMI, N. SAIFPOUR. *Diplomatic History of Persia 1917–1923: Anglo-Russian Power Politics in Iran*. New York, 1952.

FRYE, RICHARD NELSON. *Iran*. New York, 1953.

GAIL, MARZIEH. *Persia and the Victorians*. London, 1951.

GIBB, H. A. R. *Modern Trends in Islam*. Chicago, 1947.

GIBB, H. A. R. and BOWEN, HAROLD. *Islamic Society and the West: A Study of the Impact of Western Civilization on Muslim Culture in the Near East*. London, 1950.

GROSECLOSE, ELGIN. *Introduction to Iran*. New York, 1947.

HAAS, WILLIAM S. *Iran*. New York, 1946.

HADARY, GIDEON. "The Agrarian Reform Problem in Iran", in *Middle East Journal*, v (spring, 1951), 181–96.

IQBAL, MUHAMMAD. *Iran*. Madras, 1946.

IRANOV, M. S. *Babidskoye vostaniya v iranye: 1848–1852*. Moscow, 1939.

IRANOV, M. S. *Ocherk istorii irana*. Moscow, 1952.

IRANOV, M. S. *Iranskaia revoliutsiia 1905–1911 godov*. Moscow, 1957.

KEDDIE, NIKKI R. "Religion and Irreligion in Early Iranian Nationalism", in *Comparative Studies in Society and History*, IV, no. 3 (April 1962), 265–95.

KEMP, NORMAN. *Abadan: A First Hand Account of the Persian Oil Crisis*. London, 1953.

KHORASSANI, HADI. *Le régime douanier de l'iran*. Paris, 1937.

KOHN, HANS. *Western Civilization in the Near East*. New York, 1936.

LAMBTON, ANN K. S. "Some Aspects of the Situation in Persia", in *Asiatic Review*, XXXIX, no. 140 (October 1943), 420–5.

LAMBTON, ANN K. S. *Landlord and Peasant in Persia*. New York, 1953.

LAMBTON, ANN K. S. *Islamic Society in Persia*. London, 1954.

LAMBTON, ANN K. S. "The Impact of the West on Persia", in *International Affairs*, XXXIII, no. 1 (January 1957), 12–25.

LAMBTON, ANN K. S. "Secret Societies and the Persian Revolution of 1905–6", in *St Antony's Papers*, no. 4 (New York, 1959).

LEE, LESTER A. *The Reforms of Reza Shah: 1925–1941*. (Unpublished Master's thesis.) Stanford University, Stanford, California, 1950.

LENCZOWSKI, GEORGE. "The Communist Movement in Iran", in *Middle East Journal*, no. 1 (1947), 29–45.

LENCZOWSKI, GEORGE. *Russia and the West in Iran, 1918–1948: A Study in Big-Power Rivalry*. Ithaca, N.Y., 1949.

LENCZOWSKI, GEORGE. *The Middle East in World Affairs.* New York. 1956.

MALCOLM, Sir JOHN. *The History of Persia.* 2 vols. London, 1815.

MALEKPUR, 'ABDOLLAH. *Die Wirtschaftsverfassung Irans.* Berlin, 1935.

MATINE-DAFTARY, AHMAD. *La suppression des capitulations en Perse,* Paris, 1930.

MELZIG, HERBERT. *Resa Shah, der Aufstieg Irans und die Grossmachte.* Stuttgart, 1936.

MILLSPAUGH, ARTHUR C. *Americans in Persia.* Washington, 1946.

MOTTER, T. H. VAIL. *The Persian Corridor and Aid to Russia.* Washington, 1948.

PAYNE, ROBERT. *Journey to Persia.* London, 1951.

POLACCO, ANGELO. *L'Iran di Reza Scia Pahlavi.* Venice, 1937.

RICE, C. COLLIVER. *Persian Women and Their Ways.* London, 1923.

ROSS, Sir E. DENISON. *The Persians.* Oxford, 1931.

SAVORY, R. M. "Persia from the Constitution", in *Islamic Near East* (1960), pp. 243–61.

SHUSTER, W. MORGAN. *The Strangling of Persia.* London, 1912.

TRIA, V. *Kavkazskie sotsial'-demokraty v Persidskoi Revoliutsii.* Paris, 1910.

UPTON, JOSEPH M. *The History of Modern Iran: An Interpretation.* Cambridge, Mass., 1960.

WATSON, R. G. *A History of Persia.* (From the beginning of the nineteenth century to the year 1858.) London, 1866.

WILBER, DONALD N. *Iran: Past and Present.* Princeton, 1950.

YOUNG, T. CUYLER. "The Problem of Westernization in Modern Iran", in *Middle East Journal,* II (January 1948), 47–59.

II. LITERARY

(*a*) *Persian sources*

AFSHĀR, ĪRAJ. *Nathr-i Fārsī-yi Mu'āṣir* (*Contemporary Persian Prose*). Tehran, 1951.

AFSHĀR, ĪRAJ. "Jamālzāda", in *Yaghmā,* no. 12, 337–40.

AFSHĀR, ĪRAJ. "Muṭāli'āt-i Hidāyat dar Adabīyāt-i Guzashta va Farhang-i 'Āmīyāna" ("Hidayat's Research into Folklore and Classical Literature"), in *Jahān-i Naw,* no. 6, 45–6.

ĀL-I AḤMAD, JALĀL. "Hidāyat va Būf-i Kūr", in *'Ilm u Zindigī,* no. 1, 65–78.

'ALAVĪ, BUZURG. "Ṣādiq Hidāyat", in *Piyām-i Naw,* I, no. 12, 25–9.

'Aqāyid va Afkār dar Bāra-yi Ṣādiq Hidāyat (*Views and Ideas about Sadiq Hidayat*). (A collection of articles published in the Persian Press after the death of Hidayat.) Tehran, 1954.

BAHĀR, MUḤAMMAD TAQĪ. *Sabk Shināsī yā Taṭavur-i Nathr-i Fārsī* (*A Study of Styles or the History of the Development of Persian Prose*). 3 vols. Tehran, 1942.

BIHRŪZ, ZABĪHULLĀ. *Zabān-i Īrān: Fārsī yā 'Arabī?* (*The Language of Iran: Persian or Arabic?*) Tehran, 1943.

ḤIKMAT, 'ALĪ-AṢGHAR. *Pārsī-yi Naghz* (*Pure Persian*). Tehran, 1951.

JAMĀLZĀDA, MUḤAMMAD 'ALĪ. "Sharḥ-i Ḥāl" ("Autobiography"), in the *Nashrīya-hi Dānishkada-yi Adabīyāt-i Tabrīz*, vol. VI, no. 3 (1954).

KHĀNLARĪ, PARVĪZ NĀTIL. "Nathr-i Fārsī dar Dawra-yi Akhīr" ("Persian Prose in Recent Times"), in *First Congress of Iranian Writers* (1947), pp. 128–75.

KHĀNLARĪ, PARVĪZ NĀTIL. "Marg-i Ṣādiq Hidāyat" ("The Death of Sadiq Hidayat"), in *Yaghmā*, no. 4, 106–13.

KHĀN MALIK SĀSĀNĪ, AḤMAD. "Mīrzā Ḥabīb-i Iṣfahānī", in *Armaghān*, no. 10, 110–20 and 268–72.

MALKOM KHĀN, MĪRZĀ. *Majmū'a-yi Āthār* (*Collected Works*). Tehran, 1948.

MUDARRISĪ, TAQĪ. "Mulāḥiẓa-'ī dar Bāra-yi Dāstān-Nivīsī-yi Nuvīn-i Fārsī" ("Note on the New Persian Story-Writing"), in *Ṣadaf*, pp. 913–20 and 977–91.

MU'ĪN, MUḤAMMAD. "Tarjuma-yi Aḥvāl-i Dihkhudā" ("Dihkhuda's Biography"). The introduction to the latter's *Lughatnāma*, pp. 379–94.

MU'ĪN, MUḤAMMAD. "Chirāghī ka Khāmūsh Shud" ("The Light that Extinguished"). (An appreciation of Dihkhuda.) In *Yaghmā*, no. 9, 294–301.

NAFĪSĪ, SA'ĪD. *Shāhkārhā-yi Nathr-i Fārsī-yi Mu'āṣir* (*Masterpieces of Contemporary Persian Prose*). Tehran, 1951.

Nakhustīn Kungira-yi Nivīsandigān-i Īrān (*The Verbatim Report of the First Congress of Iranian Writers*). Tehran, 1947.

QĀ'IMĪYĀN, ḤASAN. *Dar Bāra-yi Sādiq Hidāyat, Nivishta-hā va Andīsha-hā-yi ū.* (Persian translation of V. Monteil's *Sâdeq Hedâyat* with additional notes and commentary by the translator.) Tehran, 1952.

QĀ'IMĪYĀN, ḤASAN. *Intiẓār* (*Longing*). (An appreciation of Ṣādiq Hidāyat.) Tehran, 1954.

ṢADR-HĀSHIMĪ, MUḤAMMAD. *Tārīkh-i Jarāyid va Majallāt-i Īrān* (*A History of Press and Periodicals in Iran*). 4 vols. Isfahan, 1948–53.

ṢAFĀ, ẔABĪḤULLĀ. *Tārīkh-i Adabīyāt dar Īrān* (*Literary History of Iran*). 3 vols. Tehran, 1957.

SHAFAQ, RIẒĀZĀDA. *Tārīkh-i Adabīyāt-i Īrān* (*Literary History of Iran*). Tehran, 1936.

SURŪSH-ĀBĀDĪ. *Barrisī-yi Āthār-i Ṣādiq Hidāyat* (*A Review of Sadiq Hidayat's Works*). Tehran, undated.

ṬABARĪ, IḤSĀN. "Ṣādiq Hidāyat: Shakhṣīyat-i ū, Afkār-i ū, Jāy-i ū dar Ḥayāt-i Adabī va Ijtimā'ī-yi Mu'āṣir" ("Sadiq Hidayat: His Personality, his Ideas and his Place in the Contemporary Socio-Literary Life"), in *Mardum*, First Year, v, no. 10 (1947), 42–7.

UMĪD, A. "Ṣādiq Hidāyat", in *Shīva*, no. 1, 14–25.

YĀSAMĪ, GHULĀMRIẒĀ RASHĪD. *Adabīyāt-i Mu'āṣir* (*Contemporary Literature*). Tehran, 1937.

YĀSAMĪ, GHULĀMRIẒĀ RASHĪD. "Ṭālibuff va Kitāb-i Aḥmad" ("Talibuff and the book of Ahmad"), in *Īrānshahr*, II, 283–97.

(*b*) *Foreign sources*

"Actualities in Persia", in *Times Literary Supplement* (5 August 1955).

ALAVI, BOZORG. *Geschichte und Entwicklung der modernen Persischen Literatur*. Berlin, 1964.

ARBERRY, A. J. *Modern Persian Reader*. Cambridge, 1944.

ARBERRY, A. J. *Classical Persian Literature*. London, 1958.

AVERY, P. W. "Developments in Modern Persian Prose", in *Muslim World*, XLV (October 1955), 313–23.

BAUSANI, A. "Europe and Iran in Contemporary Persian Literature", in *East and West*, no. 11 (1960), 3–14.

BAUSANI, A. *Storia della letteratura Persiana*, pp. 847–65. Milano, 1960.

BERTELS, E. E. *Ocherk Istorii Persidkoy Literatury*. Leningrad, 1928.

BERTELS, E. E. *Persidskij istoricheskiy roman XX veka*. Leningrad, 1932.

BINDER, LEONARD. *Iran: Political Development in a Changing Society*. Berkeley, 1962.

BORECKÝ, MILOŠ. "Persian Prose since 1946", in *Middle East Journal*, VII, no. 2 (spring 1953), 235–44.

BOYLE, J. A. "Notes on the Colloquial Language of Persia as recorded in Certain Recent Writings", in *Bulletin of the School of Oriental and African Studies*, no. 14 (1952), 451–62.

BROWNE, EDWARD GRANVILLE. *The Press and Poetry of Modern Persia*. Cambridge, 1914.

BROWNE, EDWARD GRANVILLE. *A Literary History of Persia*. 4 vols. Cambridge, 1924.

BURK, ATA KARIM. "Qā'im-Maqām: His Life and Works", in *Indo-Iranica*, 7iv (1954), 27–37.

CHAIKINE, K. *Kratkiy ocherk noveyshey persidskoy literatury*. Moscow, 1928.

Charisteria Orientalia. (Dedicated to J. Rypka.) Edited by F. Tauer, V. Kubīčkovā and I. Hrbek. Praha, 1956.

CHRISTENSEN, ARTHUR. *Contes Persanes en langue populaire*. Copenhagen, 1918.

COOK, NILLA CRAM. "The Theatre and Ballet Arts of Iran", in *Middle East Journal*, III (October 1949), 406–20.

DONALDSON, BESS ALLEN. *The Wild Rue: A Study of Muhammadan Magic and Folklore in Iran*. London, 1938.

GELPKE, R. "Politic und Ideologie in der Persischen Gegenwartsliteratur", in *Bustan*, no. 4 (Vienna, 1961).

GELPKE, R. *Persische Meistererzähler der Gegenwart*. Zürich, 1961.

JAUKACHEVA, M. "Problema osvobozhdeniya zhenshchiny v sovremennoy perskoy proze", in *Kratkie Soobshcheniya Instituta Vostokovedeniye*, XXVII (1958).

KOMISSAROV, D. S. "Obraz polozhitelnogo geroya v sovremennoy persidskoy hudozhestrennoy proze", in *Kratkie Soobshcheniya Instituta Vostokovedeniye SSSR*, XVII (Moscow, 1955).

KOMISSAROV, D. S. "O zhizni i tvorchestve S. Hedayat" in *Sovietskoye Vostokovedeniye*, no. 6 (1956), 56–70.

KOMISSAROV, D. S. "M. Hejazi i ego *sereshk*", in *Kratkie Soobshcheniya Instituta Vostokovedeniye*, 1958.

KOMISSAROV, D. S. "O realisticheskoy tendentsii v sovremennoy persidskoy literature", in *Sovietskoye Vostokovedeniye*, III (1958), 57–65. (English summary, p. 65.)

KOMISSAROV, D. S. *Ocherki sovremennoj persidskoj prozi*. Moscow, 1960.

KUBĪČKOVĀ, VĚRA. "Novoperská literatura xx. století", in J. Rypka's *Dějing perské a tádžieké literatury*, pp. 270–320. Praha, 1956.

KUBĪČKOVĀ, VĚRA. "Die neupersische literatur des 20. jahrhunderts", in J. Rypka's *Iranische literaturgeschichte*. Leipzig, 1959.

LAW, HENRY D. G. *Persian Writers*. Special number of the *Life and Letters*, LXIII, no. 148 (1949).

LAW, HENRY D. G. "Sadiq Hedayat", in *Journal of the Iran Society*, I, no. 3 (London, 1950), 109–13.

LESCOT, ROGER. "Le roman et la nouvelle dans la littérature iranienne contemporaine", in *Bulletin d'Etudes Orientales de l'Institut Français de Damas*, no. 9 (Beirut, 1942), 83–101.

LESCOT, ROGER. "Deux novelles de Sâdegh Hedâyat", in *Orient*, no. 8 (1958), 119–54.

LEVY, R. *Persian Literature, an Introduction.* Oxford, 1923.

LEVY, R. *The Persian Language.* London, 1951.

MACHALSKI, F. *Historyczna Powieść Perska.* Kraków, 1952.

MACHALSKI, F. "'Šams et Toghrâ': roman historique de Moḥammad Bāqir Hosrovî", in *Charisteria Orientalia*, pp. 149–63. Praha, 1956

MACHALSKI, F. "Principaux courants de la prose persane moderne in", *Rocznik Orientalistyczny*, no. xxv (1961).

MASSÉ, H. "La littérature persane d'aujourd'hui", in *L'Islam et l'Occident* (1947), pp. 260–3.

MONTEIL, V. *Sâdeq Hedâyat.* Published by L'Institut Franco-Iranian. Tehran, 1952.

MOSTAFAVI, RAHMAT. "Fiction in Contemporary Persian Literature", in *Middle Eastern Affairs*, II, nos. 8–9 (August–September 1951), 273–9.

NAFISI, SA'ID "A. General Survey of the Existing Situation in Persian Literature", in *Bulletin of the Institute of Islamic Studies*, no. I (Aligarh, 1957).

NIKITINE, B. "Le roman historique dans la littérature persane actuelle", in *Journal Asiatique*, no. 223 (1933), 297–336.

NIKITINE, B. "Les thèmes sociaux dans la littérature persane moderne", in *Oriente Moderno*, XXXIV (Rome, 1954), 225–37.

NIKITINE, B. "Sayyed Mohammed Ali Djemalzadeh, pionnier de la prose moderne persane", in *Revue des Etudes Islamiques*, no. 27 (Paris, 1959), 23–33.

"Persian Literature To-day", in *Times Literary Supplement* (12 July 1953.)

REZVANI, M. *Le Théâtre et la Danse en Iran.* Paris, 1962.

ROZANOV, G. *Rasskazī Persidskikh Pisateley.* (Preface by E. E. Bertels.) Moscow, 1959.

ROZENFELD, A. Z. "O Hudozhestvennoy Iranskoy Literature XX Veka", in *Vestnik Leningrad*, no. 5 (1949).

ROZENFELD, A. Z. "Sadek Khedayat" ("Opuit Kharakterristiki Tvorchestva"), in *Kratkie Soobshcheniya Instituta Vostokovedeniye*, no. 17 (1955), 66–72.

ROZENFELD, A. Z. "A. P. Chekhov i Souremennaya Persidskaya Literature", in *Pamyati I. I. Krachovskoyo* (1958), 73–9.

RYPKA, JAN. *Iranische Literaturgeschichte.* Leipzig, 1959.

SCARCIA, G. "'Ḥājī Āqā' e 'Būf-i Kūr', i cosiddetti due aspetti dell'opera dello scrittore contemporaneo Persiano Ṣādeq Hedāyat", in *Annali dell'Instituto Universitario Orientale di Napoli*, no. VIII (1958), 103–23

SHAFAQ, REZAZADE. "Drama in Contemporary Iran", in *Middle Eastern Affairs*, IV, no. 1 (January 1953), 11–15.

SHAKI, MANSOUR. "An Introduction to the Modern Persian Literature", in *Charisteria Orientalia* (Praha, 1956), 300–15.

SHOYTOV, A. M. "Rol' M. F. Ahundova v Razvitii Persidskoy Progressivnoy Literatury", in *Kratkie Soobshch. Inst. Vostokovedeniye*, no. IX (1953).

SHOYTOV, A. M. "Nekotoruie Osobennosti Tvorcheskoyo Metoda Bozorga Alavi", in *Kratkie Soobshch. Inst. Vostokovedeniye*, no. 39 (1959), 23–32.

STOREY, C. A. *Persian Literature*. (A bio-bibliographicals urvey.) London, 1927–39.

VASSIGHI, H. *M. A. Djamalzadeh sa vie et son œuvre*. (A Ph.D. dissertation of the Faculty of Letters of the University of Tabriz.) Unpublished, 1955.

WICKENS, G. M. "Bozorg Alavi's Portmanteau", in *The University of Toronto Quarterly*, XXVIII (1958).

YARSHATER, EHSAN. The Persian section of *Cassell's Encyclopaedia of Literature*. London, 1953.

YARSHATER, EHSAN. "Persian Letters in the Last Fifty Years", in *Middle Eastern Affairs*, IX (1960), 298–306.

ZOLNA, M. "Z Rozwazan Nad Forma Niektorych Utworów Sadeka Hedajata", in *Przeglad Orientalistyczny*, no. 2 (1957).

INDEX

Zand, dynasty, 7
Zand-i Vuhūman Yasn, 182, 207
Zan-i Zīyādī, 125
Zaydān, Jurjī, 28
Zaynu'l-'Ābidīn, Ḥājj, of Maragheh, 17, 40
Zen, 181
Zhivago, Dr, 181
Zībā, 74, 75
Zinda Bi-gūr, 144, 202, 204
Zola, Emile, 78
Zoroastrian, 3, 47, 49, 50, 137, 148